Expanding the Black Film Canon

Expanding the Black Film Canon

Race and Genre across Six Decades

Lisa Doris Alexander

University Press of Kansas

Published by the University Press of Kansas (Lawrence, Kansas 66045), which was organized by the Kansas Board of Regents and is operated and funded by Emporia State University, Fort Hays State University, Kansas State University, Pittsburg State University, the University of Kansas, and Wichita State University

© 2019 by the University Press of Kansas
All rights reserved

Library of Congress Cataloging-in-Publication Data

Names: Alexander, Lisa Doris.
Title: Expanding the Black film canon : race and genre across six decades / Lisa Doris Alexander.
Description: Lawrence, Kansas : University Press of Kansas, 2019. | Includes bibliographical references and index.
Identifiers: LCCN 2019006695
  ISBN 9780700628391 (cloth : alk. paper)
  ISBN 9780700628407 (pbk. : alk. paper)
  ISBN 9780700628414 (ebook)
Subjects: LCSH: African Americans in motion pictures. | Race relations in motion pictures. | Racism in motion pictures. | African Americans in the motion picture industry.
Classification: LCC PN1995.9.N4 A44 2019 | DDC 791.4308996073—dc23
LC record available at https://lccn.loc.gov/2019006695.

British Library Cataloguing-in-Publication Data is available.

Printed in the United States of America

10 9 8 7 6 5 4 3 2 1

The paper used in this publication is recycled and contains 30 percent postconsumer waste. It is acid free and meets the minimum requirements of the American National Standard for Permanence of Paper for Printed Library Materials z39.48-1992.

CONTENTS

Acknowledgments   vii

Coming Attractions   1

1. I Ain't Fit to Live with No More: *Nothing But a Man* Revisited   17

2. "Hey, Where Are the White Women At?": The Presentation of Racism and Resistance in *Blazing Saddles*   38

3. *Harlem Nights*, Awkward Framing, and Complicated Gender Politics   59

4. Who's the Real Gangsta?: *The Glass Shield* and the Politics of Black Communities and Police Relations   77

5. "If You're Going to Tell People the Truth . . . Make Them Laugh": *C.S.A.: The Confederate States of America* as Mockumentary and Truth-Telling   97

6. Ladies First: Ava DuVernay and Black-Female-Centered Narratives   119

7. Who's the Hero of the Piece?: Hollywood's Representation of Jackie Robinson's Legacy   141

8. Are We Allowed to Be Children?: Black Teen Films, Trauma, and the Race to Adulthood   163

Post-Credit Sequence   185

Notes   191

Bibliography   213

Index   235

ACKNOWLEDGMENTS

The first part of these acknowledgments is a mea culpa. I was in such a rush to finish and publish my first book, because the future of my career depended on it (publish or perish is real, my dear readers, and I needed to be employed to pay my student loans), that I did not include an acknowledgments section. So, to show that I am not a complete ingrate, these acknowledgments have two parts. As with many academic works, my first book was an outgrowth of my dissertation, and to that end, first, I would like to thank my mom, Doris Alexander, for her unconditional love and support (both financial and emotional), as well as her stubborn desire to see me graduate and finish the book. I would also like to extend my gratitude to my dissertation committee: Dr. Phil Terrie, who guided me through the process while patiently enduring my penchant for comma splices, as well as Drs. Vikki Krane and Kathy Bradshaw, who waded through endless drafts and offered their valuable insight. In addition, I would like to thank Dr. Don McQuarie, ACS program director, and Gloria Enriquez-Pizaña, for their administrative assistance.

I would like to thank Tony Miller for talking baseball with me and allowing me to live vicariously through him; Heather Surface for always letting me vent, even if it was long-distance; Tony Avruch for explaining theory to me and offering sound advice; Julie O'Reilly for validating the amount of time I spend in front of the television set and showing everyone that there is a light at the end of the tunnel; Stevie Tuszynski for introducing me to new, and much-needed, avenues of procrastination; Stefan Hall and Charlie Cuthbertson for being the pop culture gods they are; and Dustin Tahmahkera for enduring my long-winded and whiny email messages. I would also like to thank Dr. Gretchen Flesher Moon for her grammar, punctuation, and proofreading wizardry, as well as Drs. Emily Drew, Alison Butler, Ken Nolley, and Thabiti Lewis for their support and cheerleading efforts. I must also point out that Judy Fiske's proofreading efforts were amazing and cannot fully be measured. I would like to thank the 2005 World Series Champion Chicago White Sox for Grinder Rule #17: never be satisfied with what you have achieved—it pales in comparison to what you can achieve. Last, but certainly not least, I would like to thank my cat Dusty, for just being Dusty.

This time around, I need to thank the University of Nebraska Press for permission to reprint the article "The Jackie Robinson Story vs. The Court-Martial of Jackie Robinson vs. 42: Hollywood's Representations of Jackie Robinson's Legacy," which appeared in NINE: A Journal of Baseball History and Culture 24, nos. 1&2, 2015–2016. I also need to thank Taylor & Francis for granting me permission to reprint the article "Nothing But a Man Revisited," which appeared in the Journal of Popular Film & Television 41, no. 3, 2013.

It should serve as no surprise to anyone that many of the people who helped me survive writing the first book were instrumental in helping me finish this one. My mom remains my biggest fan, and continues to read chapters and offer invaluable critiques on films she hasn't seen and has no interest in ever seeing. Tony Avruch, Charlie Cuthbertson, Stefan Hall, Julie O'Reilly, Heather Surface, Stevie Tuszynski, and Peg Yacobucci continue their proofreading and pop culture discussant duties. My colleagues in the African American Studies Department at Wayne State—Melba Boyd, David Goldberg, Ollie Johnson, and Lisa Ze Winters—have offered unwavering support and advice. While Dusty is no longer my furry little life mate, Mittens has taken that mantle with great pride and indifference.

Coming Attractions

Blacks do go see mainstreams movies, but are not depicted there.

> Mia Mask, *Contemporary Black American Cinema: Race, Gender and Sexuality at the Movies*, 2012

The ultimate goal of the definition of a Black film is so that critics, theorists, causal [sic] viewers and most importantly filmmakers can better discern when Black actors are merely being used as tokens to feign racial inclusiveness as opposed to when certain filmmakers are using Black actors to be critical of the status quo, encourage racial empathy, tolerance, diversity and/or attack the general power imbalance that exists along the lines of race and class within a highly stratified society.

> Andre Seewood, "Towards Defining the Black Film: The Genuine, the Compromised, and the Token," *Shadow and Act*, 2015

In a June 2014 interview with *Variety*, filmmaker Spike Lee was asked about the "explosion" of black films that were released the preceding year and remarked, "I know. These articles come out every 10 years. Every 10 years, I get calls, 'Spike, can you speak about this new discovery of black film?' It changes that year, but then there's a nine-year drought."[1] The interviewer, Ramin Setoodeh, was asking Lee about the proliferation of black films released in the previous year, including Steve McQueen's *12 Years a Slave*, which would eventually win Oscars for Best Picture, Best Supporting Actress, and Best Adapted Screenplay and garner six additional nominations; Lee Daniels's *The Butler*; Ryan Coogler's *Fruitvale Station*, which won the Prix de l'avenir Prize at the Cannes Film Festival; Malcolm D. Lee's *Best Man Holiday*, the long-awaited sequel to his 1999 film *The Best Man*; and Brian Helgeland's *42*, which told the story of Jackie Robinson's first year with the Brooklyn Dodgers. The irony of Setoodeh's question is the fact that the recent incarnation of the black film renaissance actually began in 2012, with the release of such high-profile films as Salim Akil's *Sparkle*; Benh Zeitlin's *Beasts of the Southern Wild*, which was nominated for four Oscars including Best Picture; Sheldon Candis's independent film *LUV*; and Anthony Hemingway's Tuskegee Airmen biopic *Red Tails*. In that same year Ava DuVernay became the first black woman to win a directing award at the Sundance Film Festival for her sophomore feature *Middle of Nowhere*.[2]

Given the number of black films being released, it felt as though Hollywood was on a roll, and that the typical black film drought would be avoided. Unfortunately, just one year later, the number of black films being released decreased precipitously, which helps explain why for two years in a row, in 2015 and 2016, there were no black Oscar nominees in the major categories. The lack of nominees led to the creation of the hashtag #OscarsSoWhite on social media, which continued the discussion about the lack of inclusion in the film industry even at a time when the president of the Academy of Motion Picture Arts and Sciences was a black woman. While many people were focused on the lack of Oscar nominations for the black creative talent behind the 2015 films *Creed*, *Straight Outta Compton*, and *Concussion*, some pointed to larger systemic problems in Hollywood that prevent people of color from telling their own stories in a meaningful way. As Chris Rock joked during his opening monologue at the 2016 Oscars, "Hollywood is sorority racist. It's like, 'We like you, Rhonda, but you're not Kappa.' That's how Hollywood is."[3] Just two years earlier, Rock penned a column for the *Hollywood Reporter* in which he observed, "The best [black films] are made outside of the studio system because they're not made with that many white people — maybe one or two, but not a whole system of white people."[4]

Clearly the lack of inclusion in Hollywood has been a well-known issue for some time. It remains to be seen whether the discussion will lead to sustained change within the film industry. Though an argument can be made that there were not many Oscar-worthy black films released in 2015, the same cannot be said of 2016, which saw the release of several financially successful and critical acclaimed films, such as Barry Jenkins's *Moonlight*, Theodore Melfi's *Hidden Figures*, Raoul Peck's *I Am Not Your Negro*, and Denzel

Washington's *Fences*. The same can be said about 2017, which featured Jordan Peele's *Get Out*, Malcolm D. Lee's *Girls Trip*, Reginald Hudlin's *Marshall*, and Dee Rees's *Mudbound*. The year 2018 also saw a plethora of black films, including Ryan Coogler's *Black Panther*, George Tillman Jr.'s *The Hate U Give*, Spike Lee's *BlacKkKlansman*, Antoine Fuqua's *Equalizer 2*, Peter Ramsey's *Spider-Man: Into the Spider-Verse*, and Boots Riley's *Sorry to Bother You*. The end of the decade has seen sustained, increased interest and investment in black films.

If we reach back to the 1950s, when Hollywood began telling slightly less stereotypical stories about black people's lives, and if we assume that there was a groundswell of black films at least once per decade in addition to the handful of black films consistently released during any given calendar year, we are left with a plethora of films available for analysis. Because of either the sheer number of films or the possibility that some films fly under the radar, it is not surprising that some black films have not received the scholarly attention they deserve. For obvious reasons, scholars tend to focus on films that were deemed important creatively or politically, and/or were controversial when they were released. In a similar vein, dramas tend to receive more attention than comedies, and films that failed at the box office are not seen as relevant compared to films that attracted larger audiences. For example, there are multiple books and articles discussing black films of the 1970s. Films from the Blaxploitation movement, such as *Cotton Comes to Harlem* (1970), *Shaft* (1971), *Superfly* (1972), and *Cleopatra Jones* (1973), are typically discussed as important black films that represent the decade because they were made for black audiences. Thus, a film like Mel Brooks's *Blazing Saddles* (1974), despite being a very popular Oscar-nominated film, having a black man as the main character, and featuring Richard Pryor as one of the cowriters, does not fit into the common perception of what black films of the period should be.

What is also interesting about film scholarship is that black films overall, regardless of their critical acclaim, political importance, or box-office success, do not receive the scholarly attention they deserve. As Beretta Smith-Shomade states in the special section of *Cinema Journal* dedicated to black popular culture, "African Americans' history [is] dominated by erasures and obfuscations."[5] This erasure manifests itself in the fact that "the ground and works examined by African American [media] scholars fall outside the pale of mainstream viewership—general audiences and scholars alike," and the fact that "if one were to survey any number of syllabi for Introduction to Film or its equivalent, one would most likely find a single day dedicated to 'race and ethnicity in the media.' This might be the only time that a black media text appears in the course. What message does this send to students, other than that black media is—at best—only tangentially relevant to the critical study and appreciation of film, television, and new media?[6] Smith-Shomade's point is laid bare in the very existence of the special section of *Cinema Journal* where her piece was published. Instead of integrating black popular culture throughout the journal's volumes, the African American caucus is relegated to a separate section of one issue. This allows the contents of the remaining issues to remain surprisingly limited in their discussions of black media products without the appearance of neglect, despite the fact that, as cultural studies scholar Stuart Hall maintained, "American mainstream popular culture has always involved certain traditions that could only be attributed to black cultural vernacular traditions."[7]

It is easy to trace how embedded blackness is within Hollywood films, despite the fact that black popular culture is often relegated to the scholarly margins. As James Lowen points out in his book *Lies My Teacher Told Me: Everything Your American History Textbooks Got Wrong*, "America's first epic motion picture, *Birth of a Nation*; first talkie, *The Jazz Singer*; and biggest blockbuster ever, *Gone with the Wind*, were substantially about race relations,"[8] and more importantly, all of these films feature segments or have at the core of their narrative the subjugation of black stories and black people. For example, *Birth of a Nation* framed the Ku Klux Klan as the saviors of the pre–Civil War South, as opposed to the terrorist organization most people understand it to be. The most famous scene from *The Jazz Singer* involves Al Jolson donning blackface, a practice that was often used to perpetuate stereotypes of black communities, and *Gone with the Wind* paints a magnolia-myth version of the post–Civil War South that was not the reality for many black communities during that time.

It is easy to dismiss these examples as being from bygone eras; however, there are more contemporary examples. In the 2010s, Hollywood's flavor of the month (for lack of a better phrase) was comic book films. Since 2010, there have been approximately fifty superhero films released, and of those, only three feature black characters as the primary protagonist or antagonist (*Men in Black 3* [2013], *The Amazing Spider-Man 2* [2014], and *Black Panther* [2018]). Four others feature black characters as a prominent member of an ensemble (*Fantastic Four* [2015], *Suicide Squad* [2016], *Doctor Strange* [2016], and *Justice League* [2017]). The lack of racial diversity in these films could lead some to believe that race does not play a role in science fiction/fantasy or comic book films; however, Pulitzer Prize–winning author Junot Díaz points out that:

> Look, without our stories, without the true nature and reality of who we are as People of Color, nothing about fanboy or fangirl culture would make sense. What I mean by that is: if it wasn't for race, *X-Men* doesn't make sense. If it wasn't for the history of breeding human beings in the New World through chattel slavery, *Dune* doesn't make sense. If it wasn't for the history of colonialism and imperialism, *Star Wars* doesn't make sense. If it wasn't for the extermination of so many indigenous First Nations, most of what we call science fiction's contact stories doesn't make sense. Without us as the secret sauce, none of this works, and it is about time that we understood that we are the Force that holds the *Star Wars* universe together. We're the Prime Directive that makes Star Trek possible, yeah. In the Green Lantern Corps, we are the oath. We are all of these things—erased, and yet without us—we are essential.[9]

Despite how essential race is to the science fiction/fantasy genre, the films and television shows within those genres have been, and continue to be, overwhelmingly white, and have not embraced the "secret sauce" of race and racism that Díaz argues is the underpinning of the genre. This lack of racial and financial self-awareness, particularly where sci-fi/fantasy is concerned, is why some analysts and executives were shocked in 2018 when *Black Panther* became the highest-grossing film of that year. As Scott Mendelson from *Forbes* argued, "It's unfortunate that it took this long, as Hollywood may have finally figured out the value of 'not a white guy' movie stars. . . . I have long argued that Hollywood erred badly by spending a decade trying to find the next Tom Cruise when it should have been looking for the next Will Smith."[10]

Given the erasures Smith-Shomade and Díaz write about, it is no surprise that many black films have eluded critical analysis. This is not to say that an academic canon of black films does not exist. On the contrary, a reliable collection of black films have received scholarly critiques and regularly find their way into most courses focusing on black films. Examples are Oscar Micheaux's *Within Our Gates* (1919), Andrew Stone's *Stormy Weather* (1954), Sam Petrie's *A Raisin in the Sun* (1961), Gordon Parks's *The Learning Tree* (1969), Melvin Van Peebles's *Sweet Sweetback's Baadasssss Song* (1971), Charles Burnett's *Killer of Sheep* (1978), Spike Lee's *Do the Right Thing* (1989), Julie Dash's *Daughters of the Dust* (1991), John Singleton's *Boyz n the Hood* (1991), and Haile Gerima's

Sankofa (1993). One or two of these films might even be discussed during the one day that Intro to Film courses devote to "race and ethnicity in media" that Smith-Shomade pointed to. Of course, there is often a disconnect between films that attract critical attention and films that attract popular attention. In 2016, partially in response to the #OscarsSoWhite campaign, *Slate* gathered a panel of experts to create the Black Film Canon, which included many of the films discussed above but also added more recent examples, as well as films that have received less attention from academics, including Michael Schultz's *Cooley High* (1975), Marlon Riggs's *Tongues Untied* (1989), Ernest Dickerson's *Juice* (1992), Carl Franklin's *Devil in a Blue Dress* (1995), F. Gary Gray's *Friday* (1995), Kasi Lemmons's *Eve's Bayou* (1997), and Ryan Coogler's *Creed* (2015). This book seeks to build the academic film list with films that would typically be restricted to the popular list. By expanding the number of and types of films analyzed, we can chart the increasing number of voices that tell black stories, and we can examine ways in which the representation of black characters and black communities have progressed and regressed over time.

The first part of this book will discuss one underexamined film per decade, starting in the 1960s, using aspects of black feminist thought and critical race theory (CRT) to analyze what each film tells us about the status of black people and race relations in the United States at the time the film was released. As discussed earlier, Hollywood's modus operandi concerning black films historically has been to allow a handful of black films and/or black filmmakers to be recognized each decade before shuttling them to the side until the next decade. This is the reason why the first part of the book focuses on one film to represent a particular decade. As we moved into the 1990s, the number of black films and black filmmakers increased, and many of those filmmakers refused to be pushed aside. The beginning of (hopefully) the end of the ten-year renaissance cycle is the reason why the second part focuses on particular themes and traces them through multiple films. By doing so, we can further expand the black film canon. In addition, this book will demonstrate the importance and complexity of black popular culture and provide a road map for thinking about black film in the future.

This book straddles a scholastic fence. It is not a straight history of black representation in film in the vein of Donald Bogle's *Toms, Coons, Mulattoes, Mammies, & Bucks: An Interpretative History of Blacks in American Film*, nor is it a traditional film studies text that focuses on a specific thesis or genre and follows that thread throughout, such as Novotny Lawrence and Gerald R.

Butters Jr.'s *Beyond Blaxploitation* or Adilifu Nama's *Black Space: Imagining Race in Science Fiction Films*. This book combines the two approaches by taking a longitudinal view of the changing representations of black communities, and by discussing each film within its specific historical context. Going back to *Blazing Saddles*, for example, it makes sense to discuss the film within the context of both the 1970s Blaxploitation movement as well as the era that saw the decline of the Western as a dominant film genre. At the same time, it makes sense to discuss the film within the larger history of parody and satire, and to focus on how Brooks told the story of a 1970s black sheriff in an 1870s setting. This method focuses on the films themselves, allowing for speculation as to why the film is important and why it has not received sufficient scholarly attention. It also highlights the diversity of the films and illustrates the multitude of ways scholars can discuss black films.

As the field of cinema studies has continued to grow and include scholars whose primary research is in traditional disciplines, new interdisciplinary theories and methodologies for analyzing and critiquing film continue to be introduced.[11] In my previous book, *When Baseball Isn't White, Straight, and Male: The Media and Difference in the National Pastime*, I found that even though neither black feminist thought nor critical race theory was designed to critique professional sports in general and Major League Baseball specifically, the two were extremely helpful both in understanding how "power relations [operated] along the lines of race, class, gender, and sexuality" and in "exploring the meaning of specific events in order to illustrate the persistence of inequities with American society."[12] Because Hollywood films, like professional sports, bring in many billions of dollars per year, are exported around the globe, and are grounded in a historical and contemporary practice of racial inequality, critical race theory and black feminist thought can provide useful theoretical insights into how race, class, and gender operate in popular film.

For example, one of the issues theorist Patricia Hill Collins discusses in her foundational work *Black Feminist Thought: Knowledge, Consciousness, and the Politics of Empowerment* is the notion of controlling images. She writes about "the gender-specific depiction of people of African descent within Western scholarship and popular culture" that is then used "to make racism, sexism, poverty, and other forms of social injustice to appear natural, normal, and inevitable parts of everyday life."[13] We see these controlling images appear repeatedly in Hollywood films as black actors are typically cast as toms, coons, mulattoes, mammies, and bucks, to quote the title of Donald Bogle's seminal text—and that list does not even include the more contemporary controlling images such as jezebels, magical Negroes, and strong black women. To show how pervasive and how beloved these controlling images are, it is worth noting that of the nine black women who have won Oscars for leading or supporting roles, at least five portrayed characters who could easily be classified as one of the aforementioned controlling images. Black men have received praise for slightly more varied representations, as there is an even split among the ten roles played by black actors who have won Oscars for leading or supporting roles, with five that can easily be classified as a controlling image. The films analyzed in this book offer more nuanced representations of black characters, and confront, negate, or parody the controlling images that have plagued black filmic characters for decades.

One of the key components of both critical race theory and black feminist thought, the concept of intersectionality, can also provide valuable insight into film analysis. While black women have been discussing the ways in which their race and gender impact their everyday circumstances for decades, critical race theorist Kimberlé Crenshaw has brought the concept of intersectionality to the forefront of popular discourse. Crenshaw argues

> many of the experiences black women face are not subsumed within the traditional boundaries of race or gender discrimination as these boundaries are currently understood, and that the intersection of racism and sexism factors into black women's lives in ways that cannot be captured wholly by looking separately at the race or gender dimensions of those experiences.[14]

Failing to acknowledge these intersections can lead to skewed interpretations regarding the state of women, people of color, and particularly women of color in the United States. For example, in 2016, the University of Southern California's Annenberg School for Communication and Journalism released a study titled "Inequality in 800 Popular Films: Examining Portrayals of Gender, Race, & LGBT Status from 2007 to 2015." As one can imagine, the study found that the level of inclusion in popular films is quite grim. Of the hundred top-grossing films in 2015, only thirty-two featured a female lead or co-lead, which is disappointing.[15] However, when intersectionality is factored into the analysis, the numbers are even more dire: of those thirty-two female leads or co-leads, only three were female actors from underrepresented racial or ethnic groups.[16] While women in general are underrepresented in popular film, women of color are almost invisible.

Of course, these intersections are not limited to race and gender, as socioeconomic class, sexual orientation, gender identity, age, and immigration status are intersecting identities that also can produce discriminatory treatment and less than fully realized representations in popular media. While race is the primary identity discussed in this text, the overwhelming majority of the films analyzed here also deal with intersecting identities including gender (chapters 1, 2, 3, 6, and 7), class (chapters 1, 2, and 6), and sexual orientation (chapter 8).

Critical race theory began as a legal theory devoted to understanding "the historical centrality and complicity of law in upholding white supremacy (and concomitant hierarchies of gender, class, and sexual orientation."[17] Though there is not a rigid set of boundaries that define CRT, it is often "characterized by frequent use of the first person, storytelling, narrative, allegory, interdisciplinary treatment of the law, and the unapologetic use of creativity."[18] Though CRT initially focused solely on the law and jurisprudence, it since has been adopted by scholars in a variety of disciplines. As the quote from Cornel West at the beginning of this paragraph points out, the legal system is complicit in upholding white supremacy, but the law is not the only system that reifies hierarchies of privilege. Certainly popular culture broadly, and film specifically, have been and continue to be used to reinforce stereotypes that perpetuate white supremacy.

Many critical race theorists disagree with the commonly held notion that "laws are or can be written from a neutral perspective [and they argue that] not all positioned perspectives are equally valued, equally heard, or equally included."[19] Likewise, film has never been and should never be viewed as coming from a neutral perspective—the audience is viewing the world that has been created from the standpoint of the writer, director, and editor. Because those who make, finance, and distribute films are predominately white males, "some positions have historically been oppressed, distorted, ignored, silenced, destroyed, appropriated, commodified, and marginalized—and all of this, not accidentally."[20] The "universal" narrative in Hollywood films has always been assumed to be a white character, and writers and directors who wish to tell stories from a different perspective have been rebuffed. For example, when director Kasi Lemmons was shopping her script for *Eve's Bayou*, she was asked "to put in white characters, I mean, even if they were negative white characters – just any white character," a move that would have changed the entire tenor of the film.[21] In 2014, Chris Rock maintained that "I couldn't have made *Top Five* at a studio. First of all, no one's going to make a movie with a prince so little and artsy: a star putting out a movie and getting interviewed by a woman from The New York Times. I would have had to have three two-hour meetings explaining that black people also read The New York Times."²² In 2016, veteran actor Don Cheadle directed the film Miles Ahead, which focused on the life of jazz legend Miles Davis. Cheadle spoke openly about the fact that after he crowdsourced some funding for the film, he "only cleared the final financing hurdle when he wrote in a fictional Rolling Stone reporter and cast Ewan ("young Obi-Wan") McGregor in the role."²³ When George Lucas, whose films have grossed over a billion dollars at the box office, wanted to make the film Red Tails (2012), about the Tuskegee Airmen, according to an Entertainment Weekly article, "no major Hollywood studio was willing to finance a World War II epic featuring an all-black cast, meaning that he had to pull out his own pocketbook if his take on the pioneering African-American fighter squad was ever going to get made."²⁴ When writers and directors want to tell stories about black communities, the financial gatekeepers often force them to include white characters in an effort to appeal to white audiences.

Even if filmmakers manage to forgo centering on or adding whiteness to their narratives to get their stories financed, there are still racial repercussions. In 2015, DreamWorks released its first full-length animated feature starring a female of color in the leading role. Home followed the story of a young black girl named Tip, voiced by singer Rihanna, who was searching for her mother following an alien invasion. Tip befriended an alien named Oh, and the two, along with Tip's cat, set off for adventure. When the film was released, writers noticed something interesting about the film's advertisements: "In predominantly Asian, Latino, and white neighborhoods, billboards for HOME featured just the cat and the alien. In black neighborhoods, Tip and the alien were featured prominently."²⁵ This segregated advertising occurred a year after the Italian advertisements for the film 12 Years a Slave featured Brad Pitt and Michael Fassbender but excluded the film's black star Chiwetel Ejiofor.²⁶ Finally, even if a film is made, released, and advertised appropriately, when film scholars do not critically engage with black films, their marginalization continues, highlighting the myriad ways that white supremacy within the film industry is perpetuated. Calling attention to how privileges are preserved is one of the main themes of critical race theory. Moving from the status of black folks in front of the camera to their status behind the camera, it becomes clear that race is intimately associated with the types of stories that society allows filmmakers to tell.

Out of the 700 top-grossing films made between 2007 and 2014, only 45 had black directors, and not surprisingly, "Of the films with a Black director, 40.2% of all characters were Black. When the director was not Black, only 10.6% of all on screen speaking or named characters were Black."[27] Whether this disparity is a function of black directors being more interested in telling stories that reflect their personal realities, or a function of the fact that black directors are hired to helm films with diverse casts, is unknown. This is not to say that white filmmakers cannot tell stories about black characters; on the contrary, a few of the films discussed here have white writers and/or directors. At the same time, white writers telling black stories can cause complications. First, there is the fear that if white writers and directors are being hired to tell black stories, then it will be even more difficult for black writers and directors to gain employment. In a piece for the *Hollywood Reporter*, John Singleton related the sentiment of a screenwriter who said: "'Hollywood feels like it doesn't need us anymore to tell African American stories.' The thinking goes, 'We voted for and gave money to Obama, so [we don't need to] hire any black people.'"[28] On the other hand, there does not seem to be a need to fear an avalanche of white writers and directors clamoring to tell black stories. As the research shows, white directors are far less likely to tell stories about non-white protagonists. Second, there is a fear that even though the story might be about black communities and their struggles, white directors may choose to place white characters at the centers of those stories. This type of storytelling can be found in many acclaimed Hollywood films, including *Glory* (1989), which told the story of the all-black 54th Massachusetts Volunteer Infantry through the eyes of a white commanding officer; *Mississippi Burning* (1988), which dramatized the violence to which civil rights workers were subjected through the eyes of two white FBI Agents; *Amistad* (1997), which looked at the mutiny aboard a slave ship through the eyes of the white lawyers defending one of the formally enslaved men; *The Help* (2011), which looked at black domestic workers in the South through the eyes of a white female writer; *Django Unchained* (2012), which followed a freed slave's quest to rescue his wife through the eyes of the white bounty hunter who freed him; *Race* (2016), which documented Jesse Owens's masterful performance at the 1936 Olympics and focused on the relationship between Owens and his coach Larry Snyder; and *Green Book* (2018), which followed the black pianist Dr. Don Shirley and his white chauffeur through a concert tour in the 1960s South.

As mentioned earlier, Hollywood studios often want white characters that white audiences can relate to, in an effort to make black stories more "universal." Unfortunately, most of the men who directed the aforementioned films, including Steven Spielberg, Quentin Tarantino, Robert Zwick, and Alan Parker, were all established directors who had the clout to feature a black protagonist at the center of the film but chose not to.

That being said, this text does not simply look at films that have black protagonists, because films with black main characters can reinforce stereotypes. The definition of black film is complicated since "Black film is not a national cinema; black film is a cinema whose borders are variously defined by multiple audiences, diverse scholars, different generations of students, and the changing priorities of the popular press."[29] Instead, this book is more interested in films that conform to Andre Seewood's definition of a black film as

> a film with a majority Black cast that situates Whites, if any, in peripheral or non-influential roles where the narrative resolves itself by giving more dramatic attention to the emotions and circumstances of the Black character(s) [and films in which] the concept of dramatic agency (the ability of the character(s) to directly influence and change the circumstances within a story and survive the outcome of those circumstances) is explicitly exercised by the Black characters who are integral to the film's plot and theme.[30]

As Seewood's definition intimates, while having one or more black characters in leading roles is certainly a step in the right direction, it is not the only step. Some films, for example, include black characters who unfortunately have little influence over the film's narrative, or simply exist to further the white character's story arc (such as the aforementioned *Amistad*, *The Help*, and 2018's *Green Book*). Though having a black writer and/or director at the helm increases the chances that black characters will play larger roles in a given film, the race of the writer or director is not enough to classify a film as a black film by Seewood's definition. Of course, black directors have helmed films with predominantly white casts; examples include Carl Franklin's *One True Thing* (1998), Spike Lee's *Summer of Sam* (1999), and Antoine Fuqua's *King Arthur* (2004)—and there is no reason to pigeonhole black directors to solely making black films.

The films selected for this book reflect several criteria. First, each can be defined as a black film within the parameters of Seewood's definition. Second, with *Blazing Saddles* being the one exception, none of the films discussed here have been analyzed in any depth in other studies of black films, and one goal of this project is to jump-start discussions about films that have escaped scholarly attention. In that vein, the titles within Spike Lee's filmography are not included, given that his films have been discussed in two edited anthologies and a plethora of journal articles. Though they have not received the same volume of attention, given the gravity of their work, Haile Gerima's and Julie Dash's films also have received critical analysis. A film like Ivan Dixon's *The Spook Who Sat by the Door* (1973), based on Sam Greenlee's book, has not been the subject of widespread scholarly coverage; however, the attention it has received from Christine Acham and Elizabeth Reich, among others, is quite extensive. Third, the films had to have a theatrical release in the United States. While access to established distribution avenues has long been an issue for black filmmakers, films that do secure a theatrical release are typically—although not always—those that have a greater visibility to audiences writ large, and to scholars who have greater access to those titles. Unfortunately, the preceding criteria exclude some fascinating films, such as William Greaves's *Symbiopsychotaxiplasm* (1968) and Robert Townsend's made-for-TV biopic *10,000 Black Men Named George* (2002), about the union activist A. Philip Randolph. Fourth, the films included here are all U.S.-based productions. Every nation-state has its own sets of opportunities and challenges when it comes to financing, production, and distribution. In order to establish a common ground between the films for the sake of comparison, it seemed wise to focus on films produced in the United States, despite the fact that this criterion eliminates films such as Anthony Harvey's *The Dutchman* (1967) and Amma Asante's *Belle* (2014), both of which were produced in the United Kingdom. Finally, the films presented here stand apart from other black films released during the same time period, making interesting statements about the intersections of race, class, and gender.

The first part of this book focuses on individual films. Chapter 1 discusses the 1960s with Michael Roemer's *Nothing But a Man* (1964). *Man* provides audiences with a realistic account of the effects white supremacy can have on an individual and those around him, and articulates the divides along racial, class, gender, and generational lines to expose the effects of white supremacy on black folks in the United States. The chapter analyzes the messages the film conveys about race, class, and gender, and discusses how its themes continue to be relevant in the twenty-first century.

Chapter 2 moves into the 1970s with Mel Brooks's satire *Blazing Saddles*

(1974). While *Nothing But a Man* looks at the effects of white supremacy on black people in the UnBted States, *Blazing Saddles* seeks to examine the ways in which black people subvert white supremacy, a trait the film shares with many Blaxploitation films released during the same time period. The chapter discusses the ways in which *Blazing Saddles* calls attention to and mocks stereotypes about black men, how it uses the quintessential American genre, the Western, to critique American racism, and how the tenets of critical race theory can be used to read *Saddles'* subversive racial politics.

Chapter 3 moves into the 1980s; while this was arguably the decade of Eddie Murphy, the one film of his that has received little critical analysis is *Harlem Nights* (1989). Widely considered to be both a critical and box-office failure, the film is not usually brought up in discussions of the 1980s black film renaissance. One of the unique aspects of the film was that it featured three generations of black comedians—Murphy, Redd Foxx, and Richard Pryor—and was grounded in black comedic stylings. Unfortunately, white audiences, who were used to seeing Murphy alongside white costars, were not impressed with *Nights* and its predominately black cast. (Murphy's film *Coming to America*, released the previous year, also received a lukewarm reception from critics.) Because *Nights* was framed as a failure, the film has not been discussed in terms of the messages it sends to the audience. As it stands, the gender politics of the film are quite complicated. The chapter uses black feminist thought to discuss the female characters in the film, all of whom use or are defined by their sexuality, and to ask whether this is an empowering step forward for representations of black women, or a misogynistic step backward.

In the 1990s the black film renaissance, dubbed New Black Realism, was predicated on films that focused on black poverty, gangs, and drug culture, such as *Boyz n the Hood* (1991), *New Jack City* (1991), *Juice* (1992), and *Menace II Society* (1993). Charles Burnett's *The Glass Shield* (1994) takes the critiques of the justice system contained in New Black Realism and subverts them by removing black criminality from the equation and making the primary protagonist a black police officer. Chapter 4 analyzes what *The Glass Shield* brings to the table in terms of our perception and understanding of how and why violence against black bodies by law enforcement continues to occur. The chapter considers what factors contributed to the film's lack of acclaim and visibility, how its tone and subject matter relate to other black films released during the same time period, and how the film fits into a twenty-first-century discussion around Black Lives Matter, police violence against black bodies, and the racial bias not just of individual police officers but of the entire criminal justice apparatus.

Chapter 5 discusses the 2000s through the eyes of Kevin Willmott's *C.S.A.: The Confederate States of America* (2004). While *Nothing But a Man* and *The Glass Shield* are straightforward dramas and *Saddles* and *Harlem Nights* are over-the-top comedies, *Confederate States* is a mockumentary: a genre that uses a documentary style to present fictitious events. Willmott's film hypothesizes where the United States would be if the South had won the Civil War. The fact that many of the contemporary events presented in the film are not entirely fictitious adds to the humor and the horror of the film. The chapter analyzes how *C.S.A.* critiques and calls attention to racism, history, and popular culture's role in reinforcing the American racial project.

The chapters in the second part discuss multiple films in order to analyze characterizations and themes across time. The one aspect that all of the previously discussed films have in common is that the main protagonists are black men. In the twenty-first century, the number of films that feature black female protagonists, particularly in nuanced roles, is relatively low. Filmmaker Ava DuVernay has made it clear that she wants to focus on telling stories about black women, and her first two films, *I Will Follow* (2010) and *Middle of Nowhere* (2012), do just that. Chapter 6 analyzes what messages DuVernay's films send about black women, their circumstances, and their humanity, as well as how these women resist the controlling images usually placed on black female characters in Hollywood films.

Chapter 7 tackles Hall of Fame baseball player Jackie Robinson via the three filmic adaptations of his life: *The Jackie Robinson Story* (1950), *The Court-Martial of Jackie Robinson* (1990), and *42* (2013). The chapter analyzes the ways in which race and racism in the United States were framed at the time of each film's release.

Chapter 8 discusses black coming-of-age films. The teen film has been a Hollywood staple for several decades, arguably reaching its apex in the 1980s with the proliferation of John Hughes films such as *Sixteen Candles* (1984), *The Breakfast Club* (1985), and *Ferris Bueller's Day Off* (1986). There have been black coming-of-age films going back at least to *Cooley High* (1975); however, more contemporary black coming-of-age films that deal with black teenagers growing up in inner cities have been perceived more as gangsta films rather than teen films—see *Boyz n the Hood* or *Menace II Society*. That being said, there have been a handful of black coming-of-age films that focus on serious, yet less dire teenage angst and activities. The chapter will analyze three generations of such films: the Hudlin brothers' *House Party* (1990), Gina Prince-Bythewood's *Love & Basketball* (2000), and Dee Ree's *Pariah* (2011). We will use these to discuss the evolution of the genre and how the portrayal of black teenage life has evolved from the 1990s to the 2010s.

This book is an attempt to move the conversation forward, to show that black films can be analyzed from various points of view, and to highlight the fact that even films that look trivial on the face can be read in profound ways. Each of the films discussed here makes compelling statements about the intersections of race, class, gender, and sexual orientation. By analyzing these films, we can gain a sense of how portrayals of black folks, race relations, and racism have evolved over the course of six decades; help maneuver the study of black film away from the margins and closer to the mainstream of film studies; and broaden our ideas of what films are deemed worthy of discussion.

1

I Ain't Fit to Live with No More
Nothing But a Man Revisited

A film about civil rights that was made at the height of the modern civil rights movement and yet contains only oblique references to it? This is an interesting vision through which to consider the politics of history in a film that seemingly does not even acknowledge its own profoundly important historical context.
> David C. Wall and Michael T. Martin,
> *The Politics and Poetics of Black Film:*
> *Nothing But a Man*, 2015

In a world filled with the literal and physical signs of discrimination and apartheid, the system doesn't always have to be expressed or made visible in order to be enforced. Everyone already knows his or her place within the hierarchy. The behavior we see in our characters reflects the social forces that we don't see.
> Robert Young, *The Politics and Poetics*
> *of Black Film: Nothing But a Man*, 2015

The 1960s ushered in an age of "black-themed movies—movies featuring storylines about the lives of black people and the challenges facing black communities."[1] After decades of writing black characters as stereotypes and caricatures, or ignoring black actors and the nation's system of racial apartheid altogether, Hollywood films were beginning to present more complex black characters and attempting to continue the racial discussions that were playing out in the streets and on television sets across the United States as the civil rights movement gained momentum. While these films were steps forward in terms of representation, "they tout[ed] integration and social assimilation for blacks largely in terms that were palatable to dominant white tastes."[2] Some of the most influential films of the 1960s conform to these ideas, including *To Kill a Mockingbird* (1962), *The Dutchman* (1967), and *The Learning Tree* (1969) as well as an assortment of Sidney Poitier features including *A Raisin in the Sun* (1961), *In the Heat of the Night* (1967), and *Guess Who's Coming to Dinner* (1967). These films addressed race and racism head-on, and in many cases were unapologetic in their analysis that racism was a significant problem that needed to be dealt with.

At the same time, in the majority of these films black characters were required to share a large portion of the narrative with white characters. In Norman Jewison's *In the Heat of the Night*, while Sidney Poitier's Virgil Tibbs initiates the slap heard 'round the world to protect his honor, it was Rod Steiger's performance as Gillespie, the bigot who overcomes his racism to solve a murder, that won the Oscar for Best Actor. The character of Tibbs is more educated and forthright than the character of Homer Smith in *Lilies of the Field*, which Poitier won the Oscar for in 1963. Most of the narrative space in *Guess Who's Coming to Dinner* focuses on Spencer Tracy's and Katherine Hepburn's characters as the blindsided parents of a daughter engaged to be married to a black doctor. Though *To Kill a Mockingbird* focuses on the trial of Tom Robinson, played by Brock Peters, the main protagonist of the story is Atticus Finch, the lawyer who represents Robinson; Gregory Peck won an Oscar for this performance. Douglas Petrie's *A Raisin in the Sun*, Gordon Parks's *The Learning Tree*, and Jules Dassin's *Uptight* (1968) engaged in questions of race and racism, and all could be classified both as racially significant films and genuine black films because they reserved the majority of the narrative for black characters and allowed those black characters "to directly influence and change the circumstances within a story and survive the outcome of those circumstances."[3] Unfortunately, the films that provided significant narrative space for black characters did not receive the same critical acclaim as the films that revolved around white characters.

Another film that fits the description but is usually left off the list of racially significant films that focus primarily on black characters is Michael Roemer's *Nothing But a Man*. Though *Man* won the San Giorgio prize at the Venice Film Festival in 1964, an award given to films "considered especially important for the progress of civilization," because it was independently financed, it was marketed as an art film and received minimal distribution.[4]

Roemer has argued that the film was dismissed because "white audiences weren't interested in what they viewed as a depressing story about blacks in the South."[5] According to Robert Young, one of the writers and producers of the film, "The distributor wouldn't allow us to put photos of the cast in the ads . . . they wanted *Nothing But a Man* to be seen as an art film, which was to ghettoize it."[6] Instead, the Greek masks symbolizing comedy and tragedy were used in the film's posters.[7] Roemer remembered talking to an exhibitor in Philadelphia about why *Man* was only being shown in the suburbs, and the exhibitor informed him that black audiences were not wanted in city theaters.[8] Because *Man* was released before Hollywood actively courted black film audiences, it was not until it was later released on 16mm that black audiences found this film through rentals to schools, churches, and community centers.[9] Still, *Nothing But a Man* seemed destined to obscurity.

Thankfully, in 1993 *Nothing But a Man* was rediscovered by mainstream audiences; the film was restored and began touring the black film festival circuit. Hal Hinson of the *Washington Post* remarked that "it may be that the best film to come out so far in 1993 was actually made in 1964."[10] *Man* was placed on the National Film Registry in 1994 and later received a fortieth anniversary DVD release. In 2012, *Black Camera, an International Film Journal* devoted a special issue to discussing the film. In 2013, a newly restored 35mm print of the film began showing around the world and even more people began speaking up about the film. Oscar-winning editor Richard Chew commented, "I saw this film that made a monumental impact on me called *Nothing But a Man* [and] when I saw it I realized film could be a social document, like a novel; it could tell you something about the society you live in and that's what appealed to me."[11] Director Ira Sachs brought up *Man* in a 2014 interview when he was asked if there were any films that had the same feel as his work *Love Is Strange*. He answered: "There is a movie called *Nothing But a Man* from the mid-1960s. It's about an African-American couple who get married in the south, and the film follows how the marriage dissolves. So much of it seems as if their love is corroded by the culture they live in."[12]

Even though *Nothing But a Man* did not have mainstream success when it was released, it clearly had an impact on those who were able to view it. This chapter will discuss *Nothing But a Man* using elements of black feminist thought and critical race theory to analyze which messages it conveys about race, class, and gender. Though it is not framed as being as explicit as other racial message films produced during the 1960s, it touches on many themes that continue to be relevant in the twenty-first century.

Famed sociologist William Julius Wilson begins his text *The Declining Significance of Race: Blacks and Changing American Institutions* by arguing that in contemporary American society, "The life chances of individual blacks have more to do with their economic class position than with their day-to-day encounters with whites."[13] While that may have been the case when Wilson wrote his text in 1978, *Nothing But a Man* links the main character's interaction with whites and his socioeconomic class position, and argues that the two could not be separated in the 1960s. *Man* opens with the sights and sounds of the working-class world: the sound of jackhammers punctuates the image of men driving spikes and laying and removing railroad tracks. The audience is introduced to Duff (Ivan Dixon), a veteran who served in Japan, presumably during the Korean War, and who now works as a section hand on the railroad. Duff and his coworkers, including Frankie (Leonard Parker) and Jocko (Yaphet Kotto), live in a cramped barracks without indoor plumbing, where they play cards and checkers with homemade pieces. Their idea of a night out consists of a visit to the local bar, where they are on a first-name basis with the local prostitute, Doris (Helene Arrindell). In the next scene, the rail worker's existence is contrasted with the immaculately dressed congregants at a local church. The middle-class status of the church members is highlighted by the clothing and jewelry adorning the female parishioners. Duff politely crashes the church's evening picnic and meets Josie (Abbey Lincoln), the preacher's daughter. There's an immediate attraction between the two, although Duff acknowledges the difference in their socioeconomic status right away when Josie mentions that's she's a teacher; his response is "Oh, you've been to college," and he prefaces asking her out on a date with, "Well, I don't know what you've been told about section hands." The presumptions based on class continue later in the film as Josie's father and stepmother express their disapproval with Josie's growing relationship with Duff. According to Josie's father, Reverend Dawson (Stanley Greene), "Well, we have a position in town, Josie; we have to remember that. There are lots of other young men." Her stepmother Susan chastises Josie by remarking, "There's just one thing you can be looking for in a man like that."

It would be easy to assume that such class animosity exists only in the middle-class black communities who look down upon their working-class counterparts, but *Man* shows that the assumptions based on class come from all directions. During their first date, Duff asks Josie, "Are you slumming or something?" to which Josie responds, "You don't think much of yourself, do you?" Even Duff buys into the notion that romantic relationships should not cross socioeconomic class lines. In his eyes, middle-class people would obviously be dating beneath themselves if they went out with working-class partners, and therefore, even though Josie does not see economics as a roadblock to their relationship, she does acknowledge their differences when she finally answers Duff's question of why she goes out with him with the remark: "Most of the men I know, they're kinda sad. When I met you the other day I had the feeling you were different." In the same way that Duff assumes Josie has heard negative stories about section hands due to their occupation and class, Josie plays into a characterization of middle-class black men being sad or somehow not black enough. Judging a person's blackness based on socioeconomic class is not a new phenomenon; "poor and working-class Black culture [has been] routinely depicted as being 'authentically' Black whereas middle- and upper-middle class Black culture was seen as less so."[14] This discussion surrounding who is black enough plays itself out later when Duff implies that he has had the more authentic black experience because of his class status, telling Josie she's "never been a nigger" because of her middle-class upbringing. While race is inextricably linked to class, it would be a mistake to assume, as Duff does, that white supremacy is only experienced by poor and working-class black communities, particularly during a time period when de jure segregation forced all black citizens, regardless of their education or socioeconomic status, into the same communities and subjected them to the same virulent racism. Josie's reaction to Duff's comment shows the audience just how inaccurate she thinks it is.

Old School v. New School

Socioeconomic class isn't the only basis for the intraracial conflict present in *Man*. Though the effects of racism are at the heart of *Nothing But a Man*, the film also highlights the growing generational divide that occurs whenever members of the next generation reach the point when they can advocate for their own agenda. During the 1950s, while many older blacks chose to exist under the status quo, some younger blacks were not interested in simply surviving under Jim and Jane Crow: they wanted to upend the status quo. Reverend Dawson certainly fits into the category of the older black generation that existed in survival mode, while Duff seems to want more—whether he verbalizes it or not. Though Duff does not come across as someone who would actively participate in civil rights demonstrations, this is not a knock against him, because it is clear that he possesses not only racial consciousness but class consciousness as well. As a character,

Duff sees the inequalities, is not content with those inequalities, and also seems to understand how to challenge those inequalities. At the same time, his words and actions characterize a person who either does not believe in himself enough to realize that he is capable of enacting change, or someone who does not believe that change can come from the grassroots.

After Duff and Josie are married, Duff stops working for the railroad and takes a job at the local mill. Duff quickly witnesses the intersection of race and class at his new job when, during a lunch break, a white worker boldly takes a piece of a black worker's sandwich out of his hands without asking. The older black worker, Barney (Alfred Puryear), says and does nothing as he watches the white worker eat his sandwich and verbally insult him. After learning that Barney has four kids, the white worker remarks that Barney's wife "can cook, too. Now it's no wonder you've been dragging your tail on the job; you've been doing your best work at home." Barney simply looks down at the floor and the camera shifts to Duff, who is annoyed by the situation but continues to eat his lunch. The white worker turns his attention to Duff and they exchange words:

> WHITE WORKER: What's the matter, boy? Don't you ever smile?
> DUFF: I smile when it's funny.
> WHITE WORKER: It wasn't funny, huh? Well, I thought it was. What do you say, Barney, wasn't it funny?
> BARNEY: Yeah, it was funny.
> WHITE WORKER: Sure, what do you say, boys? Wasn't it funny?
> BLACK WORKER: Sure, yeah.
> WHITE WORKER: The trouble with you, boy, is you ain't got no sense of humor. You oughta smile more.
> DUFF: I know.

When the white worker leaves, the other black workers lecture Duff on how to survive; he is told to watch himself and to "act [like] a nigger," suggestions that Duff finds reprehensible. He responds by saying, "If you fellas stuck together instead of letting them walk all over you, they might not try it." This strategy almost certainly worked for the railroad workers, as we do not witness any racial hostilities in their workplace and it is mentioned that the section hands make a good living. Unfortunately, the strategy does not work in Duff's new workplace; he is fired for even suggesting that the workers unionize, and then is blacklisted from the other mills in town because he is seen as a union agitator and troublemaker. The backlash that

Duff encounters from the black workers regarding unionizing and racial solidarity highlights "the obstacles to and the possibilities for mobilizing black opposition to white supremacy"[15] and promotes ideals forwarded by union organizer and civil rights activist A. Philip Randolph.

While it was easy for Duff to suggest mobilization as a method to combat racism because he had seen it work before, it proved far more difficult to actually convince people that solidarity was worth the risk, especially because the whites of the town viewed blacks as "expendable capital—a workforce that may be put aside if broken (read: standing up for themselves) or causing trouble (read: being vocally political),"[16] and because the black workers knew exactly what was at stake—which is why at least one of them sold Duff out to the white bosses. Duff was the sacrificial lamb used to ensure that the other black workers would keep their jobs and be left alone, although by all accounts, the black workers will continue to experience harassment regardless of Duff's presence.

The roadblocks preventing Duff from achieving sustainable employment lead to one of the most poignant moments in the film. Reverend Dawson visits Duff's and Josie's home to discuss the couple's future in light of the fact that Duff has been unable to secure steady employment. Though most of the film is played in wide and medium shots, most of this scene consists of close-ups. The camera remains still through most of the scene—there are no sweeping camera movements. Instead of using the traditional shot/reverse-shot setup, the scene plays out in longer takes that heighten the intensity between the characters. The scene cuts between Duff's and Dawson's conversation and Josie's activities in the kitchen. In the beginning, Duff is sitting while Reverend Dawson stands and takes up most of the frame. Duff seems small, as he is at a loss to explain how he is going to support his family, and he jokes about robbing a bank. Eventually, as the conversation becomes more heated, Duff stands, and he insults Reverend Dawson by calling him "a white man's nigger." After that exchange, it is now Duff who takes up more of the frame, and the reverend who appears small because Duff's assessment is at least partially correct. Earlier in the film, Josie has told Duff that a lynching took place in town eight years prior, and, while Reverend Dawson knew who participated, he did not reveal that information. The camera now cuts to an extreme close-up of the reverend's face as Duff tells him, "You been stooping for so long you don't even know how to stand straight no more. You're just half a man." The reverend's face is full of anger at what Duff says, but also sadness because, again, the statement is not entirely without merit. Earlier in the film we see the white school superintendent enlist Dawson to talk a black family out of suing for their child to attend the white school. In exchange for Dawson's cooperation, the superintendent agrees to talk to the mayor about building a new school for black children. Dawson knows this is not right—the film is set nearly ten years after the U.S. Supreme Court ruled that separate educational facilities were unconstitutional—but he tells Duff, "You've got to go slow," because the town has not had any problems for eight years, a reference to the lynching. The scene continues with a cut to a close-up shot of Josie kneeling on the kitchen floor, crying. The audience does not know whether she is crying because she cut her finger on a shard of glass she is picking up off the floor, or because of the conversation occurring in the living room—presumably it is a combination of the two.

The generational conflict exists not only between Duff and Reverend Dawson but also between Duff and his estranged father. The often-quoted phrase "Those who do not know history are destined to repeat it" best sums up Duff's relationships with his family. The audience casually learns that Duff has a four-year-old son, James Lee, living in Birmingham, whom he has not seen in a few years. Whether it is finally being in closer proximity to the boy or Josie's influence, Duff visits James Lee only to learn that his mother has abandoned him to the care of a neighbor who can scarcely afford to take care of her own children. Seeing James Lee prompts Duff to visit his own father Will (Julius Harris), who also abandoned him as a child. Meeting Will and his girlfriend Lee (Gloria Foster) provides the catalyst for Duff to change his behavior and gives the audience a glimpse of how badly Duff's and Josie's relationship could turn out if Duff is not able to find a job. One could write this off as yet another portrayal of a dysfunctional black family, marred in what Daniel Patrick Moynihan described as the "tangle of pathology,"[17] but, again, it is not that simple. Unfortunately, most discussions of Moynihan's analysis place the blame for female-headed households squarely on the shoulders of black women. According to black feminist theorist Patricia Hill Collins:

> The Black matriarchy thesis argued that African American women who failed to fulfill their traditional "womanly" duties at home contributed to social problems in Black civil society. . . . As overly aggressive, unfeminine women, Black matriarchs allegedly emasculated their lovers and husbands. These men, understandably,

either deserted their partners or refused to marry the mothers of their children. From the dominant group's perspective, the matriarch represented a failed mammy, a negative stigma to be applied to African-American women who dared reject the image of the submissive, hardworking servant.[18]

That is not the scenario that happens here. Josie can be described using a myriad of adjectives, but aggressive, unfeminine, and emasculating do not apply. In fact, Josie tries to create a two-parent family by suggesting, before they are even married, that Duff's son should come live with them. Suffice to say, neither the relationship between Josie and Duff nor the relationship between Lee and Will fails due to a stereotypical caricature of a domineering black woman. In fact, going back to director Ira Sachs's comments about the film, these romantic relationships fail not because of individual choices or some sort of pathology inherent to black communities, but because white supremacist *society* has failed black communities, making it difficult to sustain healthy and functional relationships.

Returning to Duff's relationship with Will, it would be an understatement to call their initial meeting brief and acrimonious. When Will, Duff, and Lee arrive at the local bar, Will immediately demands to know what Duff wants from him. When Lee stands up for Duff, Will switches to a tirade about women only wanting money from men—an observation particularly ironic since the audience already knows that Will has been unemployed for several months due to a work-related accident, meaning Lee must be supporting him financially. As a final insult, Will makes a brief mention of Duff's mother having a relationship with the white man she worked for, but Lee stops that train of thought before Will can lash out any further. The symmetry in Will's comment is apparent because when Duff told Josie about his son James Lee, he also made a passing mention that he did not completely believe that James Lee was his son. It becomes obvious that Will's behavior is not new—Lee seems more exhausted than surprised by his verbal abuse. John Nickel, author of "Disabling African American Men: Liberalism and Race Message Films," makes the argument that *Nothing But a Man* presents Will as "a black body out of control and dangerously diseased, an image reinforced by his disability."[19] On the contrary, Will appears less like an out-of-control and dangerous black man and more like a black man who is broken physically, mentally, and emotionally. While Reverend Dawson deals with racism by collaborating with those in power in an effort to secure a sliver of safety for his family and effect small changes on behalf of his community, Will's response is to dull the pain with alcohol and to lash out at those closest to him. Again, the audience does not know if Will's alcohol abuse began before or after his accident, though Lee's remark that "he's been hitting it pretty hard" implies that he drank before the accident, and that it served as an impetus to increase his destructive behavior. Seeing Will's condition provides a catalyst for two major choices Duff makes in an effort to not end up like his father. First, it is after meeting Will for the first time that Duff asks Josie to marry him, and second, it is after watching his father die that Duff returns to Josie with his son.

White Supremacy, Patriarchy, and Power

While the racism Duff experiences is clearly the main driving force of the film, it is through his relationship with Josie that the audience witnesses the emotional and psychological effects of racism. Despite the fact that *Man's* main protagonist is Duff, there is plenty of room for Josie within the narrative. Most mainstream Hollywood films have created black female characters who were "maids, mammies, mulattoes, and mistresses. At best, they were cast as entertainers—singers, dancers, and musicians—and only that,"[20] and most of these characters were never fully formed individuals. That is not the case with Josie, despite the fact that her primary function in the film seems to be to frame Duff's evolution. Though the first ten minutes of the film focus solely on class conflicts within black communities, it does not take long for the subject matter to shift slightly. Toward the end of their first date, Duff and Josie retreat to Frankie's car, where two white men accost them by shining flashlights in their faces and on Josie's breasts. The tension and danger introduced by the assailants is palpable and made even bolder due to the fact that the assault takes place close enough to the bar that the audience can faintly hear the upbeat Motown music coming from the jukebox. The upbeat and cheerful emotions conveyed by Stevie Wonder's "Fingertips" at the beginning of the scene are diametrically opposed to the emotions being expressed by Duff and Josie while they are being harassed. The only reason the white perpetrators do not attempt physical and/or sexual assault is because they recognize Josie and do not want the high-profile trouble that could come from attacking the daughter of a well-known minister, who obviously has powerful white friends.[21] The scene ends with Duff putting away his well-hidden switchblade and remarking, "They don't sound human, do they?" As with the scene between Duff and Reverend

Dawson, the interpretation of the ending of the date scene is complicated. On the one hand, audiences are relieved to know that Duff was prepared to defend himself and Josie against the racist assailants if the confrontation had become physical. On the other hand, the fact that Duff was armed could also mean that the situation could have escalated rapidly and ended more violently than originally feared.

Though the confrontation discussed above is a matter of race, gender, and power, all of the subsequent confrontations highlight the intersection of race and class. Duff knows what he must do to find employment; the black mill workers make it explicitly clear that acting like a nigger is required, but there are lines that Duff is not willing to cross even if it means not being financially viable. Unfortunately, Duff "equates his masculinity with being able to work and support his family. Without work, he feels he is nothing, not even a man."[22]

This connection between economics and social justice was made explicit during the civil rights movement. Before he was assassinated, Dr. Martin Luther King Jr. was in Memphis supporting striking sanitation workers in their effort to obtain better wages and working conditions. While there, King called on black communities to boycott businesses with unfair labor practices; he paraphrased fellow activist Jesse Jackson when he said, "Only the garbage men have been feeling pain; now we must kind of redistribute the pain."[23] Though King is often framed as being diametrically opposed to Malcolm X, the latter espouses a similar ideal in his famous "Ballot or Bullet" speech when he points out that "Once you can create some—some employment in the community where you live it will eliminate the necessity of you and me having to act ignorantly and disgracefully, boycotting and picketing some 'cracker' someplace else trying to beg him for a job. Anytime you have to rely upon your enemy for a job, you're in bad shape."[24] Both men understood the importance of economic stability to the larger fight for human rights and for an individual's sense of self.

In the film, Duff's frustration arises out of his "inability to hold a job in a white-controlled environment and still assert his right as an equal human being," and this frustration builds over the course of the film even though "it is the racism that Duff suffers that challenges or confronts his notions of what it means to be a 'man' and forces him to consider what that means."[25] As mentioned earlier, Duff's father, Will, copes with racial and economic oppression by lashing out at the people closest to him—particularly Lee, a woman who by all accounts understands the reasons for his behavior and tries to be supportive. Unfortunately for Josie, as the stress mounts, Duff begins to emulate his father's behavior and directs his anger and frustration toward her. Throughout the remainder of the film, the scenes alternate between Josie's and Duff's conversations and the racism Duff encounters. After a scene that contains a montage of shots showing Duff being rejected for work, the film cuts to a scene of Duff and Josie on their back porch, discussing their financial situation. The scene begins with a close-up of Josie, who shows understanding of how gender impacts economic opportunities as she tells Duff, "It's not as hard on a girl; they're not afraid of us." From there the camera switches to a two-shot so the audience can see that Josie and Duff are in close proximity to each other; they are on the same page, so to speak. While Josie explains that they have enough money to last for a while, it looks like Duff is trying to fix a chair. The action moves to the traditional shot/reverse-shot as Josie suggests that she could do day work after their baby is born, an idea Duff rejects. As he describes the way he sees white people looking at Josie, the camera moves back into a wide shot to show Duff suddenly take an ax and break the chair. Josie is startled and jumps up. Now there is a distance between them that was not present in the earlier two-shot. When Josie attempts to walk away, Duff grabs her and the camera moves in closer to the couple. They are close together, facing each other, as Josie explains, "I can't stand to see you like that; I know you can't help it;" to which Duff replies, "Stop being so damn understanding." The scene ends with a close-up of Duff as he walks down and out of the frame. This is the first scene where the audience witnesses Duff emulating his father's behavior. The downward trajectory Duff takes to exit the frame signals the beginning of his spiral out of control.

Another interesting aspect to this scene is the fact that while Josie understands that the socioeconomic impact of racism was felt most directly by black men, Duff acknowledges the added burden of sexual violence that black women were often subjected to, explaining why he is opposed to her working as a domestic. Even if the film does not say so outright, it highlights the fact that white supremacy is intersectional in that it affects people differently based on gender and socioeconomic class. As such, the film "features labor and gender politics as key elements both of racial subordination and liberation."[26] While the concept of intersectionality is almost a given in the twenty-first century, to see it play out in a film from the 1960s is quite progressive.

The next discussion between Duff and Josie is even more heated and is

Josie and Duff

preceded by the "half a man" confrontation with Reverend Dawson discussed earlier in this chapter. The scene, which lasts for a little over one minute, is a two-shot done in one take with Josie and Duff sitting close to one another; again, they are on the same page at the beginning of the scene. While Duff is looking directly at Josie, she is looking down, filing her nails—Duff is taking up more room in the frame than she is. Josie explains that she is not afraid of white people, because "They can't touch me inside." Duff stands up, again moving away from Josie in the moments before he lashes out with, "Like hell they can't. They can reach right in with their big white hands and turn you off and on." Josie is in the foreground of the shot, but since Duff is standing, he towers over her as he tells her to shut her mouth. With her back turned to Duff, Josie continues to look down while Duff walks away. Because both Josie and Duff remain in frame throughout the entire scene without any cuts, "The threads of power and violation [are] spread out before the viewer, with no evasion, no faces hidden, no obliquely angled reaction shot to serve as a screen."[27] The framing is also very tight, showing that neither of them have any room to maneuver; "Their response is resolutely to avoid seeing each other see the other. Once again Josie is afraid, but now she is deeply alone, even by Duff's side."[28]

Josie tries to offer comfort and methods of coping internally with white supremacy, but Duff rejects both.

When Duff discusses the white community's ability to turn him on and off, he is not talking solely about physical violence: the only physical and potentially violent confrontation that has occurred at this point in the film is during his first date with Josie. Instead, he is talking about economic violence; a type of violence described by critical race theorist Derrick Bell, who writes: "A major function of racial discrimination is to facilitate the exploitation of black labor, to deny us access to benefits and opportunities that would otherwise be available, and to blame all the manifestations of exclusion-bred despair on the asserted inferiority of the victims."[29] The economic violence is in addition to verbal violence, where hearing racial insults "is like receiving a slap in the face. The injury is instantaneous."[30] Duff's manhood is continually challenged not only by closing off his ability to work but by the fact that everyone calls him "boy," including his father and father-in-law, two men who arguably should know better. In Charles Lawrence III's discussion on regulating racist speech, he points out the fact that "many victims do not find words of response until well after the assault when the cowardly assaulter has departed." This is what happens to Duff: we see that he wants to respond to the assaults as they occur, but, given the nature of white supremacy, particularly in the South at that time, Duff cannot respond in the moment given the possibility of fatal consequences, and unfortunately, he responds by inflicting similar verbal abuse on Josie, the one person in the film who arguably has even less power than Duff has.[31] The irony here is that despite her education, Josie's economic options are just as constrained and subject to the whims of patriarchal white supremacy as Duff's; in his anger, however, he cannot recognize their shared fate. At the same time, Josie does not recognize that because of her gender and economic status, her experiences do not directly compare to Duff's, and her coping mechanisms may not be appropriate for him. Roemer highlights the idea that "the man who has no way of supporting his family turns his violence against those who are closest to him and against himself."[32]

Duff's and Josie's final confrontation occurs after a group of white patrons verbally threaten Duff, and also Josie, though she is not present, by saying "I bet she's a sly little nigger. I wouldn't mind a piece of that myself," and threaten to burn down the gas station where Duff works if he is not fired immediately. Similar to the date scene, the incident nearly escalates to physical violence; however, this time Duff is no longer willing to simply accept the verbal attacks without responding. Duff is despondent over being fired from the job Reverend Dawson arranged for him, as well as the verbal harassment he has endured at the gas station. Again, when he goes home, Duff lashes out at the person who has even less power than he does, Josie. She explains that she loves him, and Duff's only response is to push her to the ground. We switch to a close-up of Duff's face, where the audience sees a mixture of anger and horror over what he's done. Going to the traditional shot/reverse-shot, we switch to Josie on the floor crying. After Duff leaves the room, the camera stays on Josie as she picks herself off the floor. The shot dissolves to another image of Josie lying on the bed with Duff packing a bag in the background. Duff does not look at Josie or the camera as he explains, "I ain't fit to live with no more. It's just like a lynching; maybe they don't use a knife on you, but they got other ways." Duff exits the room, and the scene ends with a wide shot of Josie alone on the bed. The scenes between Duff and Josie, as the former continues to endure the onslaught of racism, highlight film philosopher Noel Carroll's argument that Man shows "how racism causes conditions in which self-destruction and cruelty flourish."[33] Duff's comments also link racist acts of physical violence and racist acts of verbal and/or psychological violence, and Carroll makes the argument that the latter can be just as effective as the former. Though this film was released roughly ten years before the phrase "racial microaggressions" came into prominence, Duff is nevertheless referencing the idea that "brief and everyday slights, insults, indignities and denigrating messages" or "conscious and intentional discriminatory actions: using racial epithets, displaying White supremacist symbols," which psychologist Derald Wing Sue defines as microassaults, are "potentially more harmful because of their invisibility."[34] A lynching is a physical act of terror designed to intimidate black communities into submission. The suppression of economic choices, verbal harassment, and microaggressions all serve the exact same purpose.

Can We Live Happily Ever After?

At this point, much of the discussion about Nothing But a Man has focused on Duff, but it is equally important to spend some time analyzing Josie. Contemporary reviews of Man describe Josie as "sheltered," "sweet, idealistic," "understanding," and "demure but strong-willed," and, while each of those descriptions has some modicum of truth, they also seem lacking.[35] While the vast majority of the themes and situations in this film appear to be relatively straightforward, Josie's characterization is more difficult to frame. On the one hand, Josie comes across as "a Black woman who actually understood the plight of her husband. She understood what it meant to be a Black man in America. She stood by her man."[36] This portrayal is a welcome change of pace from the contemporary controlling images of black women who are portrayed as "bitches [who are] aggressive, loud, rude, and pushy."[37] On the other hand, while being supportive of one's romantic partner is certainly noble, a portrayal that advocates staying with an abusive partner is problematic. During screenings of this film, there is a palpable shift in mood in the audience when Duff tells Josie to shut her mouth, and there are usually audible gasps when he pushes her to the floor. Thankfully, Duff has the presence of mind to recognize the escalating abuse and to remove himself from the situation. If Duff and Josie's relationship had continued on the trajectory in which it was headed, it is likely that Josie would have become a mirror image of Lee, who has been described as a "long-suffering woman who understands [Will], sometimes to her regret."[38]

It is not until the end of the film that Lee shows any emotion. When Duff leaves Josie because he's "not fit to live with no more," he visits Will and Lee, where we see Will in what looks like a drunken stupor. When Will goes to take a drink, he drops the glass, and, as he begins to fall down, Lee grabs him and pushes him onto the bed. She violently lunges across his body, demanding that he lay down and get some sleep, and quietly sobs as she stoops to pick up the broken glass—a shot that mirrors an earlier one of Josie doing the same thing. Lee is clearly frustrated by the situation that has, in her words, been going on for days, and, like almost every other black character in the film, she feels trapped. The audience does not know why Lee chooses to stay with Will. It is not out of financial necessity, since she is the sole breadwinner in the home; they are not married and do not have any children. Arguably, much like Josie, Lee understands the effect white supremacy has had on Will and she neither wants to contribute to that effect nor does she want to abandon him. On the one hand, Lee represents the "strong black woman" controlling image in that:

> She confronts all trials and tribulations. She is a source of unlimited support for her family. She is a motivated, hardworking breadwinner. She is always prepared to do what needs to be done for her family and her people. She is sacrificial and smart. She suppresses her emotional needs while anticipating those of others. She has an irrepressible spirit that is unbroken by a legacy of oppression, poverty, and rejection.[39]

The strong black woman image can seem like an improvement from the mammy, jezebel, and sapphire images that proliferated popular culture previously; however, like these, the strong black woman also has real-world consequences in that "her titanic strength does violence to the spirits of black women when it becomes an imperative for their daily lives. When seeking help means showing unacceptable weakness, actual black women, unlike their mythical counterpart, face depression, anxiety, and loneliness."[40] Toward the end of the film, Lee departs slightly from the strong black woman image by showing the audience the consequences of her life with Will as she hints at her motivations for staying with him. In her final conversation with Duff after Will's death, Lee invites Duff to stay with her until he gets back on his feet. Lee tells Duff and the audience, "It's just that I hate empty rooms." While black women are often portrayed as independent superwomen, Lee's statement portrays a loneliness that is rarely seen in characterizations of black women within popular culture. Yes, Lee could have lived without Will; she simply chose not to for her own emotional reasons. Both Lee and Josie are complicated characters, though we have to ask ourselves where the line is drawn between being supportive and being a victim.

While this chapter has spent the last several pages pointing out everything that was wrong with Josie's and Duff's relationship, what the beginning of Nothing But a Man did show was a loving relationship: "a Black woman and a Black man who actually loved one another [and] Hollywood had never done that before."[41] Writer-Director Ava DuVernay called the film "my personal cinematic inspiration" because "It's one of the rare films that shows black love steeped in honesty and hardship and everyday beauty."[42] In discussing the difference between "chick flicks" and romance films, one reviewer points to Nothing But a Man as an example of the latter by writing, "The film is about a lot of things—the psychological and emotional toll of racism, and just being black in America. But at the core of the film, is a love story. Actually . . . the 2 leads are totally wrong for each other. But they see that each other has something in them that they desperately need."[43] After they are married, Josie cooks dinner, and Duff playfully sniffs the food and says, "Smells like something crawled up there and died." While this could come across as mean-spirited, Ivan Dixon just barely maintains a straight face while delivering the line, and, directly afterward, the couple embraces and he admits, "You're the best thing that ever happened to me." The playfulness continues as Duff teaches Josie how to box in their back yard; to underscore the lightheartedness of the scene, Mary Wells's "You Beat Me to the Punch"

Happily married Duff and Josie

is playing in the background. The fun is interrupted by Barney, the man whose sandwich was eaten by the white mill worker, looking down as his wife yells at him, but, instead of ending on that dire note, the scene continues by showing Josie and Duff in bed together. Again, the film shows a physical intimacy between black characters that was rare in films of this era.

In a sense, the "narrative [focuses on] those heartbreakingly commonplace situations of married couples everywhere: the courtship, marriage, new home (or shack), the quarrel, separation and reunion, and the imminent baby."[44] This does not mean that Duff and Josie were conceived as characters that just happen to be black; on the contrary, producer Robert Young mentions that "one thing that was so surprising to me was the reactions of some [white] people. The scene that got them the most was Ivan and Abbey in the kitchen and in the bedroom. They couldn't imagine that black people are the same as white people in intimate situations."[45] By showing how happy and stable their relationship was in the beginning, the film allowed audiences to witness a first-hand account of the psychological effects and economic consequences that white supremacy has on individuals and families. The film locates the dysfunction associated with black families within larger racist societal forces and not with individual black people.

At the end of the film, Duff does not have any solutions to the problems he faces; all he can do is be the best man he can be given the circumstances. Visiting his father for the second time cements Duff's fate. Duff and Lee believe they are witnessing yet another drunken stupor; unfortunately, by the time they realize that Will needs medical attention, it is too late, and Will dies in the back seat of Duff's car on the way to the hospital. Though the film does not come out and say it, Will does not drink himself to death as many believe.[46] Julius Harris's subtle performance shows a man who is having a stroke: on two occasions in the scene he grasps the back of his head, and, when Lee moves off him, he whispers, "I couldn't get the words out before." When discussing arrangements with the funeral director, Duff realizes that he doesn't know where his father was born or how old he is. Realizing that he does not want to end up the same way, Duff decides to "make me some trouble in that town." When Lee says that they will simply run him out of town again, he provides the best and only answer he can give in this situation: "No, they won't." Duff collects his son and returns to Josie; the film ends with the couple embracing and Duff telling Josie, "It ain't gonna be easy, but it will be okay. I feel so free inside." This is not a happy ending in the traditional Hollywood sense, and some have said that it amounts to no ending at all.[47] The writers were cognizant of how polarizing the film's ending would be, but in the end, they felt having Duff return to Josie and stay in the South was the stronger decision:

> He's saying that if he has to chop cotton, "I'm going to chop cotton, but nobody is moving me out of this place. This is my woman and this is my place and I'm taking this kid whom I rejected, copping out that maybe he's not mine. But sure he's mine and I'm going to get him and we're going to be here, and you [white racists] are going to have to deal with us." That's prevailing. That's in a deep sense of prevailing . . . I'm nothing but a man. I'm a man and you're not running me out of here.[48]

While the audience has no idea whether or not Josie and Duff stay together or whether Duff is able to find steady employment without sacrificing his self-worth, there is hope that the pair will succeed. By ending with Duff and Josie together again, the film sends the message "that to sustain a marriage it is necessary to resist white supremacy."[49] In retrospect, that is an extremely heteronormative way of framing how resistance to white supremacy should look. Given the film's intersectional lens, it might be more progressive to interpret the film as saying that a family or a supportive and loving community of any kind is necessary to resist white supremacy.

When the film was originally released, author and educator Hoyt Fuller made the argument that *Man* "lets the White South off the hook. Its white villains are of the variety calculated to be irrelevant—hoodlums and straw bosses. The source of the viciousness which pinions the Negro hero against the wall is never probed, never even suggested."[50] However, the manner in which *Man* portrays white supremacy makes it far more relevant today than other films of the time period. First, the film captures "the daily indignities and larger psychic costs of racialization," a topic that is rarely addressed in mainstream popular culture.[51] Second, and probably more importantly, many people who were not alive during the 1960s have a very specific idea of what white supremacy looked like at that time: George Wallace standing on the Alabama Capitol steps declaring "segregation now, segregation tomorrow, segregation forever," dogs and fire hoses being used against children, lynchings, and other violent acts of state-sanctioned or state-excused terror. If that is one's primary definition of white supremacy, and because many of these particular acts are no longer acceptable in mainstream society, it becomes difficult to convince people that white supremacy still exists. But the reality of the situation is that structural, institutional, and individual acts of racism work together. Duff and Josie being harassed on their date by white hoodlums is an individual act (and in many ways a structural one, since the hoodlums probably would not harass black folks if they thought local law enforcement would stop them). Duff being fired from his job, despite the fact that he had been told that he was doing good work, is both institutional and individual (the foreman performs the individual act on behalf of the institution). Supervisors at the second mill readily admitting they need workers, but denying Duff because he has been blacklisted, is again institutional and individual (and structural, since this is before civil-rights and labor-law protections that would prohibit this type of action). By focusing on individual acts of degradation, *Man* does not let white supremacy off the hook; it is hiding in plain sight throughout the entire film, which is how white supremacy is able to continue in the real world. Also, as Judith E. Smith points out in her discussion of *Nothing But a Man*, by having the film end with Duff and Josie together and committed to a nuclear family structure, the film "clears away any alternative personal explanations for his fate, squarely blaming institutional forms of white supremacy for the black laboring man's condition."[52] Much like the film's treatment of white supremacy, which is visible though not overtly discussed throughout the film, structural racism is also dealt with, though again, the discussion is subtle yet pervasive.

Curtain Call

During the 1960s, Hollywood films began to study "the state of being black and finding fulfillment in the narrow confines determined by a hostile white world."[53] *Nothing But a Man* certainly fits that description. The film is not only an interesting example of a racial "significant film" from the 1960s, it also provides insight into how racism continues to operate in the present. *Man* articulates the divides along racial lines, class lines, gender lines, and generational lines to expose the effects of white supremacy on black folks in the United States and illustrates "the ways in which the southern economy's oppression of black life stifles outward resistance to the daily realities of segregation in the South."[54] The film does not give audiences a happily-ever-after ending, but it does end with a note of hope: hope that Duff and Josie's relationship will remain solid, and that they will be able to navigate the terrain of white supremacy without abusing each other or their children. This hope does not obscure the fact that "the major problem developed by the narrative—the incompatibility of sustaining a black household and maintaining one's self-esteem—has not been resolved."[55] *Man* does not present any feel-good solutions to the problems of race and class in the United States, making for a realistic if depressing tone. Other scholars have observed that it also declines to "provide a sympathetic white character as a point of identification for white audiences. It did not presume the goal of assimilation into white society. Instead the narrative incidents represented the obstacles to and the possibilities for mobilizing black opposition to white supremacy."[56] The truth of the matter is that we didn't have a solution for white supremacy then, and we don't have a solution now. Providing one would have been false, and this film is anything but false.

2

"Hey, Where Are the White Women At?"

The Presentation of Racism and Resistance in *Blazing Saddles*

Well, now, if that don't beat all. Here we take the good time and trouble to slaughter every last Indian in the West, and for what? So they can appoint a sheriff that's blacker than any Indian. I am depressed.

Blazing Saddles, 1974

You've got to remember that these are just simple farmers. These are people of the land. The common clay of the new West. You know—morons.

Blazing Saddles

In 1998, the American Film Institute (AFI) began commemorating 100 years of cinema, and as part of the celebration released its "100 Years" series, which sought to highlight the top 100 American films, reflecting a wide variety of categories. The list included *Citizen Kane* (1941), *Casablanca* (1942), and *The Godfather* (1972) as its top three, and contributors went out of their way to explain why D. W. Griffith's 1915 Ku Klux Klan recruitment film, *Birth of a Nation*, also managed a spot. In 2000, the AFI released its "100 Years, 100 Laughs" list, ranking the best American comedies. Mel Brooks's 1974 film *Blazing Saddles*, a parody of classic Western films and a scathing indictment of racism in the United States, earned the number-six spot. While this canonization would suggest that *Saddles* is highly regarded and respected, not everyone agrees: in 2008 the University of Wisconsin issued a formal apology to a black student who was shown a clip from *Saddles*, which "contained racial slurs and black workers being told to 'sing like slaves.'"[1]

Saddles, written by Mel Brooks, Norman Steinberg, Andrew Bergman, Richard Pryor, and Alan Uger, is difficult to describe from a plot standpoint. The late film critic Roger Ebert opined that *Saddles* is "a crazed grabbag of a movie that does everything to keep us laughing except hit us over the head with a rubber chicken.... The story line, which is pretty shaky, involves some shady land speculators who need to run a railroad through [Rock Ridge], and decide to drive the residents out. The last thing they want there is law and order, and so the crooks send in a black sheriff figuring the townspeople will revolt."[2] Though *Saddles* has received numerous accolades, including a spot in the National Film Registry, which recognizes films that are "considered culturally, historically, or aesthetically significant," and ranks forty-ninth on the list of highest domestic-grossing films adjusted for inflation, there has been little critical attention paid to this film, especially where depictions of racism and representations of black characters are concerned.[3]

Most analyses of black participation in the film industry during the 1970s focus on the Blaxploitation movement, and films such as *Cotton Comes to Harlem* (1970), *Sweet Sweetback's Baadasssss Song* (1971), *Super Fly* (1972), and *Foxy Brown* (1974) are typically discussed as important black films that represent the decade. This leaves black-themed films from the 1970s, such as *Saddles*, *Lady Sings the Blues* (1972), *Sounder* (1972), and *The Bingo Long Traveling All-Stars and Motor Kings* (1976), that do not fit neatly into the overly broad category of Blaxploitation, lacking in critical attention. According to Novotny Lawrence, the basic conventions of films produced as part of the Blaxploitation movement usually include

> a black hero or heroine who is both socially and politically conscious; feature a variety of African American supporting characters who are integral to the plot; are set in predominantly black urban spaces; feature whites who are often cast as villains who feel the wrath of black justice; show black heroes and heroines using any means necessary to overcome the oppressive establishment and are sexually liberated characters; include contemporary rhythm-and-blues soundtracks that match the filmic images in theme and content; and often contain plot themes that address the black experience in America.[4]

While the majority of films from the Blaxploitation movement featured predominately black casts and were targeted toward black audiences, the films were often "written, directed, and produced by whites . . . shot on shoestring budgets, were badly directed, were technically poor [and] played on the needs of black audiences for heroic figures without answering those needs in realistic terms."[5] *Saddles* uses parody and satire to embrace some of the tenets of the Blaxploitation era and to turn them on their heads at the same time: it was a big-budget production with mainstream whites as its target audience, yet it also provides a black heroic figure and partially addresses the needs of black audiences by highlighting the black experience in the United States, albeit in comedic terms. This chapter will discuss the ways in which *Blazing Saddles* utilizes trickster motifs to effect change, calls attention to and mocks stereotypes about black men, and uses the quintessential American genre, the Western, to critique American racism.

As partially noted in Ebert's review, *Blazing Saddles* tells the story of a railroad worker, Bart, played by Cleavon Little, who becomes sheriff of Rock Ridge. He is given this opportunity by an unscrupulous politician, Hedley Lamarr, played by Harvey Korman, who wants to force the residents to leave their town so he can run the railroad through it, and who figures that the sight of a black sheriff will be enough to cause the racist townspeople to flee. Lamarr enlists his assistant Taggart (Slim Pickins); a large brute by the name of Mongo (Alex Karras); a showgirl named Lili Von Shtupp, played by Madeline Kahn (who earned an Oscar nomination for her performance); and a plethora of stereotypical villains to help intimidate people out of their homes. Sheriff Bart is joined in his fight by an alcoholic named Jim (Gene Wilder), who used to be a famous gunslinger named The Waco Kid. Mel Brooks plays the hapless Governor Lepetomane. Just because the writers could do it, all the residents of Rock Ridge are named Johnson, a choice that has comedic value and also shows how insular the town really is. *New York Times* critic Vincent Canby noted that *Saddles* "is every Western you've ever seen turned upside down and inside out [and] braced with a lot of low burlesque," and in her discussion of the film's fortieth anniversary, Nadya Faulx writes, "Gone are the earnest, long-winded speeches about racial harmony that characterized movies like *The Defiant Ones*; instead, the film, co-written by Richard Pryor, tackles race and racism head-on and with humor. (It's so un-PC that Brooks told Jimmy Kimmel in 2012 he wouldn't be able to make the film today.)"[6] *Saddles* "was, at the time, far and away the most successful comedy ever made,"[7] and the film garnered three Oscar nominations for Best Film Editing, Best Original Song, and Best Supporting

Actress. Forty years after its initial release, Blazing Saddles remains popular, funny, and thoroughly—and purposely—offensive.

Before diving into the analysis of Blazing Saddles, it is worth noting that technically the film does not conform to Andre Seewood's definition of a Genuine Black Film, which is

> a film with a majority Black cast that situates Whites, if any, in peripheral or non-influential roles where the narrative resolves itself by giving more dramatic attention to the emotions and circumstances of the Black character(s) [and films where] the concept of dramatic agency (the ability of the character(s) to directly influence and change the circumstances within a story and survive the outcome of those circumstances) is explicitly exercised by the Black characters who are integral to the film's plot and theme.[8]

On the one hand, the film is centered on the emotions and circumstances of a black main character, Bart. In addition, Bart possesses all of the dramatic agency in the film, since the other characters respond to his actions, making him the focal point of the film's themes. At the same time, Bart is one of only two black characters with significant speaking roles in the film, which complicates the framing of Saddles as a black film. Seewood's other black film categories include the Compromised Black Film, which involves white savior tropes and/or black characters who do not survive the circumstances within the story, as well as the Pseudo-Inclusive White Film, characterized by black tokenism where "more often . . . the white characters control, change and survive the circumstances within the story than do the black characters."[9] Neither of these definitions describes Saddles. The film does not contain any white saviors; on the contrary, Bart is the savior of the film. Bart cannot be characterized as a token character, either, because he both controls the narrative actions in the film and survives them.

Based on this, Blazing Saddles should be framed as a Genuine Black Film. Since Brooks set out to mock racism in the United States, it makes perfect sense that the majority of the characters in the film needed to be white, because racism and white supremacy are largely perpetuated by white people and white institutions.

Blaxploitation and the Trickster Motif

Despite the fact that films of the Blaxploitation movement span multiple genres, one of the hallmarks shared by them is the precept that the black characters in these films deviated from representations that audiences were accustomed to seeing on the big screen. In Melvin Van Peebles's *Sweet Sweetback's Baadasssss Song*, the film usually framed as the starting point for the genre, the main character is a male sex worker who intervenes when the police attempt to murder a young black militant. Sweetback spends the remainder of the film running from the authorities, and it ends with him making it to Mexico but vowing to return and "collect some dues." Gordon Parks Sr.'s *Shaft* also features a character working outside the traditional legal establishment. As Isaac Hayes's Oscar-winning theme song points out, the protagonist, Shaft, is a "private dick that's a sex machine to all the chicks." Throughout the film, he moves alongside, between, and against black mobsters, white mafia kingpins, black nationalists, and the police in order to solve his case. Pam Grier's *Foxy Brown* is a similar protagonist: she poses as a prostitute to investigate her boyfriend's murder, and in the process helps remove black women from an exploitative modeling agency. Gordon Parks Jr.'s *Super Fly* follows Priest, a drug dealer who decides to make one final score before retiring, but encounters aggressive law enforcement officials and personal betrayal on his way out of the game. These characters embody aspects of modern tricksters who are "suave, urbane, and calculating."[10] The protagonists in many Blaxploitation films usually act "with premeditation [and are] always in control of the situation."[11] In addition to working outside the law, Sweetback, Shaft, and Foxy Brown, in one way or another, are working toward helping people within working- and lower-class urban black communities.

Tricksters embody a variety of different characteristics; however, those stemming from African folk traditions, like the Blaxploitation protagonists, are

> ostensibly disadvantaged and weak in a contest of wills, power, and/or resources, [and yet] succeed in getting the best of their larger, more powerful adversaries. Tricksters achieve their objectives through indirection and mask-wearing, [and] through playing upon the gullibility of their opponents. In other words, tricksters succeed by outsmarting or outthinking their opponents.[12]

As the protagonist in *Saddles*, Bart embodies many of these characteristics; however, he forges a slightly different path than other characters in his cohort. While the overwhelming majority of Blaxploitation films take place in urban environments, *Saddles* is set in the Old West, a decidedly more rural setting; however, the conceit of the film is that while the events take place in 1874, the story assumes it is actually 1974, a time when the West has already been "tamed."[13] Because the film imports 1970s sensibilities and references into the Old West, there are multiple urban and contemporary touches throughout. For example, when Bart rides toward Rock Ridge to accept his post as sheriff, he passes the Count Basie Orchestra playing "April in Paris." Bart stops to listen to the music and then gives Count Basie, playing himself, some dap before continuing his journey. The cameo adds a nice note of sophistication, random and out of place though it may be, to the Western motif and reminds the audience that even though the sets make it look like the film takes place in the 1800s, we are really witnessing events from the 1970s. Andrew Bergman, one of the screenwriters, noted that these urban touches were deliberate. When he envisioned the character and the story, he commented, "We have Eldridge Cleaver riding into town on a pony and you make the joke with a Gucci bag that he's hip and that's it and you don't examine it."[14] This scene does provide a short close-up of the Gucci saddle bag on Bart's horse as he approaches Count Basie's orchestra. The urban versus rural aspect of Bart's character is summed up when Jim asks him, "What's a dazzling urbanite doing in a rustic setting like this?" The writers have taken an urban character who would be perfectly at home in a Blaxploitation film and transported him into the 1870s—but let him keep his 1970s mentality, which complicates the urban aspect of films produced during that time.

Like any trickster, Bart finds a way to control the situation even when it appears that everyone else is in control. When he arrives in Rock Ridge, the residents are at first happy to see their new sheriff and cheer his arrival—until they notice he is a black man. Before he looks up to actually see the sheriff and take in this fact, Howard Johnson, the chairman of the welcoming committee, delivers his practiced welcome speech, saying, "As chairman of the welcoming committee, it is my privilege to extend a Laurel-and-Hardy handshake to our new . . . nigger." The marching band stops playing and the welcome sign retracts as the townspeople stare in confusion. Bart ignores the silence as he extends the welcome sign to its original position and heads to the stage to address the crowd. As Bart reads his orders, the townspeople draw their weapons and prepare to shoot him. Thinking quickly, Bart draws his gun and threatens to shoot himself if anyone makes a move. The townspeople drop their weapons as Bart takes himself hostage and threatens to "blow this nigger's head all over this town." He then responds to himself in an exaggerated and stereotypical tone of voice: "Oh Lawdy Lawd, he's desperate, do what he say!" Bart then walks himself to the safety of his office as one lady asks, "Isn't anyone going to help that poor man?"—a sentiment that was absent only seconds before, when the townspeople were ready to shoot him themselves. Like the protagonists in multiple Blaxploitation films, and like any trickster, Bart successfully outsmarts his well-armed opponents and uses their gullibility against them.

Throughout the film, Bart uses the trickster "mentality as a strategy for survival with dignity as well as a strategy for political intervention."[15] As discussed in the previous chapter, Duff in *Nothing But a Man* is told by fellow black workers that he has to "act [like] a nigger" if he wants to survive, and the film shows multiple instances of black men being humiliated by white men. Duff rejects this treatment and is punished by being fired and then blackballed from every decent job in town. Bart employs trickster strategies as do the black mill workers in *Nothing But a Man*; however, Bart is never humiliated or framed as inferior when he does so. On the contrary, each time Bart resorts to trickster techniques, they highlight his intelligence, ingenuity, and sense of humor while at the same time pointing a finger at the ignorance and gullibility of the white racist characters. Bart's actions highlight the difference between the audience laughing *with* you and the audience laughing *at* you. Brooks's intention with the film is for the audience to laugh *with* Bart and *at* the white racist characters because they are the butt of the jokes, not Bart. Once Bart successfully uses the trickster persona to save his own skin when he first arrives in Rock Ridge, he employs a similar strategy later when the unscrupulous land grabbers unleash Mongo onto the town.

Mongo is described as "more of a what than a who," and when Bart reaches for his gun to confront Mongo, he is told, "No, no, don't do that. If you shoot him, you'll just make him mad." Mongo punches a horse, tears the doors off the saloon entrance, and is seen pushing a piano with ten struggling townspeople behind it. As any trickster would, the sheriff realizes that if he cannot defeat Mongo with pure strength, he must outsmart his opponent. Bart quite literally puts on his trickster mask as he dresses up like a telegram deliveryman and gives Mongo a candygram. Bart then saunters out of the saloon to the Looney Tunes theme song, and places his fingers in his ears because the candygram is rigged with enough explosives to incapacitate Mongo. The ruse works on two levels: first, Mongo is no longer able to wreak havoc on Rock Ridge; and second, the townspeople are forced

Bart leads railroad workers in song

to acknowledge the sheriff's authority and ingenuity. One little old lady visits the sheriff and backtracks her earlier racial hostility by saying, "Good evening sheriff, sorry about the earlier 'Up yours, nigger.' I hope this apple pie will in some small way say thank you for your ingenuity and courage in defeating that awful Mongo." This admiration is short-lived as the lady ends her conversation by saying, "Of course, you'll have the good taste not to mention that I spoke to you." This exchange highlights the notion that while playing the trickster might be successful in terms of survival, there are limits to its effectiveness as a tool for widespread and long-term political and social change. The sheriff does garner the townspeople's respect, but only on the down-low, as he remarks, "I'm rapidly becoming an underground success in this town." The question becomes whether the private respect is sufficient or whether Bart's actions must also lead to public, sustained respect for the trickster behavior to be worthwhile.

While the overwhelming majority of protagonists in Blaxploitation films operate outside the establishment, Bart has his feet in both worlds, since he begins in the film as an outsider before rising in status to become sheriff of Rock Ridge. When the audience is first introduced to Bart, he is, like Duff in Nothing But a Man, a railroad worker. In the scene that caused the University of Wisconsin to issue an apology, Bart one-ups his white supervisor, Lyle, when the latter requests that the workers entertain him, remarking that "When you were slaves, you sang like birds. Come on, how about a nice nigger work song." While his fellow workers are ready to revolt, Bart chooses comedy and humiliation instead of violence. The workers huddle together and conspire to give Lyle exactly what he has asked for, in a manner of speaking, as they perform a verse from Cole Porter's "I Get a Kick Out of

You." Calling upon a cappella harmonies reminiscent of a 1950s doo-wop group, the railroad hands mock the supervisor by changing the lyrics: "I get no kick from champagne / mere alcohol doesn't thrill me at all / so tell me then why should it be true / that I get a belt out of you / some get a kick from cocaine." The song selection again highlights the fact that even though the film is set in the 1870s, the characters have their feet squarely in more contemporary settings, since this song was originally written in the 1930s. Lyle and his fellow supervisors are clearly confused by this musical selection and demand a more "appropriate" choice. When the railroad workers then feign ignorance of the lyrics to "Swing Low, Sweet Chariot," the white supervisors proceed to make fools of themselves by performing "Camptown Races," much to the amusement of the railroad workers. A violent response to Lyle's racist query may have been satisfying at first, but it would have certainly led to injury and/or death for the railroad workers. Bart's solution not only adds levity to the situation but saves lives as well. Once again, Bart employs trickster tactics to achieve his goals and to one-up his opponents.

Why Am I Asking You?

The trickster motif connects *Blazing Saddles* to Blaxploitation films released during the 1970s, and at the same time, *Saddles* also contains elements of both parody and satire. Michael Tueth defines parody as a work "that broadly mimics another work of art or another artist's characteristic style and hold[s] the original up for ridicule, which is usually affectionate but may sometimes prove hostile."[16] *Saddles* takes the conventions of the Western genre and turns them on their heads. For example, as Pat Dowell points out in the essay "The Mythology of the Western," "One of the Western's most enduring concern [sic] [is] masculinity and its prerogative of violence."[17] One of the more popular storylines within the genre involves a story similar to the one presented in *Saddles*: a town is terrorized by the "bad guys," and the sheriff, cowboy, or sympathetic gunslinger must use violence in order to solve the problem. The masculinity Dowell points to is always embodied by the Western hero, usually portrayed by an actor with a "tough guy" persona.

In *High Noon* (1953), Gary Cooper plays the retiring sheriff, who must face an outlaw he arrested years earlier. *Shane* (1953) tells the story of a former gunslinger, played by Alan Ladd, who attempts to settle down but is brought into a violent conflict between ranchers and settlers. James Stewart plays a less-than-reputable bounty hunter trying to capture a murderer in *The Naked Spur* (1953). Burt Lancaster and Kirk Douglass play Wyatt Earp and

Doc Holliday, respectively, in *Gunfight at the O.K. Corral* (1957). Much like the previously mentioned protagonists, Earp attempts to leave his violent career behind but is forced to face a band of thieves. Though it is a remake of Japanese filmmaker Akira Kurosawa's seminal film *Seven Samurai* (1954), *The Magnificent Seven* (1960) is a classic Western that tells the story of a town being harassed by bandits; the townspeople fight back by hiring a group of gunslingers to protect them. Any discussion about Westerns as a genre would be incomplete without mentioning John Wayne, the embodiment of western masculinity. In *El Dorado* (1966), Wayne joins Robert Mitchum to help save a rancher and his family from their rivals. Each of these films ends with some kind of physical altercation between the protagonist(s) and the antagonist(s) involving fists, bullets, or both. In the end, violence always begets violence, and violence solves all problems.

Hollywood's current climate does not embrace Westerns in the same way that it did in the 1950s and 1960s, and in the last twenty years or so only a handful of films could be classified as Westerns, including Clint Eastwood's *Unforgiven* (1992) and three remakes: *3:10 to Yuma* (2007), starring Russell Crowe and Christian Bale; *True Grit* (2010), starring Jeff Bridges and Matt Damon; and *The Magnificent Seven* (2016), starring Denzel Washington. Because there are so few Westerns being released today, many aspects of the genre that *Saddles* parodies are lost on contemporary viewers. This would help explain why *Saddles* is framed as being offensive and racist when shown in classrooms, as opposed to being viewed as making fun of racists, which was the film's original intent.

Saddles can also be framed as satire that employs "humor, often quite sophisticated, to attack what its author considers stupid or immoral."[18] One of the film's primary goals is to ridicule racism, placing the film squarely within satire territory. However, as discussed in the previous paragraph, because Brooks sends up the Western genre in his comedic sandbox, parody is also in play. As Wes Gehring points out, "Spoofing has affectionate fun at the expense of a given form or structure; satire more aggressively attacks the flaws and follies of mankind. . . . *Blazing Saddles* makes pointed satirical comments on racism and violence in the one-time glorified American West."[19] One way *Saddles* uses parody to make satirical comments is by breaking the fourth wall to acknowledge the audience's presence throughout the film, and to literally call the audience's attention to the ridiculousness of racism. For example, as mentioned earlier, when Bart arrives in Rock Ridge, the townspeople are less than enthusiastic about the idea of a black man as their sheriff. When he uses trickster techniques to get himself to the safety of his office, Bart remarks to himself: "Oh baby, you are so talented," and then looks straight into the camera to add, "And they are so dumb." This moment not only reinforces the fact that Bart is clearly smarter than everyone else in the film, but that he is well aware of this fact and wants to make sure the audience is, too.

Another example of the film breaking the fourth wall occurs as the sheriff begins decorating his new office, hears a noise off-screen, and looks into the camera to explain to the audience that "The drunk in number two must be awake." At this point, the audience is introduced to Jim, who becomes Bart's sidekick for the rest of the film. As Jim moans and hangs upside down in his cell, the two have the following exchange:

> BART: Are we awake?
> JIM: We're not sure. Are we . . . black?
> BART: Yes, we are.
> JIM: Then we're awake. But we're very puzzled.

While interracial buddy films had their moment in the 1960s with *The Defiant Ones*, and would come back again in the 1980s with films such as *48 Hrs.* (1982), *Running Scared* (1986), and the *Lethal Weapon* series (1987–1992), the relationship between Bart and Jim is quite different as "there's no tension to overcome, no soul-searching or come-to-Jesus/Kumbaya moment. Bart and Jim are never pitted against each other; they're allies right off the bat, and the enemy, in this case, is white racism."[20] In addition, in most interracial buddy films, the white character is clearly the main protagonist, but in *Saddles*, Bart is the primary character. Because Bart breaks the fourth wall to tell the audience what is happening, we know that Jim must be an important character to the story, and we have the added bonus of Bart performing a shout-out to his previous interracial exploits with him singing an over-enunciated version of "Camptown Races" as he goes to meet Jim.

Though it may not be an intentional breaking of the fourth wall, there is another scene where Bart engages the viewing audience. As he walks through town on his first full day as sheriff, feeling happy and wearing a welcoming smile on his face, he encounters an elderly white woman and attempts to engage her in conversation:

> BART: Good morning ma'am, and isn't it a lovely morning?
> WOMAN: Up yours, nigger.

Bart and Jim's reaction to racial slur

The scene fades and we move to the next scene where Bart is back in his office. There is a close-up of Bart's face looking forlorn and, though he is facing the camera, his eyes are slightly off-center. Jim has his arm around Bart and attempts to console him. Slurs of every kind permeate the dialogue of this film; this is one of the only scenes where the audience sees the negative effect language has on a character. Though the popular mantra of "sticks and stones may break my bones, but words can never hurt me" is often accepted as a truism, many critical race theorists reframe these racial slurs as fighting words or words "'which by their very utterance inflict injury or tend to incite to an immediate breach of peace,' and which are commonly understood to convey direct and visceral hatred or contempt for human beings on the basis of their sex, race, color, handicap, religion, sexual orientation, or national and ethnic origin."[21] Most would never expect such language from a little old lady, which heightens the tension and surprise.

As black feminist theorist Patricia Hill Collins points out in her discussion of fighting words, "Although fear, rage, and shock may characterize the victim's reaction, she or he may not think of an appropriate response until much later. Moreover, the effect of dehumanizing language is often flight rather than fight."[22] The audience sees this framing in action as Bart's face is frozen with his original smile as the woman walks away. We do not know how much time passes between when Bart is verbally assaulted and when he is back in his office with Jim; however, the audience does know that Bart either would not or could not respond to the fighting words. Bart continues to look distraught as Jim attempts to comfort him: "What did you expect? Welcome, sonny? Make yourself at home? Marry my daughter? You've got to remember that these are just simple farmers. These are people of the land. The common clay of the new West. You know—morons." Jim uses humor to defuse the situation, but the use of close-ups to reinforce Bart's injury shows that even though *Blazing Saddles* is a comedy, the effects of racism are real. Arguably, this is another example of Bart breaking the fourth wall even though it is not verbalized as it is in previous examples. The blank expression Bart has on his face as he faces the camera illustrates how hurtful the little old lady's words were, and signals to the audience the silent question of, Can you believe what just happened to me? By repeatedly breaking the fourth wall, Brooks acknowledges that the story takes place in a film, and that he is inviting the audience to laugh along as he makes fun of racists and racism.

The Fool's Gonna . . . I Mean, the Sheriff's Gonna Do It!

While Bart uses trickster tactics as a tool for survival with dignity, their utility for achieving sustained social and political change is less certain. This diminished effectiveness has to do with critical race theorist Derrick Bell's concept of interest convergence. Bell notes that "the interest of blacks in achieving racial equality will be accommodated only when it converges with the interests of whites"[23] and uses the landmark *Brown v. Board of Education* school desegregation case as an example. In Bell's view, the U.S. Supreme Court did not strike down school segregation because segregation was wrong or unconstitutional, nor because the Court was interested in the welfare of black children. Instead, the *Brown* decision was a political calculus designed to

> provide immediate credibility to America's struggle with Communist countries to win the hearts and minds of emerging third world peoples. . . . [It] offered much needed reassurance to American blacks that the precepts of equality and freedom so heralded during World War II might yet be given meaning at home . . . [and because] segregation was viewed as a barrier to further industrialization in the South."[24]

Bart's fate in *Saddles* follows a similar trajectory. After performing "I Get a Kick Out of You," Bart and fellow railroad worker Charlie are sent ahead of the crew to check for quicksand. Unfortunately, they do find quicksand, become mired in it, and are left to die by Lyle and Taggart. Thankfully, Bart and Charlie are able to rescue themselves and, while violence may not have been an appropriate answer to Lyle's "sing like slaves" request, being left to die is another matter entirely. Despite Charlie's pleas, Bart hits Taggart in the head with a shovel. Because of this assault, Hedley Lamarr sentences Bart to death. When Bart is about to be hanged, Lamarr hatches his plan to steal Rock Ridge from the residents using Bart as the bait. When the citizens of Rock Ridge request a sheriff to counter the villains Lamarr has sent to harass them, a move that would interfere with his plans to take over the town, Lamarr wonders "if [he] can find a sheriff that so offends the citizens of Rock Ridge that his very appearance would drive them out of town." Lamarr assumes that the townspeople will be so racist toward Bart that they will either undermine any efforts Bart makes to try and restore law and order, or will simply leave the town outright. This is the textbook definition of interest convergence. Lamarr does not save Bart because he cares about Bart's life or because he thinks Bart's action was justified. In this instance, Bart benefits from the fact that his interest in living converges with Lamarr's interest in scaring the townspeople out of their property.

We see interest convergence in play again toward the end of the film. The townspeople decide to flee after discovering a help-wanted ad requesting "heartless villains for destruction of Rock Ridge." Bart devises a plan to save the town: they will build an exact replica of the town, and when the "heartless villains" come to destroy it, the townspeople will strike. Since they only have twenty-four hours to complete construction, Bart enlists the help of his former railroad colleagues, who want a plot of land to homestead in exchange. The townspeople initially agree to "give some land to the niggers and the chinks, but we don't want the Irish." The railroad workers balk at the discrimination against the Irish workers and demand that everyone be included in the agreement. The townspeople eventually agree. In this case, the townspeople are not accepting the black, Chinese, and Irish railroad workers because it is the right thing to do, although their exposure to Bart has at least lessened some of more virulent racism. Rather, the townspeople accept the railroad workers because it is the only way to keep their town from being destroyed. This scene not only highlights how flexible racial animus can be but also demonstrates the fluidity of whiteness. The townspeople eventually, albeit begrudgingly, accept the black and Chinese workers into their town; however, they draw the line at the Irish, who, at this point in American history, have not fully completed their journey to "becoming" white. The situation is a bit ironic because, as historian Ronald Takaki points out in his book *A Different Mirror*, Irish immigrants were originally "compared to blacks" and "were imagined as apelike and 'a race of savages,' at the same level of intelligence as blacks."²⁵ Many Irish immigrants established their white bona fides by attacking blacks and "thus, blacks as the 'other' served to facilitate the assimilation of Irish foreigners."²⁶ In Brooks's universe, it is the black workers who stick up for the Irish immigrants. In this scene, Bart is able to secure a substantive intervention for his people, as the railroad workers will now have inroads toward better economic opportunity and a community that, while initially reluctant, is ultimately supportive of their presence. While trickster tactics help in the short term, interest convergence is the key to long-term, sustained change.

Hey, Where Are the White Women At?

One of the criticisms of "significant films" of the 1960s, particularly those starring Sidney Poitier, is that they rarely acknowledge black male sexuality. Part of this avoidance was due to a fear of black male sexuality, and part of it was due to a desire to distance the more contemporary storytelling from the hypersexual portrayals seen in films such as *Birth of a Nation*. Donald Bogle remarks that Griffith's *Birth of a Nation* portrayed three varieties of blacks, one of which was the black bucks, who were "always big, baadddd niggers, over-sexed and savage, violent and frenzied as they lust for white flesh."²⁷ Blaxploitation films exist on the opposite end of the spectrum, as they were often unapologetic about portraying black male sexuality. In *Sweetback*, the main character is a sex worker who is, by all accounts, quite skilled at his craft. At one point in the film, a biker gang confronts Sweetback and challenges him to a duel. Allowed to choose the method of confrontation, Sweetback chooses "fucking"—with a white woman no less. In *Shaft*, the main character is described as "a sex machine with all the chicks": these words are, in fact, in the first line of the film's theme song. This unabashed treatment of black sexuality was a double-edged sword. On the one hand, portraying black love and black sexuality was a rebuff of previous representations that framed black male characters as either savage or sterile.²⁸ On the other hand, the explicit portrayal of black sexuality raised the ire of many critics who felt that sex was portrayed for pure shock value.

In that same vein, *Saddles* does not shy away from black male sexuality, and it also pokes fun at the stereotype of the hypersexual black male. Going back to the scene where Bart arrives at Rock Ridge, Bart ignores the stares of the residents, heads to the stage, and prepares to address the crowd. At that point he reaches into his pants pocket to pull out his speech and quips, "Excuse me while I whip this out." The townspeople are shocked: the women scream and faint, children hide their eyes, and the men look on in horror as they all assume that Bart is about to expose himself. Of course, the joke is on the townspeople, as Bart does nothing to provoke their response and there is nothing explicitly sexual about his statement, even if the phrasing certainly constitutes a double entendre. The townspeople, inculcated with stereotypes of black men as sexual predators, particularly where white women are concerned, infer sexual connotations where none exist, and therefore react poorly, looking ridiculous in the process.

Bart's sexuality comes into play again later in the film as Lamarr, having failed to conquer Bart with Mongo the beast, decides to send in the beauty. Lili Von Shtupp, billed as the Teutonic Titwillow within the film, is charged with the task of first seducing and then abandoning Bart. Things do not go quite as planned when Lili invites Bart to her dressing room and turns out the lights; after a quick joke about not being able to see the sheriff in the darkened room, she asks Bart, "Is it true what they say about the way you people are . . . gifted?" We hear the sound of a zipper and Lili exclaims, "Oh it's true, it's true, it's true!" Lamarr's plan is thwarted as Von Shtupp falls in love with the sheriff and decides to help him instead of Lamarr. In this instance, it isn't Bart who is lusting after a white woman, it is the white woman lusting after him. Instead of being savage and violent as the black buck stereotype would lead the audience to believe, he is romantic and gentle. When he leaves the dressing room, Lili comments, "What a nice guy." As Van Jordan remarks in his "Ode to Blazing Saddles," the joke relies not only on the audience's knowledge of the sexual stereotypes but also on them being able to recognize how the scene works against those stereotypes: "A black man *shtupping* a German floozy, who tries to ensnare him between her legs, but gets hoisted by her own garter petard? Well, that's just some funny *scheiße*."[29] The film does not desexualize Bart, nor does it portray him as a hypersexual character; it deconstructs the hypersexual stereotype by "having Bart return to the jail a physically wasted lover" who turns down an opportunity for more sex.[30] The sex scene is not actually shown; everything is left to the viewers' imaginations, which forces them to confront their preconceived notions about black male sexuality. By not showing an explicit sex scene between Bart and Lili, the film acknowledges Bart's sexuality but does not offend the sensibilities of those who criticized some Blaxploitation films for their explicit treatment of sex.

The final scene that plays with sexual stereotypes also manages to combine the trickster tactics discussed earlier. After the townspeople reveal the advertisement for villains willing to destroy Rock Ridge, Bart and Jim go undercover to discern Lamarr's plan. Because Bart would be recognized, they need a disguise and find two Klansmen waiting in line, both of whom have the phrase "Have a nice day" with a smiley face imprinted on the backs of their robes. Jim hides Bart behind a giant rock and calls the Klansmen over, and when Bart pops out from behind the rock, he exclaims, "Hey, where are the white women at?" Once again, the film and the characters bank on the audience's familiarity with established stereotypes and use this to their advantage. Bart and Jim know that Klansmen would be incensed at the idea of a black man lusting after a white woman, and use this knowledge to trap and defeat them. To further enforce the idiocy of what the Klan stands for, when Bart and Jim reach the front of the line and are discovered, before making their hasty exit, Bart exclaims, "And now, for my next impression, Jesse Owens." Bart could invoke anyone, but he chooses the four-time Olympic gold medalist who is primarily known for dismantling Adolph Hitler's notion of white racial superiority at the 1936 Olympic Games in Berlin. In the end, Bart's character runs counter to the stereotypes usually assigned to black men because he is "a supercool dude; he is elegant and urbane, a connoisseur of fine wines and good food; he is sensuous and erotic."[31]

You'd Do It for Randolph Scott

Though race prejudice and the pervasiveness of antiblack stereotypes drove the narrative of *Blazing Saddles*, the fact that the film is a Western is equally important. Frederick Jackson Turner's seminal talk, "The Significance of the Frontier in American History," which he delivered during the 1893 World's Columbian Exposition in Chicago, was a pivotal moment in shaping how we viewed the American character and the West's contribution to that narrative. According to Turner, the "expansion westward with its new opportunities, its continuous tough with the simplicity of primitive society, furnish the forces dominating American character."[32] The American character that Turner alludes to is more complicated, as NBA Hall of Famer and author Kareem Abdul-Jabbar notes: "[It] was not only rooted in democracy and individualism, but it also grew from white racism, violence, and intolerance."[33] From the 1903 short *The Great Train Robbery* to the 2016 feature film *Hell or High Water*, Westerns, as a genre, embraced this image of the Western frontier, which "promoted individualism, self-reliance, practicality, optimism, and a democratic spirit that rejected hereditary constraints."[34] Though Westerns date back to the early days of film, their heyday spanned the 1950s and 1960s, and during that time, the genre served as "a vehicle for American self-definition. It was the cultural production that continuously refurbished a national foundation myth of agrarian equality for a twentieth-century superpower with imperial ambitions."[35] Westerns were the quintessential American film genre, and though some were produced outside the United States, the American project placed its stamp on the genre. In that same vein, though racism has many forms and exists in multiple places and contexts, it can be said that racism in the United States is unique and, much like the Western, shapes how we define the American character. If someone is going to show how ridiculous racial prejudice is, it makes sense to use a genre that is ingrained into the American mythos. It seems fitting that Westerns began their decline in the 1970s, just as the Blaxploitation movement was beginning its period of dominance. *Saddles* mixes the frontier sensibilities of the fading Western genre with the hallmarks of the Blaxploitation movement—trickster mentalities and urban sensibilities.

Bart is not necessarily interested in using violence to achieve his goals; he prefers cunning, guile, and subterfuge to defeat the bad guys. There are exactly two gunfights in the entire film. The first time Bart returns to the railroad after his promotion to sheriff, he encounters his old friends and his former antagonists. Taggart recognizes Bart as the person who hit him in the head with a shovel and remarks, "Now, what in the hell do you think you're doing with that tin star, boy?" Bart replies, "Watch that 'boy' shit, redneck; you're talking to the sheriff of Rock Ridge." That tin star has placed Bart in a position of power and authority over Taggart, and Bart uses that advantage to push back against racist language and disrespect. Lyle volunteers to have his boys "shoot that nigger dead" to make Taggart feel better about Bart's promotion. In this situation, Bart does not make any moves to get his gun; he simply warns the potential shooters that drawing their weapons would not be a good idea. When Lyle's men fail to heed Bart's warnings, Jim shoots the guns out of their hands. Here, it is not the hero that resorts to violence, it is the sidekick, and Jim does not kill the antagonists; he simply disarms them. While some later Westerns, such as Sergio Leone's *Man with No Name* trilogy and *The Wild Bunch* (1969), seemed to delight in the level of carnage they could portray on the screen, *Saddles* shies away from the physical violence typical to most Westerns.

Because *Saddles* is a parody that enjoys calling attention to its status as a film, the characters are not only aware of all of the conventions of the Western genre, they are perfectly aware that they are in a Western. When the townspeople learn that Lamarr is enlisting villains to destroy their town, they all decide to flee and sheriff Bart tries to change their mind:

> BART: Well, can't you see that's the last act of a desperate man?
>
> MAYOR JOHNSON: We don't care if it's the first act of *Henry V*. We're leaving.
>
> BART: Now, wait a minute. Wait just one doggone minute here. Just twenty-four hours to come up with a brilliant idea to save our town. Just twenty-four hours, that's all I ask.
>
> TOWNSPEOPLE: No!
>
> BART: You'd do it for Randolph Scott.

With the evocation of Scott's name, the townspeople remove their hats, cover their hearts, and exclaim with reverence, "Randolph Scott"; what sounds like a gospel choir sings his name as well. An actor whose name, like John Wayne, is almost synonymous with the Western genre, Scott appeared in a multitude of films for almost four decades, usually playing the hero. The respect the townspeople have for Scott and what his characters represent is clear as they give Bart the twenty-four hours he has requested.

In the final minutes of the movie, when Rock Ridge is attacked, *Saddles* again breaks the fourth wall, literally, by having the Rock Ridge fight scene between the townspeople and the hired villains spill into what looks like the set of a musical. The Western villains do battle with stereotypical white, gay, male dancers in tuxedos. The fight spills over again into the studio commissary for a pie fight, where extras from a variety of films engage in fisticuffs. Lamarr escapes the fighting by hailing a cab and requesting, "Drive me off this picture." Bart follows the cab on his horse and confronts Lamarr in front of the iconic Grauman's Chinese Theatre, where *Blazing Saddles* is shown on the blinking marquee. Lamarr and Bart reenact their version of the gunfight at the O.K. Corral, and in the end, Lamarr is killed. This is the only time Bart resorts to using a weapon, arguably not because he *wants* to shoot Lamarr, but simply because that is how Westerns are supposed to end. The genre dictates Bart's actions in this case, and though the character has avoided or made fun of the genre's tropes up to this point, it isn't a Western without some sort of gunfight. If Brooks wanted to stick with the black buck stereotype, he could have made Bart overly violent and aggressive. Instead, when Lamarr initially says that he is unarmed, Bart lays down his weapon instead of shooting the bad guy outright. Brooks ends the film by reinforcing Bart's urban sensibilities and sending up one last Western convention: Bart and Jim ride off into the sunset on their horses, but after several seconds, they dismount and depart the picture in a limousine. While many Westerns end with the protagonists heading west in search of their place on the vanishing frontier, Bart and Jim are in Los Angeles and therefore about as far west as a person can go without ending up in the Pacific Ocean; the limousine serves to remind the audience that this film actually takes place in the 1970s.

Curtain Call

In his discussion about the film, Mel Brooks notes that "the engine that drove the movie was the hatred of the black; it was race prejudice. Without that, the movie would not have had nearly the significance to force to dynamism and the stakes that were contained in the film."[36] If the audience does not know the stereotypes or even acknowledge that racism exists, then it is not possible to laugh at the ridiculousness of racism and racists. It can certainly be argued that by making fun of racism and racists, *Blazing Saddles* in some respects delegitimizes the real-world impact that racism has on black people, and the physical, emotional, and economic harm that racist words and actions can inflict. On the other hand, if racism is indeed permanent, as critical race theorists argue, dissecting racism from every angle, including comedic ones, cannot hurt—and the film does not completely gloss over the effects of racism. The film also shows that discussions about the effects of racism and methods of dismantling white supremacy need not always be dry and dire. During a time when stories dealing with black people's lives were often dismissed as black exploitation fare, *Blazing Saddles* went in a slightly different direction. Taking elements from classic Westerns, Blaxploitation films, and over-the-top comedies, *Saddles*, in the words of co-star Gene Wilder, "smashed racism in the face . . . but they're doing it while you laugh."[37] At the same time, *Saddles* can also be read as "a Blaxploitation film *par excellence* [insofar as] the film's obsessions, with the traditions of the American Western, and its comic, irreverent, and trickster approach, are aspects of Blaxploitation cinema at its finest."[38] Though *Saddles* embodies most characteristics common to films in the Blaxploitation movement, save the urban setting and the rhythm-and-blues soundtrack, it feels more accurate to say that *Saddles* straddles and toys with the categories of Westerns, Blaxploitation, comedy, parody, and satire.

Bart embraces elements of a modern-day trickster and a hard-boiled Blaxploitation protagonist while toying with stereotypes of black male hypersexuality. The film uses the Western, a genre intimately connected with ideals about the American frontier character, and skewers racial prejudice and the people who perpetuate it, a choice that is ironic because racism, too, is intimately connected with the American character. After forty years, some of the film's references may be dated; however, *Blazing Saddles* remains an offensive, crude, hilarious classic that makes race prejudice look like the idiotic thing that it is.

3 Harlem Nights, Awkward Framing, and Complicated Gender Politics

SUGAR RAY: Damn, I'm sure gonna miss that place
. . .
QUICK: Man, there's other cities. Find someplace else to start all over again.
SUGAR RAY: But there's no place like Harlem.
                                         Harlem Nights, 1989

It was like there were two different things. There were the people that watched it and enjoyed it and then there were the critics who hated it. It was like the divide with this film. It's like they didn't see the movie at all.
                              Joel G. Robertson, Forgotten Flix
                                                  Remembers, 2015

As part of the video for his 2002 single "Pass the Courvoisier, Part II," Grammy-nominated artist Busta Rhymes included an homage to the 1989 Eddie Murphy film *Harlem Nights*. The homage featured Rhymes, Sean Combs, Pharrell, and Mo'Nique dressed in 1930s period clothing, reenacting an alley fight sequence from the film. Fast-forward fourteen years, and at the end of the April 18, 2016, episode of his series *News One Now*, host Roland Martin wished actress Lela Rochon a happy birthday and referred to her as Sunshine, the name of the character she played in *Harlem Nights*. One of the members of his panel, Republican political consultant Shermichael Singleton, admitted that he had never seen the film, much to the horror of Martin and the other panelists, Joia Jefferson Nuri and Quentin James. Martin, half-teasing and half-serious, threatened to revoke Singleton's "black card," and said he would not be welcomed back on the show until he had seen the film and could pass a quiz proving so. After Singleton made several attempts to justify this gap in his black film knowledge, Martin finally dismissed Singleton's excuses by stating "Get off of my set." The shaming continued on Twitter as Martin encouraged his followers to "put @Shermichael on blast. He hasn't seen *Harlem Nights*? He is barred from all summer cookouts, Maze concerts, [and] MLK events." Singleton finally relented and agreed to watch the film. The hip-hop homage and public shaming may seem like a strange reaction to a film that is almost thirty years old and was framed by mainstream critics as a box-office disappointment; at the same time, they point to the affection that black audiences have for the film.

The mainstream reviews of *Harlem Nights* were not particularly kind. Roger Ebert maintained that "there is not an original idea in the movie from one end to the other."[1] Desson Howe of the *Washington Post* wondered: "Will anyone notice, above the inevitable jocularity, that nobody worked too hard on the thing?"[2] Hal Hinson, also of the *Post*, began his review of *Harlem Nights* with the missive "'Written and Directed by Eddie Murphy'—these are words that will forevermore strike fear in the hearts of moviegoers everywhere. These are frightening words. Words to make the bravest man shiver. Once there was Freddy. Once there was Chuckie and Jason and Howard the Duck. Now there is the scariest of them all. Now there is *Harlem Nights*."[3] Susan Stark of Detroit's *Free Press* titled her review "Is This Racist, Sexist Garbage, or Simply Entertainment?" and argued that "*Harlem Nights* is a movie that would assure you of the complete moral and intellectual worthlessness of the human race."[4] These are not the reviews of a beloved film. In fact, *Nights* won the Razzie Award for Worst Screenplay, and Eddie Murphy was nominated for Worst Director. Ironically, the film was also nominated for an Oscar for Best Costume Design. Because there were so few mainstream black film critics during the 1980s, it is difficult to make comparisons between how white critics and black critics responded to the film. At the same time, we have to acknowledge the possibility that the film, which was made with black audiences in mind, did not resonate with critics who were not African American, and that their privilege influenced how they received *Harlem Nights*. Though mainstream critics were not fond of *Nights*, fans have been less harsh. It is interesting that according to Rotten Tomatoes, critics gave the film a dismal 21 percent fresh rating, while audiences gave the film an 81 percent fresh rating—which is quite good.[5] In a podcast on forgotten films, one commenter said that Harlem Nights is "worth remembering until your dying day."[6] The reviews feel bifurcated: people either loved it or hated it.

In addition to the lackluster reviews, Harlem Nights also met with some controversy. During a screening in a Southfield, Michigan theater, a gunman opened fire. Two people were injured and the gunman was shot by police. The theater canceled screenings of the film for the rest of the day and, in the wake of the event, had metal detectors installed.[7] There were two other shooting incidents in California, and in Boston, several fights broke out after a screening of the film. According to Boston's mayor, Ray Flynn, who tightened security at the theater where the fighting occurred, "The movie glorifies violence."[8] Some theaters stopped screening the film as a preemptive measure.[9] Such reactions were baffling considering the fact that the highest-grossing film of 1989 was Batman, which was released five months prior to Harlem Nights. There is no question that Tim Burton's Batman, and every other film in that franchise, are far more violent than Harlem Nights.[10] Given the controversy and the unflattering reception the film received from mainstream critics, why would Rhymes pay tribute to it, and why would Martin and his guests be horrified that someone, particularly a black person, was not familiar with this film? Martin's reaction highlights the disconnect between how mainstream, predominately white, viewers received the film, and how black viewers did.

At its core, Harlem Nights is a caper film in the vein of The Sting (1973), A Fish Called Wanda (1988), and Ocean's Eleven (1960 and 2001). It tells the story of Sugar Ray, played by Richard Pryor, who runs an illegal after-hours club in Harlem during the Jazz Age. His protégé, Quick, played by Eddie Murphy, helps Sugar Ray navigate mobsters, racist police, and various other threats to their business and safety. Redd Foxx plays Bennie, the craps dealer with less-than-stellar visual acuity, and Della Reese plays Vera, who is in charge of the sex workers. Bugsy Calhoune (Michael Lerner) is the mobster who wants to put Sugar Ray out of business, and Phil Cantone (Danny Aiello) is a corrupt detective who wants to extort money from Sugar Ray both for his own personal gain and for the benefit of Calhoune's bottom line.

One feature the film had going for it was that it showcased three generations of black comedy with Redd Foxx, Richard Pryor, and Eddie Murphy. According to Murphy, "This whole thing didn't happen until we all got together and cooked this up. Hollywood wasn't trying to hook us up. But I think it's just historic that I get to work with these brothers."[11] Though some black comedians, including the film's stars, had been in the mainstream public eye for more than a decade, this was one of the few *fictional* films to harness the stylings of black comedy. In addition, though Murphy was an extremely hot commodity at the time, this was not the type of comedy that mainstream audiences were used to seeing from him.

This chapter will provide background information on the making of *Harlem Nights* and the reception it received from critics and audiences. In addition, black feminist thought will be used to analyze the gender politics of the film. Roles for black women in film up to *Nights'* release were not particularly plentiful, and what roles there were often conformed to long-standing controlling images of black women. While mainstream critics were concerned about the film's quality and the amount of profanity the characters used, many failed to note the ways in which the film both amplified and discredited notions of hypermasculinity, and how the black female characters navigated and thrived within the film's universe.

Fear of a Black Planet

According to Raquel Gates, "It is Murphy's consistent quality of mainstream acceptability . . . that has led many scholars to overlook the sociopolitical significance of Murphy's work and to interpret his film and television performances as inherently apolitical."[12] Murphy was certainly one of the stars, if not *the* star of the 1980s. After a stint on *Saturday Night Live*, his filmic success came in the form of the black buddy in films such as *48 Hrs.* (1982) and *Trading Places* (1983). He parlayed these performances into recognition as one of the most bankable stars of the 1980s. These characters charmed audiences in part because of Murphy's charisma, and partly because the characters "offered a reassuring image to Whites. [They were] the Black buddy, friend, or Black sidekick that everyone wanted."[13] The character's sense of self "stemmed from his relationship to his White friend or work partner"[14] and can be seen not only in Murphy's characters but also in Richard Pryor films including *Silver Streak* (1976), *Stir Crazy* (1980), *The Toy* (1982); Gregory Hines's roles in *White Nights* (1985) and *Running Scared* (1986); and Danny Glover's character Roger Murtaugh in the *Lethal Weapon* franchise (1987–1998).

Murphy's big-screen debut was in the Walter Hill film *48 Hrs.* (1982). Nick Nolte plays Jack Cates, a cop trying to find an escaped convict named Albert Ganz (James Remar). Murphy plays Reggie Hammond, a former associate of Ganz who is upset that Ganz snitched and landed him in prison. Hammond agrees to help Cates find Ganz in exchange for a weekend out of prison. As mentioned, most black buddy roles were deemed safe for white audiences because they ignored the racial elephant in the room. In this film, however, that elephant is on full display, as the first spoken words in the film are racist remarks. When a beat-up truck approaches a prison work detail and a Native American man gets out of the car, a police officer remarks, "I wonder what reservation they let him out of." It turns out that the driver, Billy Bear (Sonny Landham), is part of Ganz's escape plan, and the policeman catches a bullet for his trouble. The racist remarks do not end there. Cates, who is supposed to be the film's protagonist, spends the overwhelming majority of the film demeaning Hammond by referring to him as "a smart boy," "watermelon," "spear-chucker," "boy," and "nigger"; by saying "I own your ass"; and by constantly calling him "convict." In the most talked-about scene in the film, Cates and Hammond go to a country-western bar with Confederate flags hanging prominently throughout, prompting Cates to remark that this is "my kind of place." At one point Cates derides the fact that Hammond is a criminal, which is ironic because Cates himself engages in criminal activity that includes falsifying a police report and beating an unarmed suspect. For the audience, the safety of Murphy's character lies in the fact that he never responds to Cates's comments, probably due to the fact that Hammond knows that Cates has the power of life and death over him because of the badge and the gun. As Ed Guerrero points out, Murphy has "no self-interest in [this] narrative, nor [does he] question or threaten the power relations of the dominant social order."[15] Toward the end of the film, Cates issues an apology/explanation of his behavior by telling Hammond he was "just doing my job keeping you down." The film goes a step further when the black police captain (Frank McRae) also calls Hammond a nigger, signaling to the audience both that it's okay to use that term and that the racial resentment police show toward black communities is embedded in the structures of authority.

John Landis's *Trading Places* (1983) stars Dan Aykroyd as Louis Winthorpe III, an overprivileged futures trader whose bosses, Randolph and Mortimer Duke (Ralph Bellamy and Don Amache), are obsessed with the nature-versus-nurture argument concerning success. The Dukes take a "perfectly useless psychopath [Murphy's Billy Ray Valentine] and turned him into a successful executive. During the same time [they] turned an honest, hard-working man into a violently deranged would be killer." *Trading Places* is far more interested in class distinctions as opposed to racial ones, though the latter makes itself known in several moments during the film. When

Winthorpe is interacting in his world, we see that he occupies wholly white spaces that are comprised of his workplace, his country club, and his circle of friends. In contrast, when Valentine moves into his upper-class home and throws a party, his "friends" come from a variety of racial backgrounds. The Dukes and Winthorpe, before he is relegated to the lower rungs of society, have a complete lack of empathy and a total disdain for working-class and poor folk. The brothers turn Winthorpe's and Valentine's lives upside down over a one-dollar bet. There are only a few instances when race explicitly enters the narrative. As Valentine proves that his abilities as an investor are as good as Winthorpe's, the Duke brothers discuss how they will end their wager. Mortimer makes it clear that he does not want Winthorpe back, and Randolph inquires as to whether Valentine will stay. Mortimer reacts in shock, saying, "Do you believe I would have a nigger run our family business?" Unbeknownst to the Dukes, Valentine is in a bathroom stall and overhears their discussion. Valentine tracks down Winthorpe, who has attempted suicide. When the latter awakes from what he thinks is a dream, he comments about the loss of his house, job, and fiancée, and blames it on a "terrible, awful Negro." Later in the film, as Winthorpe and Valentine plot their revenge on the Dukes, Winthorpe unsuccessfully disguises himself in blackface and a loc wig to fool a corrupt business associate of the Dukes. There is no discussion as to why that particular disguise was chosen, or of the racist implications of having a white person don blackface, and because Valentine is clearly in on the plan, there is a tacit approval for the costume.

In Murphy's most profitable live-action film, *Beverly Hills Cop* (1984), he played a role that was not written for him: Axel Foley was originally supposed to be played by Sylvester Stallone. In the film, Murphy plays an impoverished Detroit police detective whose childhood friend Mikey is murdered during a visit. Foley travels to Beverly Hills to find out who killed Mikey and why. The film is a traditional fish-out-of-water tale, and the humor lies in watching Foley acclimate to his new racial and socioeconomic surroundings. Because the character was not written as a black man, the lack of attention paid to race in the film is almost understandable. Director Martin Brest has said that he wanted to stay away from race because he did not want it to be an issue in the film.[16] The only scene where race is directly addressed is when Foley first arrives in Beverly Hills and tries to con his way into staying at the Beverly Palms Hotel. When Foley is rebuffed because there are no vacancies, he accuses the hotel of racism and shames the manager into accommodating him. While the scene is memorable and humorous, it is also problematic for two reasons. First, it "turns the very idea of racism into a joke," and second, it reinforces the idea that "some white Americans were complaining [that] blacks found racism in places where it did not exist."[17] The audience knows both that Foley did not have a reservation and that the receptionist is not lying when she tells Foley that the hotel has no vacancies. Since the scene is played for humor, the larger ramifications of Foley's actions are swept aside.

Though racially Foley is out of place in Beverly Hills, the film focuses more on the character's socioeconomic status than on his racial identity. Even before Foley leaves for Beverly Hills, he is not framed in racial terms, an interesting choice given his location in Detroit, a city that is often framed in racial terms; however, as Philippa Gates points out, "The black male body is offered as heroic only when it is contained by a lack of sexuality or action, isolation from a black community, or class."[18] Though his boss is black, most if not all of his coworkers are white; the best friend who is murdered is white; the suspects Foley pursues during a car chase at the beginning of the film are white; and the childhood friend he meets in Beverly Hills, Jenny Summers, is also white.

As questionable as the racial dynamics of the film's version of Detroit are, the real-world socioeconomics of Motown were also problematic. In the late 1960s, members of the Detroit Police Officers Association were the third-highest-paid police officers in the country.[19] While all public employees experienced some loss in wages during the 1980s due to the Reagan administration's cuts to city government spending and white flight, because of the relative strength of civil defense unions, this wage loss was usually quite small. Since Foley was a detective, he would have been earning more than the average patrolperson, and more than likely would have been able to afford more than the "crappy blue Chevy Nova" that was a source of comedy throughout the film. The fish-out-of-water tale would not have been as drastic and comedic if Foley was portrayed as the middle-class worker the character probably would have been in reality. The misrepresentation of Detroit is made all the more egregious given the fact that the film's producer, Jerry Bruckheimer, is from Detroit: he graduated from the middle-class high school named on the shirt Murphy wears throughout the film.[20] Murphy's performance helped propel *Beverly Hills Cop* to earn over $230 million at the domestic box office, which made it the highest-grossing film of 1984.[21] The film spawned two sequels, and a third has been the subject of rumors for several years.

You Keep Using That Word. I Don't Think It Means What You Think It Means

Mainstream discussions typically associate *Harlem Nights* with failure. As mentioned in the beginning of this chapter, it is true that critics, for the most part, did not enjoy the film; however, critical disdain does not necessarily equal box-office failure. Despite the critical condemnation rained on the film, by every other metric it was successful. According to IMDb, Murphy filmed *Nights* for $30 million, and it grossed $60 million domestically and another $35 million internationally.[22] The film ranked number one the weekend it was released, is number twenty-one on the list of the highest-grossing domestic films of 1989, and comes in at thirteen on the list of worldwide box-office earnings for that year.[23] At the time, *Harlem Nights*'s opening of $16.1 million "was the third-biggest U.S. Thanksgiving-Christmas release ever."[24] One has to wonder how a film that earned more than triple its production budget is considered a box-office failure. The framing of the film as a failure also does not take into account the controversy mentioned earlier in the chapter. If theater chains were removing *Harlem Nights* from screens due to concerns over violence, it would help explain why the film did not meet its financial expectations; as one viewer commented, a movie can't make money if it's not being shown in theaters.[25] It seems misguided to blame Murphy, or the film, for theater owners' decisions. In many ways, *Harlem Nights* continues to be judged not on its own merits but by circumstances that have little to do with the film itself.

One aspect of the film that critics focused on was the amount of profanity. In his review, Roger Ebert notes that "Murphy and Pryor are famous for their liberal use of four and 12–letter words in their comedy monologues, but did Harlem dandies in the 1930s speak like stand-up comedians in the 1980s? I don't think so."[26] Vincent Canby of the *New York Times*, whose overall review was kinder than most, opines, "The characters in 'Harlem Nights' talk dirtier than movie characters used to. Vulgarity has become a principal means of communication."[27] William Thomas of *Empire* argues that "if endlessly repeating the phrase 'motherfucker' was intrinsically amusing then *Harlem Nights* would be the funniest film ever made."[28] Almost thirty years after the film's release, a Google search for "*Harlem Nights* profanity" brings up multiple stories about the fact that some variation of the word "fuck" appears in the film 133 times. What is interesting about that criticism is that *Harlem Nights* did not even hold the record for the number of f-bombs in films released the same year. According to multiple internet sources, Oliver

Stone's *Born on the Fourth of July* has 196 variations of the f-bomb and Spike Lee's *Do the Right Thing* has 240. While both Stone's and Lee's films received some criticism, the reviews did not call attention to the use of profanity. Part of that might be because of the time period in which *Nights* take place; however, as Ebert points out, the profanity should not be surprising given the fact that Murphy uses profanity in all of his R-rated films.

Class Politics and Location

Though Murphy could have set his film during any time period, it is telling that he chose Harlem in the 1930s. An extremely important moment, particularly within African American history, "The Harlem Renaissance may best be conceptualized as a group of black writers and poets, orbiting erratically around a group of black intellectuals positioned in the N.A.A.C.P., the Urban League, and other African American political and educational institutions."[29] Some of the most influential writers in American culture emerged from this period, including Zora Neale Hurston, Langston Hughes, Countee Cullen, and Jean Toomer. Their writings "included race-building and image-building, jazz poetics, progressive or socialist politics, racial integration, the musical and sexual freedom of Harlem nightlife, and the pursuit of hedonism."[30] Jazz and blues musicians including Louis Armstrong, Cab Calloway, and Duke Ellington played at local clubs that are immortalized in *Harlem Nights*. Partly because of the artistic output of this time period, the neighborhood of Harlem holds a special allure for black communities. Legendary basketball player and author Kareem Abdul-Jabbar has said that one of his favorite quotes states: "'I'd rather be a lamppost in Harlem than governor of Georgia.' People don't understand a black American saying that but it's so true [that it's about] being someplace that you are accepted and encouraged to be at your best."[31] The location and the time period in which *Harlem Nights* exists evokes very specific racial connotations far more than any other film Murphy had been in at that point in his career.

While the film focuses on a particular historical moment, the physical setting also had personal resonance for Murphy. Sugar Ray's bar was based on a real bar in Brooklyn owned by Murphy's Uncle Ray. Murphy's uncle remembered that he "used to tell Eddie the stories about when I ran with the mafia . . . that Donnie Brascoe [sic] and all of that."[32] This aesthetic is highlighted during a conversation between Sugar Ray and Detective Phil Cantone, when Cantone describes Club Sugar Ray as "an after-hours spot" that is the "hottest spot in Harlem" where customers can "gamble, drink,

Quick, Ray, and Bennie admire Harlem

fuck, dance." It is places like Sugar Ray's bar where writers, entertainers, critics, patrons, and sometimes common folk congregated. We see this throughout the film as regular folks, both white and black, dress in their finest attire and come to dance and gamble along with celebrities such as the heavyweight champion Jack Jenkins (Stan Shaw).[33]

The racial and class divide is exposed when Cantone visits Sugar Ray at his home. Cantone compliments Sugar Ray on his suit, assuming he purchased it from Macy's. Sugar Ray corrects him, informing Cantone that his suits are custom-made and offering to provide him with the name of his tailor. When Cantone says that he buys his clothes off the rack, Sugar Ray sarcastically says he can't believe it because "your clothes fit you so well." In the previous scene, we see the employees and the customers at Sugar Ray's dressed in formal attire, and it is clear by the differences in the men's appearances that Cantone is in a much lower tax bracket than Sugar Ray. Cantone inquires how Sugar Ray is able to afford his nice home and custom-made suits, to which Sugar Ray replies that he's owned a candy store for the past twenty years. Cantone opines that there "must not be a nigger on the street with a healthy tooth in his mouth," given how successful Sugar Ray appears to be. Though Prohibition ended five years prior to the main events of the film, there is still quite a bit of illegal activity happening in Club Sugar Ray, so it is not surprising that the crew would have a front of some kind to prevent the very police interference Cantone represents. It is clear that Cantone either wants Sugar Ray to pay him off or is trying to shut the club down.

I'm an Honest Ho and All My Hos Is Honest

Though mainstream critics eviscerated *Harlem Nights*, the complaints did not touch upon the most interesting aspect of the film: the gender politics. If they are mentioned at all, the general consensus about the women in the film is summed up by Donald Bogle's brief characterization that they "seemed to spring from the imagination of a vindictive misogynist."[34] How did Bogle arrive at that conclusion? Let's go back to the scene recreated in Busta Rhymes "Pass the Courvoisier, Part II." In *Harlem Nights*, the employees of Club Sugar Ray are counting the night's receipts, and Vera is late because sex work does not end when the club closes. Quick complains that "the girls" only brought in $200, despite the fact that the club was packed. He then implies that Vera is stealing money, a charge that she does not take lightly. To defend her integrity, Vera challenges Quick to a fight. He initially treats the fight as a joke, literally laughing in Vera's face when he steps into the alley, until she punches him in the nose. Vera sends Quick flying across the alley, telling him, "You're going to have to learn to respect me" in between punches. Quick rebounds only because he grabs a trashcan lid (and shortly thereafter the entire trashcan), and hits Vera with it. Unfortunately for Quick, this does not deter Vera. As she gets up off the ground, the score from *Jaws* plays in the background, implying two things: first, that Quick has completely underestimated his opponent and messed with the wrong person, and second, that Vera is a predator. Vera shows that she is ready to defend herself by removing a switchblade from her bra as the background music switches to the theme from *Psycho*. It is interesting that Vera is framed as the "psycho" in this scene, despite the fact that it was Quick who escalated the violence in the first place. Quick takes it another step by pulling a pistol from an ankle holster and shooting Vera in her pinky toe.

There are a few ways to read this scene in terms of the gender politics. On the one hand, as discussed in the *Nothing But a Man* chapter, watching a protagonist perpetuate violence against a woman is problematic to say the least. In *Man*, the audience usually reacts with disbelief when Duff pushes Josie to the floor. Even the character is horrified at what he has done and physically removes himself from the situation before he can inflict any more damage. The scene serves as a warning that, because Duff cannot figure out how to deal with the racial and economic violence he has been experiencing, he is taking his frustrations out on Josie. The act of physical violence against Josie is framed as Duff's breaking point.

In *Harlem Nights*, the violence against women is played for comedy, but the question we have to ask ourselves is, Why is the scene funny? Some audiences assume that because Quick is a young man who is presumably the physically stronger of the two, the fight will not be a contest. In this case, both the characters and audience members underestimate Vera's strength. Other viewers assume that Vera is a force to be reckoned with, and are waiting to see Quick get his butt handed to him. Is the scene funny because, as Redd Foxx states after the fight is over, "Vera whipped your ass, and if you hadn't had that gun she'd still be whipping your ass"? If so, is it some sort of progress for gender equality that Vera was able to physically defend her honor, and ultimately lost only because her opponent escalated the violence until he could win? While that could be the case, because Vera is a *black* woman, the controlling images attached to her intersectional identity come into play. Vera's portrayal conforms to the controlling image of the angry black woman, which "depicts Black women as aggressive, loud, rude, and pushy."[35] This portrayal feeds into a long history of "ridiculing African American women as being like men [which] has long been a prominent subtext in the routines of Redd Foxx, Eddie Murphy, Martin Lawrence, and other African American comedians [some of whom] dress up as African American women in order to make fun of them [and depict] them as ugly women who too closely resemble men."[36] The *Psycho* theme music underscores the idea of black women being ridiculous. Is the message supposed to be that women are crazy for trying to defend themselves against physical violence? Is the *Jaws* theme meant to imply that Vera is less than human?

Filmmaker Spike Lee, whose films employ complicated gender politics of their own, confronted Murphy on the scene, saying that Della Reese reminded him of his grandmother, and that he felt uncomfortable watching Murphy assault a motherly figure. Murphy countered that, "It was a comic moment. Who's to say that you can't hit a woman in comedy? It was a joke ... throughout the whole scene [the audience] laughed at that. The joke was, I got my ass whipped by this old woman. That's funny. See, when you're talking about comedy, you're talking about apples and oranges."[37] In the interview, Murphy acknowledged that some audience members found the scene uncomfortable, but countered that others thought it was hilarious. He also made the distinction between comedy and real life. Della Reese herself has not been critical of the scene or the film as a whole, and does not think that the role was at odds with the faith-based turn her career took later. When asked in 2012 whether she regretted her participation in *Harlem Nights*, Reese remarked, "I thank God every day for that role in *Harlem Nights*. I

Quick apologizes to Vera

come from that kind of environment. That character that I played. I *know that woman.* I grew up with her living down the street from me. No honey, *Harlem Nights* stretched my ability to act."[38] Murphy points out that Vera was based on the character Kiss My Ass, Big Bertha, from Richard Pryor's 1971 album *Craps (After Hours)*, which is more than likely based on a person Pryor knew or heard of from his family's brothels. It is clear that at least for the actors involved, women like Vera exist in the real world and the movie afforded them an opportunity to highlight these women's experiences. As viewers and critics, how do we reconcile the fact that we do not want to support portrayals of black women that reek of misogynoir[39] with the fact that there are real-world examples of women like Vera, and we should not erase them from memory? As Sharon Harley reminds us, "Telling this story is neither to glorify nor to suggest a universal acceptance of criminal behavior."[40] The goal should be to imbue these characters with nuance regardless of whether they are paragons of virtue. By all accounts, this is exactly what Reese did with her portrayal of Vera.

Later in the film, Sugar Ray asks Quick if he has apologized to Vera for shooting her in the toe. Quick has assumed that the whole matter is forgotten, but Ray and Benny remind him that Vera is a "sweet old woman." Quick does express sincere regret when he tells Vera "I never said I'm sorry to nobody for nothing I did. . . . I appreciate everything that you've done for me." Vera doesn't acknowledge his apology but instead berates him into sending someone out for some orange juice. Quick's reply—"I love you too"—is not said in a sarcastic way. After Quick leaves the room, Vera tears up, saying, "I love that little ol' boy." It's clear there is genuine affection between all of the characters, even if they don't openly show it.

The complicated gender politics continue to be manifested later in the film as Quick goes on a date with Calhoune's girlfriend, Dominique La Rue (Jasmine Guy), after Calhoune tries to convince Quick to join his organization. Quick predictably refuses Calhoune's offer, and La Rue is sent to persuade him. She makes it clear that her interest in Quick is both business and personal. As La Rue steps into the bathroom to undress, Quick removes his jacket and goes to place a gun under each pillow. When he overturns the second pillow he discovers that La Rue also keeps a gun under her pillow, a trait he finds adorable until he realizes that La Rue has been tasked with killing him. Instead of fleeing his would-be assassin, Quick stays and has sex with her. Afterward, La Rue reaches for her gun and tries to shoot Quick, but unbeknownst to her, Quick has removed the bullets from her gun. He then shoots her in the head. Author bell hooks and filmmaker Isaac Julien are not fond of the film, and hooks characterizes this scene as an example of "the tragic vision of black heterosexuality."[41] While the film overall features some troubling aspects of black patriarchy and heterosexuality, however, this particular scene does not feel as cut-and-dried as hooks and Julien make it out to be.

Yes, it feels as though Quick is engaging in a form of toxic heterosexual masculinity when he realizes La Rue plans to kill him, but then sleeps with her anyway prior to pulling the trigger himself. However, before she tries to kill him, La Rue reminds Quick that everyone in their line of work is a criminal and can't be trusted. Is it fair to judge Quick for engaging in the exact same behavior that La Rue did? Quick and La Rue are essentially equals, and he happens to get the better of her in this situation. While Quick had hoped to learn more information about Calhoune from La Rue, there is no evidence to suggest that he intended to kill her until he learned of her plans. La Rue understood, as did Quick, that they were involved in a criminal enterprise which could have deadly consequences. Quick's actions were not self-defense by any means: he knew La Rue's gun was not loaded when he killed her, and while La Rue's actions were motivated by business, Quick made it clear that his were personal. La Rue used sex, or the prospect of sex, to lure Quick into an ambush not once but twice: earlier in the film Quick believed he was meeting La Rue for a dinner date but was instead greeted by Calhoune making a business proposition. Quick was offended that his seemingly genuine interest in La Rue was manipulated and could have cost him his life.

The toxicity here is tied to an eye-for-an-eye mentality that is connected to hypermasculinity, is a by-product of the business the characters are engaged in, or is a combination of the two. When Quick relays the evening's events to Ray, he comments that "I ain't no punk. You try to kill me, I kill you." The fact that Quick frames his need for self-preservation to not being a punk, a derogatory term used to ostracize gay men, bolsters hooks's claim that this is a form of tragic black heterosexuality. Ray corrects Quick by telling him to lay low until their plan is ready:

> I didn't come this far with you so you could prove that you ain't no punk and die. What are they gonna put on your tombstone? Here lies a man, 27 years old—he died but he ain't no punk? Hey man, that's bullshit. Okay. You know when you die when you're eighty-nine, you got your children and your grandchildren around the bed, that's cool. It ain't cool to die at twenty-seven.

Quick does embody a toxic heterosexual masculinity, but the film goes out of its way to show that Quick's approach is not what the audience should be rooting for. The notion that not being framed as a punk is worth dying for is quickly dismissed as juvenile and unhealthy. Ray also reminds Quick that violence is not what they're all about—Calhoune is the gangster, but they are businessmen. While the film presents a tragic form of black heterosexuality, it also points it out and literally calls it bullshit.

Quick's encounter with La Rue brings up another interesting aspect of gender politics: the use of sex to further one's goals, a tactic that plays a key role in the film. When it becomes clear that Calhoune is trying to put Sugar Ray's out of business, the group devises a solution to rid themselves of their problems and make a sizable amount of money. Their plan is to steal the money Calhoune was betting on the heavyweight prize fight, a plot that involves setting up the man who transports the money, Richie Vento (Vic Polizos). Ray asks Vera to spy on Richie, and asks if she has a girl who can turn him out. Vera replies, "I have got a girl whose pussy is so good, if you threw it in the air it would turn into sunshine." This is the origin of Lela Rochon's character name referenced earlier in this chapter. Ray's entire plan hinges on whether or not Sunshine can seduce and manipulate Richie. Sunshine certainly succeeds; not only do Sugar Ray's crew steal Calhoune's money, take out Calhoune and his men, and imprison Cantone, but Richie leaves his wife and children to be with Sunshine, although it is doubtful that she is still interested in him—from her point of view, their relationship was about business. Though the film ends on a somewhat somber note as the crew leaves Harlem, the fact that they have a million dollars makes it clear that they will be able to start again in a new city.

Sunshine's usefulness as a character is dependent on her sexuality, which can be read as problematic. Black women have been used as sexual labor since the United States was founded, and as Kamala Kempadoo points out, "Women of color remain in various ways racialized as highly sexual in nature, and positioned as 'ideal' for sex work."[42] Of course, the film does not address how and why Vera and or the other women engage in sex work. One can imagine that in the 1930s, there were few opportunities for women in general and black women specifically to earn a decent living. We have to keep in mind that historically and in the present, "underground, illegal, and quasi-legal economies—from gambling to prostitution and beyond—offered marginalized ways to survive and prosper within the U.S. political economy."[43] There is no evidence that Vera or Sugar Ray mistreat or disrespect the sex workers, and the notion that sex work is disreputable, even when performed by consenting adults, is a puritanical argument that I will not delve into, particularly because "sex work is an integral part of the global economy and is deeply embedded in, and cannot be easily disassembled from, many women's everyday lives, strategies, and identities."[44]

Going back to the fight between Vera and Quick, it is important to note that Vera was fighting to protect her integrity—the implication that she was stealing was an insult she could not abide. Being a madam had nothing to do with the disagreement. The point is, it can be framed as problematic that the majority of the women in the film are engaged in some form of sex work; on the other hand, such work is deemed necessary and is not degraded in any way by characters in the film. As La Rue points out, virtually everyone in the film is involved in criminal enterprises. The only possible exception is the boxer, and to be fair, boxing as a sport has historically been linked with crime as well. Since that is the realm of the film, it makes sense that the women are also engaged in some form of criminal activity just as the men are.

Curtain Call

When discussing black films of the 1980s, *Harlem Nights* is rarely mentioned, despite the fact that Eddie Murphy was one of the most popular and profitable actors of that decade. The film is also an interesting departure from Murphy's early films, which catered to white audiences. Films like *Harlem Nights*, *Coming to America* (1988), and *Boomerang* (1992) were made about black characters for black audiences without apology. *Nights* continues to be framed in awkward ways. On the one hand, it is framed as a financial failure despite the fact that its box-office revenue was triple the filming budget. Critics framed *Harlem Nights* as one of the worst films ever made, while audiences, particularly black ones, continue to view the film as a comedy classic. Seeing a discrepancy between how critics versus audiences frame a film is not an isolated phenomenon; however, the racial component is quite stark. One audience member who identified herself as a seventy-two-year-old black woman argued that white critics did not enjoy the film because "it shows a group of black hoodlums outsmarting a group of white hoodlums."[45] With all of the arguments over violence, profanity, and reception, what has gotten lost from an academic perspective is what the film says about black gender politics—and even that framing is complicated. On the surface, *Harlem Nights* feels like a caper film with men taking up the majority of the narrative space. While that is certainly true, the female characters and their place both in the narrative and in society as a whole is complicated.

All of the women in this film use their bodies to achieve their goals, and the majority of the women in the film are engaged in sex work. While that could be viewed as a controlling image meant to perpetuate the idea of black women as hypersexual, the fact that all the characters in the film are connected to underground economies alters the deleterious framing of these characters. Vera and Sunshine, specifically, are integral to the plot of the film and are never denigrated for their roles as sex workers. Certainly, probably few theorists of black feminist thought would point to the use of profanity and violence as ways to define empowering images. In this case, however, it is safe to say that Vera and Sunshine are probably the two most memorable characters in the film, and they engage in whatever activities they must in order to survive and thrive in their environment. Sometimes that means playing the sexy vixen role to snare a mark, as Sunshine does. Other times it means alternating between being a hard-ass so as not appear weak in front of one's colleagues and playing the frail old lady to entrap a rival, as Vera does. They are professionals who can take care of themselves and go toe-to-toe with the male characters in the film. Are they empowering representations of black womanhood or stereotypes of hypersexual criminals? The answer depends on one's point of view. Of course, we have to remember that "political activism and criminal behavior [are not] mutually exclusive,"[46] and that imaginary divide seems to drive much of the criticism of the film's female characters. *Harlem Nights* is a caper film, and the conventions of that genre dictate that pretty much every character will be involved in criminal activity. Critics and viewers cannot and should not expect every black character to be paragons of virtue. The film does not frame the characters' criminality as somehow wedded to their race. Vera and Sunshine engage in sex work because it's a job—it says nothing about who they are as individuals. In the end, over thirty years after its release, *Harlem Nights* continues to be judged less on its own merits and more on situations that have very little to do with the film itself.

4

Who's the Real Gangsta?
The Glass Shield and the Politics of Black Communities and Police Relations

Now if you're white you can trust the police / But if you're black they ain't nothin' but beasts / Watch out for the kill / Don't make a false move and keep your hands on the steering wheel / And don't get smart / Answer all questions, and that's your first lesson / On stayin' alive / In South Central, yeah, that's how you survive.
                    Ice Cube, "How to Survive in South Central," 1991

As a historical matter, people of color have not been the beneficiaries of effective law enforcement. In other words, the privacy losses they experience are not the price they pay for effective crime prevention and detection, but a cost of race. This suggests that people of color are under-protected even as they are over-policed. In effect, from the perspective of many people of color, the Fourth Amendment has been erased.
                    Devon W. Carbado, "(E)racing the Fourth Amendment," 2002

On August 9, 2014, Michael Brown, an eighteen-year-old resident of Ferguson, Missouri, was shot and killed by police officer Darren Wilson. His body was left on the sidewalk for four hours in full view of family and friends. Brown was unarmed and had not committed any crime when Wilson killed him. Brown's death sparked outrage from the residents of Ferguson, who, in their anger and grief, initiated several days of protests that were met by militarized police resistance. Those clashes were broadcast all over the world. Contradictory witness accounts led a grand jury to not file charges against Wilson for Brown's death, and after conducting an independent investigation, the U.S. Justice Department did not have enough evidence to pursue charges of civil rights violations against Wilson. Black communities have been decrying the harassment, abuse, and killing of unarmed black citizens by law enforcement since police forces have existed; however, with the Michael Brown case, something changed. This time brought a renewed sense of vigor, due in large part to the proliferation of social media platforms that gave ordinary citizens the ability to tell their stories, as well as to capture and disseminate video of community/police interactions.

Just one month prior to Brown's death, forty-three-year-old Eric Garner was killed by New York police officers as he was being arrested for selling loose cigarettes. The officers placed Garner in a chokehold, a move that had been banned by the New York City Police Department years earlier, and it ultimately led to Garner's death. In this case, unlike with Brown, there was cellphone video of the entire incident, which captured Garner gasping for air and repeatedly saying "I can't breathe." That video went viral on social media and was broadcast on national news. The similarity with the Brown case was that no one would be held accountable for Garner's death. The cluster of two highly publicized incidents of extrajudicial police killings of unarmed black men in such a short period of time increased awareness and resistance to the practice.

Unfortunately, it seemed as though a new incident of a black citizen being killed by police was entering the public consciousness on a regular basis: Laquan McDonald in Chicago: shot sixteen times—the majority of shots were fired into McDonald's back; twenty-two-year old Darrien Hunt in Saratoga Springs, Utah: killed while cosplaying with a sword; twenty-two-year-old John Crawford III in Beavercreek, Ohio: killed in a Walmart for carrying a BB gun sold by the store; fifty-year-old Walter Scott in North Charleston, South Carolina: shot in the back while fleeing police over a broken brake light; forty-three-year-old Samuel DuBose: shot in the head by a University of Cincinnati police officer during a traffic stop; twenty-five-year-old Freddie Gray in Baltimore, Maryland: died of spinal cord injuries sustained while in police custody; twelve-year-old Tamir Rice in Cleveland, Ohio: killed within two seconds of officers encountering him playing with a toy gun in a public park across the street from his home; twenty-eight-year-old Sandra Bland in Waller County, Texas: died under mysterious circumstances while in police custody; forty-year-old Terence Crutcher: shot with his hands up while walking away from police officers in Tulsa, Oklahoma; thirty-two-year-old Philando Castile: shot in his car in Minnesota, and whose death was live-streamed by his girlfriend. The list goes on. The deaths of Crawford, Scott, Hunt, McDonald, Rice, Crutcher, and Castile were all captured on video and were played on endless loops for the world to see. Spurred by the 2012 death of Trayvon Martin at the hands of George Zimmerman, and the seeming, yet unverifiable uptick in the deaths of unarmed black folks, Patrisse Cullors, Opal Tometi, and Alicia Garza created the hashtag #BlackLivesMatter as an "ideological and political intervention in a world where Black lives are systematically and intentionally targeted for demise. It is an affirmation of Black folks' humanity, our contributions to this society, and our resilience in the face of deadly oppression."[1] The hashtag exploded on social media and turned into a guiding principle that activists have rallied around to bring police misconduct, as well as a variety of related social justice issues that affect black and brown communities, to the forefront.

At present, the Black Lives Matter network serves as a "chapter-based national organization working for the validity of Black life"[2] and was a finalist for *Time* magazine's 2015 person of the year because of "the way it has weaponized protest. Activists strategically shut down Chicago's Magnificent Mile on Black Friday [in 2015] and blocked traffic along Washington's I-395 on one of the busiest travel days of the year. The demonstrations were chosen to maximize impact: causing discomfort is designed to make society feel the pain and frustration of living as a black person in America."[3] Though Black Lives Matter has brought attention to the killing of unarmed black folks around the nation, as of 2018 only two officers have been convicted of any crimes associated with the deaths listed above, and in several cases district attorneys and grand juries declined to even file charges. Discussions of police misconduct, brutality, and misconduct are no longer confined to black communities.

One of the more interesting and often overlooked films to deal with the relationship between law enforcement and black communities is Charles Burnett's 1994 film *The Glass Shield*. One of the most memorable and explosive events of the 1990s was the March 3, 1991, videotaped and widely publicized beating of unarmed motorist Rodney King by Los Angeles police officers, whose acquittal by an all-white jury one year later led city residents to react with rage. As such, the subject of police and community relations were in the public consciousness when Burnett's film was released. Based on true events, the film follows J. J. Johnson, the first black deputy at his sheriff's department station in California. Although Johnson had wanted to be a police officer his entire life, the audience watches as he becomes disillusioned with his career choice due to the harassment he endures from his fellow officers, as well as the rampant corruption he sees and eventually participates in. According to *New Yorker* film critic Terrence Rafferty, the film is "a thoughtful, lucid moral drama with a deeply conflicted hero and no gunplay whatsoever."[4] As Cliff Thompson argues in his overview of Burnett's filmography, "The standard equipment of Hollywood cop movies—gore, steamy sex, high-speed chases, and more gore—are refreshingly absent [in *The Glass Shield*]. What takes their place is a statement about institutionalized corruption and racism and the need to maintain one's integrity in the face of them."[5] An independent feature hampered by outside interference and overshadowed by black films that highlighted black poverty and criminality, *The Glass Shield* escaped critical attention and box-office success. Unlike the previously discussed *Nothing But a Man*, *The Glass Shield* has not enjoyed any sort of renaissance except by those who appreciate Burnett's overall body of work and recognize the film as his first studio feature. Given the increased national discussions about police misconduct, it is worthwhile to analyze what *The Glass Shield* brings to the table in terms of our perception and understanding of how and why violence against black bodies by law enforcement continues to occur. It is also useful to consider what factors contributed to the film's lack of acclaim and visibility, and how the tone and subject matter relate to other black films released during the same time period.

While the other chapters in this book use elements of critical race theory (CRT) to analyze the messages being conveyed by various films, this chapter will employ CRT in a different manner. In her article "Vulnerable, Not Voiceless: Outsider Narrative in Advocacy Against Discriminatory Policing," Nicole Smith Futrell points out that critical race theorists "have long recognized that stories and storytelling can serve as a platform for marginalized members of society to challenge the legal status quo in order to effect change. Narratives from vulnerable individuals have a particularly vital role to play in addressing the racial subordination that can be manifested in aggressive urban policing practices."[6] As such, this chapter is less about analyzing *The Glass Shield* from the viewpoint of CRT, and more about framing the film as a CRT intervention into the discussion of police corruption and violence. This film itself tells a story from the viewpoint of a marginalized member of society who seeks to address racial subordination being manifested in aggressive policing practices and to change the status quo.

New Black Realism

As Hollywood moved into the 1990s, studios "began to target multiple niche markets with a diversity of products. This shift increased the opportunities for African American filmmakers and for black-oriented films."[7] This black film renaissance, dubbed New Black Realism, featured films that "most often took as their subject matter young black men living in the inner city who sometimes engaged in deviant behavior. These young men's lives were portrayed as chaotic and nihilistic, ripe with violence and drugs. [At the same time] these filmmakers made an active attempt to imbue these young men with humanity."[8] Mario Van Peebles's *New Jack City* (1991), John Singleton's *Boyz n the Hood* (1991), Ernest Dickerson's *Juice* (1992), Albert and Allen Hughes's *Menace II Society* (1993), and F. Gary Gray's *Set It Off* (1996) are some examples from that time. Many of the films "depicted children dealing with racism and violence while growing up in urban America," and many of the films' main characters exhibit a "familiarity with the ghetto and an understanding how the youth service international commerce; the facility to move, high-tech beepers in hand and guns at the ready, adroitly between the realm of formal education and the informal crack-based economic sector."[9] Because of the focus on criminality, according to Mark A. Reid, "these films inadvertently create the 'bad nigger' as the only appropriate outlet for a community that has limited socioeconomic resources and opportunities."[10] If the main protagonists of these films are gangsters, it makes sense that one thing many of these films have in common is a depiction of young people's interactions with law enforcement.

The most successful example of New Black Realism is John Singleton's *Boyz n the Hood*. The film was nominated for two Oscars, Best Original Screenplay and Best Director; Singleton became the youngest and the first African American to be nominated for Best Director. *Boyz* follows Tre Styles (played as a boy by Desi Arnez Hines II and as an older version by Cuba Gooding Jr.), who is sent to live with his father Furious (Laurence Fishburne) after getting into a fight at school. Tre has multiple encounters with Los Angeles police officers during the film, and they are all contentious. When Tre initially moves in with his father, Furious shoots at a home invader. It takes over an hour for police to respond, and when they do arrive, a black officer (Jessie

Ferguson) laments the fact that Furious did not kill the intruder because "it's one less nigger we have to deal with." Furious takes offense at the officer's language and message, and when asked if there is a problem, replies, "Yeah, it's just too bad you don't know what it is . . . brother." Later, when Tre and Ricky (Morris Chestnut) are pulled over for driving while black, that same officer puts a gun to Tre's throat and spews a racist speech: "Scared now, ain't you? I like that. That's why I took this job; I hate little motherfuckers like you. Little niggers, you ain't shit! I could blow your head off with this Smith and Wesson and you couldn't do shit."

By having a black police officer deliver these lines while his white partner looks on without comment or protest, *Boyz* makes the argument that simply diversifying police forces will not be enough to end racist practices. In the real world, police departments that are racially diverse still enact policies and practices that have a disproportionately negative effect on black and brown communities. For example, in 2014 the New York Police Department was 51 percent white, 26 percent Latino, 16 percent black, and 6 percent Asian American.[11] Despite the fact that the racial makeup of the NYPD closely mirrored the city's overall population, this did not prevent the department from perpetuating its stop-and-frisk rules, under which a court found that "many black and Latino New Yorkers had been detained and searched by New York City police officers without the requisite level of reasonable suspicion."[12] In Baltimore, as of 2015, slightly more than half of the active duty officers were African American, Latino, Asian American, or Native American, and of the six police officers indicted in the 2015 death of Freddie Gray, three were black. The issue is not just the fact that bad actors exist in every race, but that the structures of police departments themselves perpetuate racist practices.[13] In fact, according to Paul Butler, "Racial animus is not necessary to participate in or be an accomplice to a racial subordination system."[14] Eduardo Bonilla-Silva believes this participation occurs, in the case of law enforcement, because "Police officers live in a 'cops' world' and develop a cop mentality [and] that cops' world is a highly racialized one; minorities are viewed as dangerous, prone to crime, violent, and disrespectful."[15]

Directed by Albert and Allen Hughes, *Menace II Society* paints Los Angeles as the same violent landscape that *Boyz* does. The film begins by showing the main protagonists, Caine (Tyrin Turner) and O-Dog (Larenz Tate), robbing a grocery store and killing the two owners in the process. According to Paula Massood, "The film succeeds in painting a disturbing picture of violence, one in which the characters' lack of remorse, rather than stylistic convention, shapes and colors the horror of the image."[16]

Caine's encounters with law enforcement are numerous. In one instance, he is brought in for questioning regarding his involvement with the grocery store murders. He is questioned without an attorney present, and we never see him being read his rights. When the scene begins, the detective, played by Bill Duke, is backlit with red lighting and framed in shadow. As he moves toward Caine, we see that he has his gun in his hand. He then places the gun on the table, with the barrel of the gun facing Caine, and cocks the trigger before saying, "Now, you listen to me, you little bitch." Clearly the detective does not have much, if any, respect for Caine or his rights. Later in the film, Caine's narration explicitly lays out how young black men are treated by the police. We see him being pulled over for driving while black and arrested for no reason. As the police car drives off, one of the officers is beating Caine and Sharif (Vonte Sweet) with his baton while they are cuffed, offering no resistance, and screaming in pain. We see the officers pull into an alley and throw Caine and Sharif out of the car, near where four Latinos are hanging out and drinking forties. Caine's narration explains, "That night, the cops let us have it. They dropped us off in the wrong 'hood where the esse stay. I guess they was thinking we'd get our ass kicked even more. The esses was cool, though. They took us to the hospital." It is likely that the police treat the Latino men in the same manner that they abuse young black men, so the esses were not going to play the police's game.

Films in the New Black Realism movement hearken back to the Blaxploitation movement in that they were often made on shoestring budgets, featured black protagonists in urban areas, and made huge profits.[17] Many of these films highlight the often antagonistic relationship between young black men and law enforcement, and showcase the poverty and violence that can envelop inner-city neighborhoods. While these films used "trendy rap music, rap singers turned actors, and volatile filmic action to [highlight] the political and social issues that concern African Americans . . . and appeal to the frustration and rage felt particularly by black males,"[18] *The Glass Shield* approached things another way. It took the underlying critiques of the criminal justice system contained within the New Black Realism films and turned them on their head by removing a lot of the physical violence, taking poverty and drug culture off the table, and making the primary protagonist a black law enforcement official.

Welcome to the Jungle

Burnett opens *The Glass Shield* not with the actions of police misconduct or images of urban decay, but with a fantasy that illustrates the basis of Deputy Johnson's wide-eyed optimism about being a police officer. The film begins with animated comic book pages showing the police attempting to take down two suspects who are holding a white female hostage. In the panels, one suspect is firing at officers who are ordering him to drop his weapon and surrender. Johnson is shot in the neck but is still able to shoot and kill the suspect, thereby saving the hostage and his fellow officers. While Johnson's fellow officers mourn his sacrifice, it is clear that because of his heroic actions, he now has the respect of the entire force. The lone female officer in the panels tells Johnson "You *proved* yourself. . . . Your shield is made of *gold!*" (emphasis original).

In essence, popular culture's valorization of police work is what drives Johnson to select this career path. It is telling that the pathway for a black officer to earn the respect of his colleagues is through the shedding of blood and/or death. It is also interesting to point out that the story takes place in Los Angeles, which, one year earlier, had witnessed the police beating of Rodney King—an event that apparently did not deter Johnson from his chosen career path. The look and tone of the opening scene contrasts sharply with the rest of the film. According to film critic Amy Taubin, "The garish color and pulp quality of comic book imagery carries over into the film proper, where it's offset by the intensely subjective point of view of the narrative. The mix of genres throws the viewer off balance and challenges the conventional expectation that films dealing with race will be couched in documentary-style realism."[19] The comic book panels showing Johnson's fictional sacrifice transition into a scene of semi-reality where Johnson is standing at his locker, with a similar comic book panel attached to the door, being called for service. Everything moves in slow motion, emphasizing the fact that while the audience is firmly planted in the real world, Johnson is still caught up in his fantasy world as the intercom voice-over tells him to report to Edgemar Station, saying, "Lucky you, you're about to make history." Though he is slow to see it, there is a sizable difference between the fantasy of being a cop and the reality of being a cop.

A hint of reality seeps in when Johnson arrives at his new precinct and parks in a space reserved for officers. A white officer admonishes him for parking in front of the station:

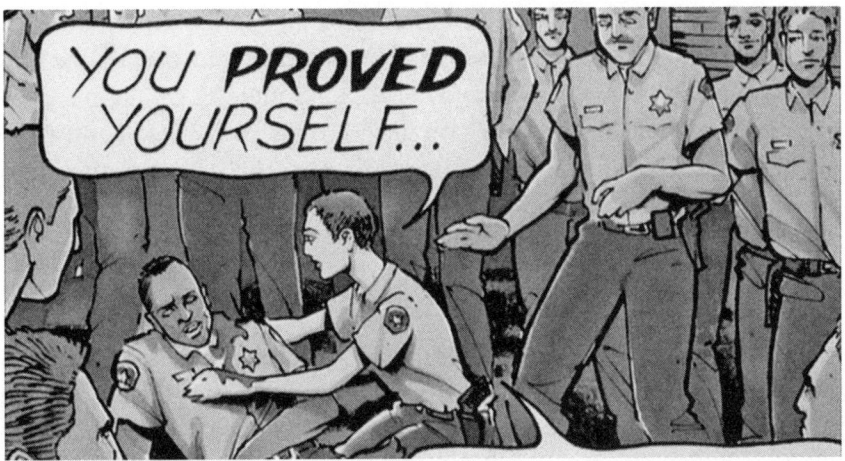

The Glass Shield *opening comic panel*

BUSH: Hey. Can't you read? It says "employees only."
JOHNSON: I am an employee.
BUSH: No. It don't mean trustees. [*Johnson smiles and flashes his badge while walking past.*]

Even the casual dismissal of the idea that he could be a police officer is not enough to shake Johnson's enthusiasm. As we watch him enter the room for the officers' roll call, the commanding officer at the podium, Massey (Richard Anderson), makes an offhand remark about how "Bush has decided to finally get rid of that rice-burnin' piece of crap and ride American." The immediate assumption that Johnson could not possibly be a fellow officer and the reference to a car made outside the United States as a "rice-burning piece of crap" lays the groundwork for how the audience is supposed to read this department: Edgemar is not a civil work environment. The dismissiveness from his fellow officers continues when Johnson is introduced to them and the officer closest to him, Deputy Bono (Don Harvey), does not shake his hand. Most of the remaining officers at least attempt to hide their disdain for Johnson's presence, though only a handful seem genuinely happy to have him aboard.

One Bad Apple or a Whole Rotten Bunch?

It is easy to dismiss the treatment Johnson endures as an individual issue versus an institutional or systemic issue; however, Burnett does not let the audience labor under that delusion for very long. Less than ten minutes into the film, the focus shifts away from Johnson and onto the larger issues between the police department and the black community. One scene opens with a lawyer, Carmen Munoz (Wanda De Jesus), at a press conference speaking about two cases in which the coroner's official report contradicts the sheriff's department findings. Reverend Banks (Tommy Hicks) stands next to her and explains that "all these young men who died while in police custody had no prior criminal records." Lastly we hear from a mother and father whose son died in the police station. We learn that there was not enough evidence to sustain charges against the sheriff's department; however, the coroner ruled that the son died at the hands of another—he did not hang himself as the sheriff department's report maintains.

This would not be the only situation where a police accounting of an incident does not mesh with reality. Of the real-world cases described at the beginning of this chapter, the police report of John Crawford's death stated that officers "shot Crawford only after repeated demands that he drop the rifle," and the 911 call that led to officers' encounter with him stated that "Crawford was pointing the gun at children."[20] However, video of the incident shows that Crawford did not point the gun at anyone and that police fired their weapons "almost immediately after encountering Crawford."[21] In the death of Walter Scott, the police's version of events stated that Scott and Officer Slager "struggled over [a Taser and] that during the struggle the man gained control of the Taser and attempted to use it against the officer." The police also alleged that "Slager 'felt threatened and reached for his department-issued firearm and fired his weapon.'"[22] According to journalist Judd Legum, "the video revealed a very different scenario. Scott, who was unarmed and fleeing, was shot in the back by Slager from a distance of at least 15 feet. After Scott was fatally shot, the video appears to capture Slager planting an object next to Scott."[23] In the case of Laquan McDonald, "A spokesman for Chicago's police union said at the time of the shooting that [Officer Jason] Van Dyke had fired his gun after McDonald lunged at him with a knife, defying an order to drop his weapon."[24] However, the dashcam footage of the incident shows McDonald running away from officers when he was shot. In the case of Samuel DuBose, Officer Ray Tensing's report said that during a routine traffic stop, "He was almost run over by the driver, and was forced to shoot the driver with his duty weapon. . . . Officer Tensing repeated that he was dragged by the vehicle and had to fire his weapon."[25] However, body camera footage shows that DuBose had both hands up when Tensing shot him in the back of the head, and that the car did not begin moving until after the fatal shot was fired. Though videos of police encounters were less prevalent when *The Glass Shield* was released, there was some precedent, and the idea that there could be a discrepancy between a police account of events and what occurred in reality was not that far-fetched. The press conference scene in the movie points to the fact that something more sinister than rude behavior is occurring at Edgemar Station.

The audience gets to witness the systemic dysfunction at Edgemar Station with the case of Teddy Woods. One evening, Johnson is sitting in his police car across the street from a gas station when a red Volkswagen Beetle pulls in. Johnson sees the vehicle but does not move to intercept the car or to call in the license plate, as there has been no suspicious activity. A second police car then pulls into the station behind the car, and Deputy Bono exits the car and asks the driver, Teddy Woods (Ice Cube), for his license. At this point, Johnson pulls his car into the gas station to assist. Bono calls dispatch to ask about the warrants out on Woods and asks where he and his girlfriend are going. Bono even asks Woods what he does for a living that he can afford the car he is driving. Woods, knowing he hasn't committed any crime, asks why he is being questioned. It turns out that Woods does have an outstanding warrant for a traffic violation, at which point the confrontation worsens:

> BONO: Do you mind if I search the car?
> WOODS: Not unless you got a warrant.
> BONO: What do you got in the car, Teddy?
> WOODS: I know my rights.
> BONO: Hey, man, if I arrest you, that car is mine! I can rip it apart, man, tear the seats out. Is that what you want? Keep your hands where I can see 'em, brother!

Woods admits to having a gun in the car, at which point Bono arrests him and Johnson arrests Woods's girlfriend. Bono's emphasis on the word "brother," coupled with his obsession with trying to figure out how Woods is able to afford such a nice car, indicates that the stop was racially motivated. Woods did not consent to the search of his car until Bono threatened him, which makes both the stop and the search illegal. The next scene shows Johnson trying to write up the arrest report and repeatedly failing—partly due to the fact that there was no justification for the stop or the search, and partly due to the fact that his commanding officer had previously criticized Johnson's paperwork.

The audience does not receive verbal confirmation that Woods's stop was racially motivated until later in the film, after Woods is charged with the murder of a white woman named Mrs. Greenspan. District Attorney Ira Kern (Erich Anderson) is prepping Deputy Bono for trial and asks him why Woods was stopped. Bono admits it was because Woods is black and proceeds to say that "it's policy," but Kern stops Bono before he can finish the sentence. The audience is meant to infer that is the department policy to stop black men who drive nice cars. Kerns tells Bono that they cannot cite any racial motive for the stop, so Bono changes his story to say that Woods committed a traffic violation, which the audience knows is a lie. Not only does the audience have a fuller understanding of the racism within the sheriff's department, they also see the district attorney suborn perjury, which anyone who has ever watched any episode of *Law & Order* or *How to Get Away with Murder* knows is illegal.

Not only does Bono testify under oath that Woods made an illegal turn that led to the stop, but Johnson backs up his story while he is on the stand as well. Johnson goes even further by saying that Woods said he "stole" his girlfriend's father's gun, although the audience hears Woods say he "got" it from his girlfriend's father. Johnson also testifies that he was in the process of calling in Woods's license plate when Bono pulled in behind Woods. Again, the audience saw Johnson paying no attention to Woods when he pulled into the gas station, so it is clear he is perjuring himself to protect Bono.

What the film illustrates is not a simple act of perjury; it is evidence of what Julia Simon-Kerr describes as systemic lying, which are "lies that participants in the legal system tell repeatedly, knowing they are lies and with the complicity of all participants, for what they see as a higher purpose."[26] The phenomenon Simon-Kerr discusses is so prevalent that it has a popular name: "testilying." Police resort to this practice "to skirt constitutional restrictions against unreasonable searches and stops [or] the falsehoods appear aimed at convicting people—who may or may not have committed a crime—with trumped-up evidence."[27] It could be argued that Bono lies because he does not want to get caught engaging in racial profiling, because he did not like Woods's attitude, or because of some combination of the two. District Attorney Kern suborns perjury to get a conviction. The audience does not know whether Kern and Bono actually believe that Woods murdered Mrs. Greenspan. Johnson is the only person that the audience knows for certain initially believes that Woods is guilty; this prompts his systemic lying because there is a disconnect between Johnson's knowledge that Woods was racially profiled and the knowledge that admitting that fact would let an accused murderer go free. At the same time, Johnson's lie was also motivated by some self-interest: he wanted to prove that he belonged at Edgemar Station, and backing up a fellow officer was a sure way to gain approval. In this case, systemic lying occurred not because of cognitive dissonance between moral beliefs and concrete outcomes, but because of a combination of self-interest, racial bias, and the knowledge that there will be no consequences.

Shortly after perjuring himself, Johnson reviews his paperwork and notices that the serial number he took from Woods's gun has been changed. When he asks his confidant Deputy Fields (Lori Petty), the only female sheriff at the station, about it, she says that "Woods is the perfect suspect. No one is going to hoot and holler if Woods is put to death." Woods's defense team learns about the changed serial number, likely through an anonymous tip from Johnson, and in an interesting turn of legal strategy, they alert the insurance company to the fact that the sheriff's department might be involved in covering up evidence about Mrs. Greenspan's murder. Because Woods's attorneys have had previous dealings with Edgemar Station, they know that justice in the Woods case has to come from outside. The audience eventually learns that Mrs. Greenspan's husband (Elliot Gould) conspired with several people at Edgemar, including Detective Baker (Michael Ironside) and Detective Hall (M. Emmet Walsh), to cover up the fact that it was Greenspan who killed his wife. The detectives altered the paperwork to make Woods look guilty. Though Baker and Hall frame Woods for the murder, Woods would not have been in police custody if Bono and Johnson had not violated Woods's Fourth Amendment rights with the racially motivated stop and the illegal search.

The Other Shoe

Teddy Woods's case is certainly the A-plot of the film; however, it becomes clear that the way the sheriff's department framed Woods was not an isolated incident. As mentioned earlier in the chapter, the audience learns at the beginning of the film that at least two black men have died in sherriff's custody under mysterious circumstances, including a young man named Ernie Marshall. Though the events leading to Marshall's death slowly unfold over the course of the film, it is helpful to outline exactly what happened to him as the circumstances surrounding his death intersect with Johnson's and Fields's investigation of the conspiracy to frame Teddy Woods.

After the press conference scene, the references to Marshall's death are vague. Marshall's parents tell their attorney that the sheriff's department is harassing them, and in a subsequent scene we see Reverend Banks handing out literature that discusses the wrongdoings that have occurred at the Edgemar Station. The most interesting—and troubling—discussion occurs during another roll call, when Massey briefs his officers on what has been happening and instructs them on how to behave:

> As you know, the attorney general's office did not agree with the findings of the Internal Affairs Commission regarding charges against this station. So I'm happy to report that the four detectives who were on leave are now back on the force. [*Cheers.*] Many of you also know two officers in the city are being sued for $7 million for wrongful death. The city council is cracking down. Budgetary reasons. They wanna take our bullets away. And as for Officer Collins, he's involved in a lawsuit, and many of you will be asked to testify. Now, remember, he's one of us, so . . . talk to no one. That's all.

After Massey dismisses the officers, one turns to Johnson and remarks, "Remember that, J. J. You're one of us, not a 'brother.'" From this exchange the audience surmises that being black is viewed as being incompatible with being a police officer. The most terrifying aspect of Massey's comments is that the audience does not know if he is referring to the Marshall case or to another incident of wrongdoing. After realizing for the first time that Woods may be innocent, and that his lies may lead to Woods's conviction and scheduled execution, Johnson visits the jail cell where Marshall died and asks the officer on duty, Foster (Linden Chiles), what happened:

> JOHNSON: How can a man hang himself in one of these cells?
> FOSTER: Give anybody enough rope, J. J.
> JOHNSON: What?
> FOSTER: J. J., don't get stickin' your nose into anything. I'm gonna tell you somethin'. There are some decent deputies here but don't go looking into a loaded gun. I hope you understand what I'm sayin'. If you know anything just keep your mouth shut. No more questions.
> JOHNSON: You never told anybody?
> FOSTER: There is no one to tell! Don't you understand?

Foster goes on to outline how the sheriff's deputies at Edgemar Station often look the other way when prominent people are suspected of a crime, and that there is some sort of reciprocity agreement for that discretion. It turns out that in exchange for erasing an arrest for the solicitation of sex from a minor, someone buried the investigation into Marshall's death. The discussion between Johnson and Foster reveals that the sheriff's department has broken protocol on more than one occasion; it cements the fact that Ernie Marshall's death was not a suicide; and it points out that the sheriff's department, as well as people outside the station, are covering up that fact. Though the audience never definitively learns who is responsible for Marshall's death, or the circumstances that landed him in jail, the fact that he was murdered by sheriff's deputies is presented as fact. While the audience has watched the events surrounding Woods's case play out on screen, even with the illegal behavior of some of the officers, some audience members might be willing to frame Woods's case as an isolated incident, or as the result of the actions of a few bad actors. The conversation between Johnson and Foster, and the questions surrounding Marshall's death, highlight just how pervasive the racist and illegal culture in the department really is. The film spins a narrative very similar to those found in films within the New Black Realism movement, saying that black and brown communities have little reason to trust law enforcement.

Going back to the idea of framing *The Glass Shield* as an intervention into the discussion of police corruption and violence, Teddy Woods's ordeal in the film serves two purposes. First, it highlights just how pervasive police corruption is. By moving the focus from Woods himself to Johnson and the other officers at Edgemar Station, we avoid the victim-blaming that surrounded the real-world cases of extrajudicial killings by police described at the beginning of the chapter. None of that matters because the audience knows that Woods has not done anything to justify Bono's stop and search, and everything that follows in the film is a direct result of those violations of Woods's constitutional rights. The audience is not required to sympathize or empathize with Woods in order to realize that he is being systematically railroaded. CRT has shown that narratives "have a vital role to play in addressing ... aggressive urban police practices"[28] in that they move us from a perpetrator-centered view of events to a victim-centered view of events, providing jurors, legislators, and ordinary people an opportunity to empathize with the victim. At the same time, the use of narratives can also have a downside because:

> Relying on empathy almost always places the onus on the
> marginalized. They must reiterate how they are—and then be—much

more like those who are not marginalized in order for their causes to matter. They must prove their pain in a way that their oppressors are willing to acknowledge. . . . Relying on empathy means black people faced with horrific levels of police brutality must make white people "feel our pain." It forces us to stream the bodies of our dead sons and daughters on a loop. It requires there to be dead sons and daughters in the first place. It always demands more spectacles of pain.[29]

The Glass Shield does not rely on empathy to sustain its point of view. On the contrary, Woods is not a particularly sympathetic character. He is combative throughout the film, to the point that his lawyer, played by Bernie Casey, is frustrated with his attitude. Again, by seeing the corruption as it happens, the audience does not need to empathize with Woods in order to understand that justice is not being served.

At the same time, the film counteracts the "stock story about the criminality of men of color. The [film] shows an alternative view that deconstructs the image of the violent, menacing thug."[30] By casting Ice Cube in the role of Teddy Woods, some audience members may have superimposed Cube's gangsta rapper persona onto their framing of Woods; however, Woods, while assertive about his rights, is not violent or menacing. As the character points out in the film, the only thing he is guilty of is being a black man—that is, "My skin is my sin."

What Went Wrong?

In some ways, *The Glass Shield* seems to fit perfectly into the aesthetic and subject matter of the New Black Realism movement discussed earlier. Films that belong to this movement feature black male protagonists in urban environments and were made on minimal budgets. They star rappers-turned-actors and deal with political and social issues concerning black communities.[31] Celeste Fisher makes the argument that gangsta films released during the 1990s used hip-hop music and artists in the theatrical trailers and "it is this aspect of the films that plays a major role in their crossover appeal."[32] *The Glass Shield* was certainly marketed to fit into the mold of *Boyz* and *Menace*. Though Ice Cube's character plays a small but important role in *Shield*, he is featured heavily in the trailer—the voice-over actually names him first in the list of actors, and his face figures prominently on the film's poster and DVD cover. It seems as though every action sequence in the film was included in the trailer, and the featured reviews of the film describe it as "a no-holds barred thriller!" featuring "heart stopping suspense!"[33] The tagline for the film proclaims that "in a world filled with violence . . . his only weapon is the truth!"

The focus on action and violence in the marketing of the film is interesting because, as the late film critic Gene Siskel pointed out, "Burnett doesn't use violence, which you would expect in a police thriller. It's one of the few police films that we've seen that doesn't have lots of gunplay in it."[34] The bait-and-switch was deliberate on the part of Miramax, the film's distributor, which initially "blocked the film's release for a full year, forced Burnett to write and direct a less blunt and despairing ending," and then sold the film "as a *Boyz n the Hood* type of action film that would appeal mainly to black males aged fourteen to twenty-four, rather than treating it as the thoughtful and morally ambiguous police drama that might attract a broader audience."[35]

Burnett's film feels less like it belongs in the neo-Blaxploitation of New Black Realism and more like it should be classified with black dramas that were released later in the decade, such as Carl Franklin's *Devil in a Blue Dress* (1995), Kasi Lemmons's *Eve's Bayou* (1997), Maya Angelou's *Down in the Delta* (1998), and Jim Jarmusch's *Ghost Dog: The Way of the Samurai* (1999). The deceptive marketing may have resulted in depressed box-office figures, as viewers went in expecting one type of film only to watch another, which could have led to bad word-of-mouth.

Because violence played such a large, albeit deceptive, role in the marketing of the film, it is important to discuss how violence is actually used in the film. The first scene that invokes violence involves Mrs. Greenspan, whose murder is the impetus for Teddy Woods's trial. Deputy Fields comes across the body, slumped in the passenger seat of her car with her head against the window. There is little blood, and it almost looks as though the victim is sleeping. The focus of the scene is not actually Mrs. Greenspan's murder; it is the dismissive manner in which Detective Baker treats Fields when he arrives on the scene. Though she tries to offer insight into the crime scene, such as the fact that the angle of the bullet seems to come from below, making the carjacking scenario Mr. Greenspan described highly unlikely, she is told to go and direct traffic. The crime scene feels sanitized and less graphic than similar scenes on contemporary television programs. While graphic gun violence and its after-effects in *Boyz*, *City*, and *Menace* are used to emphasize how little control black bodies possess, the after-effect of violence in *Shield* is not even the focal point of the scene. Instead, the focus is on the nonviolent microaggressions that Fields faces, which are supposed to make the audience uncomfortable and illustrate how biased the Edgemar officers really are.

The film ratchets up the tension from microaggressions to physical violence as the Woods case begins to unfold. While on patrol, Johnson witnesses a car run a stop sign and almost hit his squad car. As Johnson calls for backup, the car slowly begins to move in reverse toward his squad car. Stephen James Taylor's score during this scene quietly enhances the already tense atmosphere: the action takes place at night, in a poorly lit alley with an ominous blue hue. As Johnson approaches the car, the occupants open fire and there is a brief exchange of rounds before the car speeds away. Thankfully, Johnson is wearing a bulletproof vest and is not critically injured. The preceding scene showed Massey, Baker, and Hall discussing the fact that they had received subpoenas from Woods's legal team. That scene ends with Massey telling Baker to "fix it." Though it is never proven in the film, it is strongly suggested that Baker has planned this encounter in an effort to either intimidate or kill Johnson.

The final incidence of physical violence is also the most graphic and disturbing. Fields ends up in the hospital after being assaulted, presumably by members of the sheriff's department or people working on their behalf. Johnson goes to the station to confront Baker about the situation. As Johnson moves toward Baker, the latter pulls his gun. Johnson taunts Baker by saying "No, no, he can't shoot me; my hands aren't tied behind my back," and Massey states emphatically that if Baker shoots Johnson he will testify that Baker did so in self-defense. At this point in the film Johnson is unarmed, having been relieved of duty because of a fight he had with a fellow officer who wrote "nigger" on the bathroom mirror; however, being unarmed does not mean that he will not be seen as threatening or dangerous. Johnson either does not understand the danger he is in or is simply unwilling to put up with the lies anymore; in any event, he calls out Massey on his version of events, but adds, in a direct reference to the Woods case, "Well, I guess you can always find a gun to plant on me." Johnson lunges at Bono, who tells him to chill out, and as two deputies hold Johnson down on a desk, Baker places his gun in Johnson's mouth and cocks it while Johnson screams. There is a brief close-up of Johnson's face during this encounter; however, most of the scene focuses on Baker's expression as Massey gets him to stand down. It is clear from the close-up that Baker intends to pull the trigger. As Gene Siskel suggests in his review, the film "takes its energy from looks

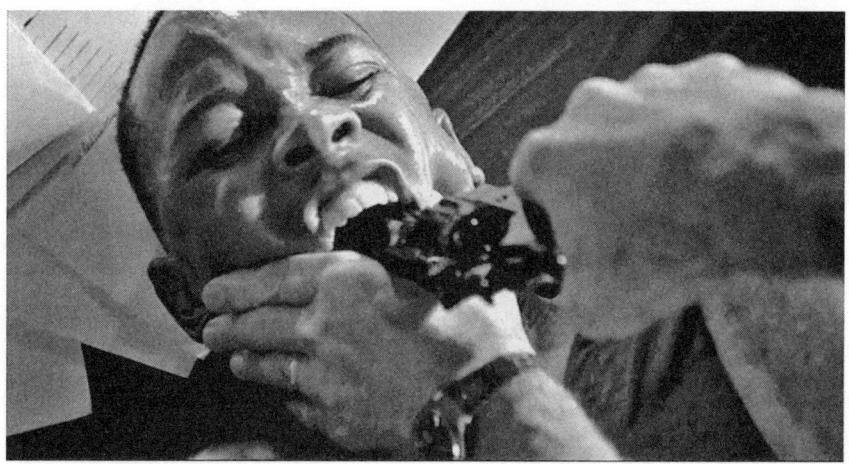

Johnson confronts Baker

in a very stylized direction, looks by the characters in their conspiracy and psychological intimidation,"[36] and that is certainly the case here. Massey and Baker have tried on multiple occasions to silence Johnson either through intimidation or attempted murder, and the audience is left to wonder if the only reason Baker does not pull the trigger is because he does not feel confident that the other officers will back him up. With one exception, all of the film's physical violence happens off-screen, and the one scene where weapons are discharged lasts for less than ten seconds. The violence in the film is psychological, a reality that does not comport with the way the film was marketed prior to its release.

Besides the deceptive marketing campaign, Shield also performed poorly at the box office because of its very limited release. In its first week, the film played in only 283 theaters, an extremely low number compared to other films; that same week, The Bridges of Madison County opened in 1,805 theaters, and Fluke opened in 1,200 theaters.[37] The films with the closest theater counts during The Glass Shield's opening weekend were Bad Boys in its ninth week of release in 384 theaters, and Tales From the Hood in 858 theaters during its second week.[38] It is certainly possible for limited-release films to gross large sums of money; however, it is not likely. Shield's limited release, combined with a deceptive marketing campaign, the year-long delay in releasing the film, and the forced edits, begs the question of whether Miramax set The Glass Shield up to be a failure.

Curtain Call

When *The Glass Shield* was released in 1994, there had been well-publicized incidents of police malfeasance, but there was no sustained national outrage; Charles Burnett wanted to call attention to police violence against black communities.[39] Fast-forward twenty years, and the barrage of videos showing the deaths of unarmed black citizens has spurned a national movement. In this context, *The Glass Shield* shows itself to be an effective tool in understanding police brutality and misconduct. While most black films of the 1990s focused on black criminality, which was used as a rationale for violent police intervention in black and brown communities, Burnett's film takes poverty and criminality off the table to expose the extent to which police departments as institutions, regardless of the individuals who occupy positions within said departments, are less concerned with protecting and serving and more concerned with intimidation and power. At Edgemar Station, it was not simply the work of one or two bad actors; the structure of the department was such that even the officers who wanted to do the right thing were forced to remain silent or, in some cases, become accomplices to misdeeds. In addition, the film shows that it is not only the police officers who are corrupt, but also the district attorneys and the entire judicial process—audiences were probably not surprised that Woods faced an all-white jury. In the end, Bono, whose racial bias set all of the film's events into motion, strikes a plea deal that keeps him out of jail and allows him to remain on the police force, while Johnson's career is ruined. Would the events in the film still have occurred if Edgemar Station had been more diverse? It is likely. Other films from the 1990s show that people of color who become police officers are capable of engaging in racially biased behavior.

The film as a whole can be framed as seeking to address the racial subordination that is manifested in aggressive police practices. By seeing the events from the police's point of view, it is possible that any racial bias that could be directed at Teddy Woods as a black suspect would be muted, and as a result, audiences are more likely to understand that the types of police practices outlined in the film cannot be tolerated.

5

"If You're Going to Tell People the Truth... Make Them Laugh"

C.S.A.: The Confederate States of America as Mockumentary and Truth-Telling

> If you're going to tell people the truth, you better make them laugh; otherwise they'll kill you.
> *C.S.A.: The Confederate States of America*, 2004, originally George Bernard Shaw, c. 1950

> The question [of who won the Civil War] implies the possibility of a counterfactual answer: The South really won the war. I have heard this argument made, and I am not persuaded. I know the logic: The racism that emerged in the postwar U.S., especially but not only in the South, looked like slavery under a different name; the South won the war of history and memory, securing the honor of the cause and forcing reunion on Southern white supremacist terms. And indeed at a certain, meta-historical level, that is hard to dispute, especially the latter point. We still do battle to displace and discountenance ancestral Confederate histories.
> Stephanie McCurry, "The U.S. Won the Civil War," 2013

For those of us who do not have a background in a STEM field, the phrase "sensitive dependence on initial conditions" probably sounds like a collection of random words haphazardly strung together. The "butterfly effect," the more common phrase, may spark slightly more recognition to nonscientists, due in no small part to the 2004 Ashton Kutcher film and the subsequent sequels that bear the name. Credited to meteorologist and mathematician Edward Lorenz in the early 1960s, the butterfly effect is explained, in layman's terms, as the idea that a butterfly flapping its wings in South America can affect the weather in New York's Central Park. To put it more broadly, Lorenz's hypothesis maintains that one unrelated and seemingly insignificant event can radically alter the world around us. Speculative fiction writers have often employed the butterfly effect in their works to create alternate histories of the world in which we currently live. In 1952, noted speculative fiction writer and Pulitzer Prize–winner Ray Bradbury penned a short story entitled "The Sound of Thunder," which posits that an accidental killing of a butterfly during a tourist's visit to the prehistoric period drastically changes the course of human history. Philip K. Dick's 1962 Hugo Award–winning novel *The Man in the High Castle* presents a world where the Axis Powers won World War II. Fast-forward almost four decades, and Pulitzer Prize–winning author Philip Roth's novel *The Plot Against America* hypothesizes what would happen if Franklin D. Roosevelt lost his third presidential bid to Charles Lindbergh. In each of these pieces, the alternate history is markedly worse than the events that occurred in history prime, a phrase that refers to the actual history of the United States as we know it.[1] These alternate histories often portray societies that are plunged into a world of fascism and terror. Though World War II can be seen as a historical nexus within speculative fiction—a hypothesis based on the sheer volume of works that deal with it—the Civil War is also a popular topic for these kinds of what-if thought experiments.

Kevin Willmott's 2004 film *C.S.A.: The Confederate States of America* is a satirical exploration of what the nation would look like if the Confederacy had won the Civil War, or, as it is retitled in the film, the War of Northern Aggression. The genius of the film, or, depending on the viewer's point of view, its problem, is that Willmott's contemporary Confederate States of America does not look much different from the contemporary United States of America. In an interview with Derrais Carter, Willmott makes the argument that "from the black point of view, I wanted to show how the Confederates *actually* won [the Civil War] and that they're still winning."[2] This film operates in a vein similar to Mel Brooks's *Blazing Saddles* by using satire and parody to critique contemporary racial politics, and that rhetorical strategy is the main reason why C.S.A. begins with the quote from George Bernard Shaw presented at the beginning of this chapter: "If you're going to tell people the truth, you better make them laugh; otherwise they'll kill you." That statement hit a bit too close to home, as Willmott revealed that he received a lot of hate mail following the release of this film, indicating that some people were prepared to take Shaw's words way too literally.³

The film is framed as a documentary produced by the British Broadcasting Company (BBC) and billed as "the most anxiously awaited television event of the decade." According to the advertisements within the film, this "controversial" documentary "shook our beloved nation and created a national scandal" and is being shown after being held from the "national airways for nearly two years." Because of the scandalous subject matter, the documentary comes complete with an advisory message that warns, "The following program is of foreign origin. The content does not reflect the views of this station and may be unsuitable for children and servants." Framed in much the same vein as Ken Burns's *The Civil War* documentary series, *C.S.A.* features "archival footage," title cards for each section, voice-overs featuring text from important historical figures, an overall voice-of-God narrator, and talking-head experts who place events in their historical, albeit fictional, context. This chapter will use elements of critical race theory (CRT) to analyze the ways in which *C.S.A.* critiques and calls attention to racism, history, and popular culture's role in reinforcing the American racial project, as well as to compare Willmott's strategies to those employed in other mockumentary films.

C.S.A. premiered at the Sundance Film Festival in 2004 before receiving a wide distribution one year later. Critics were reasonably kind. Mick LaSalle of the *San Francisco Chronicle* argued that *C.S.A.* is "a brilliant and irresistible counterfactual overview of American history" that "is ultimately not just amusing but moving because it reminds us that the Civil War was not some sectional disagreement or an argument between two equally worthy points of view, but rather a struggle for the country's moral decency and the future of democracy."⁴ Ann Hornaday of the *Washington Post* maintained that *C.S.A.* is "a piece of well-crafted righteous indignation" that reminds us that "as a country we're nowhere near coming to terms with our racist legacy."⁵ In a review for *PopMatters*, Cynthia Fuchs begins her piece with the assertion that "the most alarming thing about *C.S.A.: Confederate States of America* is how utterly unalarming it seems" and ends with the argument that the film "exposes the terrible, abiding premise that still holds up so much of today's U.S.A., that white Americans' relentless sense of privilege and rightness are not constructed, but inherent. It's a matter of faith and ownership."⁶

In the book *We Gotta Have It: Twenty Years of Seeing Black at the Movies*, Esther Iverem notes that "C.S.A. allows the thinking moviegoer, Black or White, to laugh at America's chief mental illness: its obsession with race."[7] *Boston Globe* writer Ty Burr's review straddled the proverbial fence when he wrote that "as a coherent, well-judged alternative history, the movie's a mess. As a thought-provoking and frequently hilarious jeremiad, it scores again and again, never straying far from its essential point that the South did win the Civil War to judge by the failure of Reconstruction, civil rights abuses, and a disenfranchisement that continues to this day."[8] Much like *Blazing Saddles*, not everyone interpreted C.S.A.'s satire as interesting, humorous, or even helpful: in 2014 the Dalton School in New York apologized for screening the film for a sophomore history class after parents complained about the film's tone and subject matter.[9]

How in the Hell Did We Get Here?

As mentioned earlier, several works of speculative fiction have hypothesized about how American history would be altered if the Confederacy had won the Civil War. *Bring the Jubilee*, written by Ward Moore in 1954; *If the South Had Won the Civil War*, by MacKinlay Kantor in 1960; and Harry Turtledove's novels in the Southern Victory series are a few of the most popular. In Moore's piece, the War of Southern Independence splits the nation in two. The Confederate States is a prosperous superpower while the United States is "poor, exploited, [and] backward."[10] In the years following the war, the Confederate States conquered all of Latin America and freed the slaves; however, the former slaves and Latin subjects of the Confederate States were "without franchise, and indeed for all practice purpose, without civil rights."[11]

Pulitzer Prize–winning author MacKinlay Kantor's *If the South Had Won the Civil War* imagines two events that alter the nation's history. The first is the accidental death of Union general Ulysses S. Grant, and the second is the Confederate victory at Gettysburg. With those two historical shifts, the Confederacy wins the Civil War and the nation is split in two—and then three, once Texas secedes from the Confederacy to establish its own independent nation. In Kantor's alternate history, abolitionism "was the trend of the nineteenth century and could no longer be ignored or denied"; however, despite that reality, "Texas and the Confederate States labored under the weight of an institution as unsound economically as it was repugnant spiritually."[12] In history prime the United States ratified the Thirteenth Amendment in 1865. The Confederate States in Kantor's history passed the

Liberation Act in 1885 and, in a nod to the events in U.S. history, Confederate president James Longstreet remarked, "'Had we, the Confederate States of America, gone down in defeat, there might have ensued a period of enforced amalgamation replete with every imaginable domestic horror. A common hatred directed against the Negro, which we do not now demonstrate or even possess, would have been the inevitable result.'"[13] The moral of the story appears to be that if the South had been allowed to abolish slavery on its own terms, the nation could have avoided the horrors visited upon black citizens in history prime's post-Reconstruction era.

Harry Turtledove's Southern Victory series also details an alternate timeline in which the Confederacy was victorious. The series includes the introductory book *How Few Remain*, and an additional ten novels spread across three subseries. In these works, the Confederacy is able to prevail over the Union due to the intervention of British and French forces. A Confederate victory splits the nation in two, and while official hostilities cease, conflicts along the borders in the South and West continue for decades. Taking place twenty years after the Civil War ended and told through the stories of figures such as Abraham Lincoln, Frederick Douglass, and Samuel Clemens, *How Few Remain* deals with the events leading up to and including a second war between the United States and the Confederate States, which was also won by the Confederacy. In the intervening years, "The United States had eventually emancipated the thousands of slaves still living within their borders. The Confederate States held their millions in bondage to this day."[14] Slavery was not abolished in the Confederate States until Britain and France mandated emancipation as a condition of their involvement in the second Civil War. Following that loss, the United States allied itself with Germany, which leads to interesting alternative events during World War I and World War II.

Ben Winters's *Underground Airlines* looks at a present-day United States where the Civil War never occurred. Though most of the former Confederate states eventually outlawed slavery, the "Hard Four" of Alabama, Mississippi, Louisiana, and Carolina maintain the practice. The book's protagonist, Victor, is a former enslaved person, or peeb (person bound to labor), who has turned to bounty hunting and has a very complicated relationship to his line of work. Because Victor is black, he is able to befriend runaways and infiltrate abolitionist movements to return peebs to servitude. The book follows Victor as he travels to the Hard Four states, ostensibly to recapture a fugitive named Jackdaw; however, it turns out that Jackdaw is a free-born black person who found evidence that the Hard Four is illegally selling slave-made goods to the United States, a discovery that could destroy the slavocracy.

These what-if scenarios are not the sole purview of speculative fiction writers; in 1930, British prime minister Winston Churchill penned an article entitled "If Lee Had Not Won the Battle of Gettysburg." Though Churchill acknowledges that winning at Gettysburg "could not have prevented the ultimate victory of the North" in history prime, he goes on to lay out how a Confederate victory might have been possible, and what that would have meant for world history through World War I.[15] In Churchill's alternate history, Confederate president Jefferson Davis frees all the slaves in the South in a successful effort to convince Britain and France to commit troops to the war effort.[16] After the war, the United States and the Confederate States would remain separate nations who engage in what can generously be termed a Cold War. The two nations eventually reconcile as they witness the events leading up to World War I.[17]

In 2017, the Civil War alternative history was poised to move from literary pages to the small screen when HBO announced it had greenlit a series, *Confederate*, depicting an alternative history in which the Confederates won the Civil War. The hashtag #NoConfederate went viral, and a number of pundits assessed the idea. The fact that this series was the brainchild of white men whose previous effort, *Game of Thrones*, was not known for racial inclusion in front of or behind the camera, gave a lot of people pause. Roxane Gay asked, "I wonder why people are expending the energy to imagine that slavery continues to thrive when we are still dealing with the vestiges of slavery in very tangible ways. Those vestiges are visible in incarceration rates for black people, a wildly segregated country, disparities in pay and mortality rates and the ever-precarious nature of black life in a world where it can often seem as if police officers take those lives with impunity."[18] Ta-Nehisi Coates remarked, "*Confederate* is the kind of provocative thought experiment that can be engaged in when someone else's lived reality really is fantasy to you, when your grandmother is not in danger of losing her vote, when the terrorist attack on Charleston evokes honest sympathy, but inspires no direct fear."[19]

Mockumentary and Racial Realism

In addition to having roots in speculative fiction, C.S.A. has ties to the mockumentary genre. In the book *F Is for Phony: Fake Documentary and Truth's Undoing*, Alexandra Juhasz and Jesse Lerner make the argument that "fake documentaries are a special breed of parody in that they accomplish something different, something extra; they do manage a 'link to the real.' The fake documentary is simultaneously and definitively both parody and satire, given that satire, according to [Linsa] Hutcheon, has the 'moral and social in its focus.'"[20] Cynthia J. Miller argues that mockumentaries "exist in a place where social commentary, cultural critique, and the crisis of representation collide, where humor . . . meets reflection."[21] Though it is thought to be a relatively recent invention, mockumentaries and their predecessors can be traced at least as far back as Orson Welles's 1938 radio production War of the Worlds.[22] Broadcast on Halloween, Welles's production featured a series of news bulletins reporting an alien invasion. Because of Welles's convincing performance, as well as the fact that the show ran without commercials, many listeners believed the invasion was real, and panic ensued in several cities across the country. More recent—and less terrorizing—examples include Rob Reiner's This Is Spinal Tap (1984) and Christopher Guest's films Waiting for Guffman (1996), Best in Show (2000), and A Mighty Wind (2003).

As mentioned in a previous chapter, Blazing Saddles employs strategies of parody, satire, and mockumentary broadly, and C.S.A. specifically has feet in each camp as well. According to writer and comedian Larry Wilmore, satire is about "revealing a truth. . . . The satirist's job is to shine a flashlight and say 'look at this,'"[23] and in the case of Saddles, the main focus is to shine a light on how ridiculous racism is. Like Saddles, C.S.A. also ridicules American racism; however, because the nature of racism has changed since 1974, the method of ridiculing it has also changed. The broad over-the-top humor employed in Saddles works because Brooks was dealing with overt racism. Willmott is operating in a world where overt expressions of racism are typically, but not always, frowned upon; at the same time, more subtle forms of racism, including the microaggressions discussed in the Nothing But a Man chapter, have become the norm. Therefore, the humor in C.S.A. is more subtle, just like the racism it is critiquing. In fact, C.S.A., though fictional in most respects, is far more grounded in reality because the film generally adheres to the conventions of documentaries: a viewer could accidentally stumble upon the film and take quite some time to realize that it is a mockumentary much like Welles's War of the Worlds. Because the film follows the ways in which documentaries are structured, C.S.A. can also be categorized as a parody even if its tone and premise complicate categorizing it as such. According to Thomas Prasch, C.S.A. is a "double-level mockumentary: a presumably straightforward British documentary about

American history since the southern victory, framed as a presentation on CSA-controlled network television (complete with reiterated warnings that the network is 'not responsible for the views expressed'). This allows for Willmott to play at multiple forms of parody."[24]

IMDb lists over 300 films with the keyword mockumentary; however, many are "found footage" fake documentaries such as *The Blair Witch Project* (1999), *Cloverfield* (2008), and *Chronicle* (2012) that are premised on the notion that the films feature real events captured on camera and later recovered. Though some view the mockumentary genre as being synonymous with fake documentaries, there is a distinction, as Lewis MacLeod explains: a mockumentary's "stance is always fictional, and both the film's participants and its implied viewers unproblematically recognize it as such.... The ontological status of the actors is never in doubt; they are simply pretending to make a documentary in the same way other actors pretend to be in love, work at banks, fight crime, etc."[25] Using MacLeod's distinction, *C.S.A.* fits squarely within the mockumentary genre, since the actors are pretending to make a documentary and not in fact pretending to function within an actual modern-day Confederacy. Even though *C.S.A.* feels like a mockumentary in every respect, the film is not always included in discussions on mockumentary as a genre. This omission may have something to do with *C.S.A.*'s subject matter: the overwhelming majority of contemporary mockumentary films deal with light-hearted topics: an intellectually challenged heavy metal band, a group of obsessed dog-show participants, and a small-town musical production, to name a few. Viewers can easily separate themselves from, and in many ways dismiss, the subject matter being presented in these films; if one is not involved in a heavy metal band or a participant in dog shows, the fictional nature of the film's subject matter is evident and does not impact the viewer in any real way. Despite the fact that the Confederacy did not actually win the Civil War, the realistic way racism is discussed, and the obvious connections the film makes between our actual timeline and the fictional one, makes the scenarios presented in the film seem plausible. Also, because, as one of the primary dictates of critical race theory states, "Racism is an integral, permanent, and indestructible component of this society,"[26] *C.S.A.* viewers do not necessarily have the luxury of separation, or even of the passive viewing of a film whose subject matter affects everyone whether they admit it or not.

Though *C.S.A.* may not be framed as fitting within the mockumentary genre, it certainly conforms to aspects of critical race theory. As mentioned in previous chapters, CRT "is characterized by frequent use of the first person, storytelling, narrative, allegory, interdisciplinary treatment of law, and the unapologetic use of creativity."[27] CRT scholar Derrick Bell used creativity frequently to discuss the state of race relations in the United States. One of the more popular representations of CRT remains Bell's short story "Space Traders," which offers a fictional account of what would happen if extraterrestrials landed on earth and offered the United States the solutions to their most pressing problems in exchange for the nation's black population. Bell's story ends with a horrifying image of black bodies: "heads bowed, arms now linked by slender chains, black people left the new world as their forbears had arrived."[28] C.S.A., on the other hand, begins and ends with the premise that the image of broken bodies is all there is for black folks within the Confederate States of America. Bell was not the only scholar who engaged in creative storytelling in an effort to spark discussions on white supremacy: Jerome McCristal Culp Jr.'s "The Michael Jackson Pill: Equality, Race, and Culture" hypothesizes a discussion among the black male faculty at Harvard Law School when they are told about "a pill that if taken by black people will remove all vestiges of being black," and a Massachusetts law that would "require all black residents of the state to take the Michael Jackson Pill."[29] The story looks at how race is socially constructed, the nature of racism in the United States, and how attached we are to the arbitrary and destructive concept of race. C.S.A. operates from a similar theoretical foundation as Bell's and Culp's work. When discussing the motivations behind making C.S.A., Willmott remarked, "I was trying to find a new way to tell the story, a way that did not compromise on the horrors and the difficulties of what slavery was, but at the same time was a way that could be entertaining and reach people who would normally never see a film about the Civil War or slavery or history or anything like that."[30] In addition, Willmott is not making fun of documentaries as a genre in the way that Brooks does with the Western with *Blazing Saddles*. C.S.A. is simply utilizing the form and not making any statements about the genre itself. For that reason, the film has a very complicated and uncomfortable relationship with both parodies and mockumentaries.

What Is v. What If

C.S.A. constructs an elaborate history of how the Confederate States of America came to be, and how the nation's history evolved from the War of Northern Aggression through the end of the twentieth century. Churchill's essay, and several other alternate histories, link a possible Confederate victory to the intervention of European troops at various points during the war, and C.S.A. utilizes a similar historical trajectory. In history prime, President Lincoln used the Emancipation Proclamation to frame the Civil War as a moral conflict centered on the question of slavery. In C.S.A.'s alternate history, Jefferson Davis framed the war in terms of states' rights and ignored the question of slavery entirely. Despite any misgivings Britain and France may have about the morality of slavery, the states' rights argument was compelling enough for them to commit troops to the cause. The influx of new troops led to a Confederate victory at Gettysburg, General Ulysses S. Grant's surrender to General Robert E. Lee, and President Lincoln's exile from Washington, D.C.

In the film, the primary question that dominated the political and social landscape following the Confederate victory was slavery. While Robert E. Lee supported emancipation, President Davis wanted to take a drastically different approach: former Union citizens would be forced to pay a large income tax, which would be used to rebuild Northern cities; however, "The entire tax . . . could be abated with the purchase of household or industrial slaves." A fictional congressman, John Ambrose Fauntroy, took charge of the Davis Plan. All black folks, and everyone else unable to prove pure white ancestry, were arrested and sold. Notable abolitionists such as Susan B. Anthony, William Lloyd Garrison, Harriet Beecher Stowe, William David Thoreau, Mark Twain, Ralph Waldo Emerson, and Wendell Phillips, as well as about twenty thousand other Northern whites, defected to Canada in protest of the Davis Plan.

The western expansion called for by Manifest Destiny, the continued displacement and massacre of Native Americans, and the use of Chinese immigrants to construct the transcontinental railroad existed in both history prime and the alternate history. The main difference between the historical trajectories is that in history prime, Congress passed the Chinese Exclusion Act, which prohibited Chinese workers from immigrating to the United States, while in C.S.A., the victorious Confederacy passed the Yellow Peril Mandate, which enslaved Chinese laborers. For both the United States and the Confederate States, exclusion and violence based on race were prominent and national in scope. The only major difference is that the Confederate States advanced its racist politics a step or two further than the United States did.

The Mexican-American War exists in both timelines; however, there are a few notable differences. In history prime, that war ended with the United States annexing territories that later became New Mexico, California, and Texas. In the alternate timeline, the Confederate States occupies all of Mexico, the Caribbean, and the South American continent. The Confederate States instituted a system of "apart" that resembles both the system of Jim and Jane Crow that existed in the United States from the end of Reconstruction to the passage of the Voting Rights Act in 1965, and the system of apartheid that existed in South Africa from 1948 to 1994.

In the alternate history, when the stock market crashed in 1929, the Confederate empire rebuilt its economy by reinstituting the international slave trade. According to the film's narrator, the Confederate States "acted as middleman in the new slave trade, capturing and training slaves for export. Some slaves were chosen domestically from the poor of their own country, but traditional African slaves were always preferred." With the cooperation of several African leaders, the Confederate States was able to solidify itself as an economic hegemon and bring slavery to other nations willing to participate in the peculiar institution. Though the Confederacy expanded its economic reach, it remained isolationist in every other way. When the Nazi Party began its conquest of Europe, the Confederate States "officially [supported] Germany's new Aryan racial policies" and refused to intervene militarily in any European conflict. Ironically, though the Confederate States allowed Adolph Hitler's Germany to expand unchecked, the Confederacy did not stand for an expansionist Japan—the Confederate States launched a surprise attack on the Kuril Islands on December 7, 1941. The war with Japan proved more difficult than anticipated, and as such, slaves were promised their freedom if they fought for the Confederacy.

As was the case in history prime, the Japanese surrendered after two nuclear weapons were detonated on their home soil. In the Confederate States, the slaves who fought for the Confederate States were returned to bondage, while in the United States, black World War II veterans returned to Jim Crow conditions only to be, at best, denied veterans' benefits, and at worst, lynched.

To stem the tide of abolitionism, the Confederate States erected a Cotton Curtain—a militarized wall that spanned the length of the Confederate States–Canadian border. When the Allies achieved victory against Nazi Germany, the remaining European nations instituted an embargo against the Confederate States, sending the nation into another economic depression. When John F. Kennedy was elected as the first president from the North since the War of Northern Aggression, many believed he would push for emancipation. Unfortunately, Kennedy was assassinated before he could move forward with female suffrage or slave emancipation. Though the "buying, selling, and trading of slaves pumped over $500 million into the economy" over the next three decades, the remaining Confederate timeline is surprisingly similar to the events that occurred in history prime, including the presidencies of Richard Nixon and Ronald Reagan—although the film is silent on the Watergate scandal—and at least one conflict in the Persian Gulf. In one of the commentary tracks for the film, Willmott laments how easy it was to take moments from the actual history of the United States and apply them to the Confederacy, which is why this chapter contains such a lengthy plot/historical overview.

A viewer's first response to C.S.A. might be to think that the events chronicled in the film are too far-fetched to be believed; however, the film works precisely because many of the events in the film do contain a kernels of truth, and the rest of the events are far closer to reality than most viewers would like to believe. Before the closing credits at the end of the film, several title cards illustrate just how close to history prime some of the events outlined in the film really are. Among the most interesting and unnerving is the fact that Confederacy secretary of war Judah P. Benjamin's "negotiations to win French and British support for the Confederacy lacked only a key military victory to succeed." In his Pulitzer Prize–winning book *Battle Cry of Freedom: The Civil War Era*, James M. McPherson points out that in history prime, "The main goal of Confederate foreign policy was to secure diplomatic recognition of the South's nationhood."[31] Benjamin was not the only person within the Confederacy working toward that goal: "In the quest for recognition, the Confederate State Department sent to Europe a three-man commission headed by William L. Yancey."[32] In Ken Burns's *Civil War* documentary, viewers learn that the Confederacy knew that neither Britain nor France could survive without cotton imports, and so, in an effort to pressure them to intervene, the South cut cotton production by 90 percent.[33] In both history prime and the alternate history, the Confederate States knew that the key to victory was the intervention of international forces. In history prime, that intervention did not occur, but it did in many of the alternate histories, turning the tide in favor of the Confederate States.

Another title card from C.S.A. that fits the description of truth being stranger—and uncomfortably close—to fiction notes that "Confederate leaders planned to occupy Central and South America, seizing the world's cotton and sugar supply and creating a 'Tropical Empire.'" In history prime, even before Confederate states began to secede from the Union, members of Congress were looking toward the Caribbean and South America with empire-building in mind, and arguing that "for the South to maintain sectional balance of power, new slave territory would have to be acquired to counterbalance free states regularly being admitted to the union.... Jefferson Davis expressed such reasoning when he supported a congressional bill to acquire Cuba."[34] As the threat of civil war continued, "A number of Deep South secessionists proclaimed that the South could achieve a tropical empire in a separate Confederacy."[35] When hostilities between the Union and the Confederacy officially began, U.S. secretary of state William H. Seward "wrote that there were good reasons to believe that the Confederacy had designs 'to effect either partial dismemberment or a complete overthrow of the Mexican Government with a view to extend over it the authority of a newly projected Confederacy.'"[36] Even in history prime, the Union either knew of Confederate plans to expand south or hypothesized that such an expansion would take place; in the alternate history, those plans were brought to fruition.

Even PBS Has to Sell Stuff

In C.S.A., interspersed with the history of the Confederate States of America are advertisements for products that, at first glance, would only exist within the Confederate States. This narrative choice ensures that the audience is completely immersed within the Confederacy. We get a sense of this immersion at the very beginning of the film: after the quote from George Bernard Shaw fades to black, we see a commercial for Confederate Family Insurance, which "for over 100 years [has been] protecting a people and their property." As the word "property" appears on the screen, the camera pans to an image of a young black man working in a garden and smiling into the camera behind his white owners. In the next commercial we see two men working on a car that is reminiscent of the General Lee from the popular television series *The Dukes of Hazzard*: red, with the Confederate flag on the roof and sides. One of the men laments the fact that he's "tired of eating dust" and asks, "Is there *anything* that can make this car faster?" Suddenly a third man named Duke Cooter appears and throws a bottle of motor oil toward the depressed drivers. Cooter, who is dressed in what looks like a NASCAR driver's outfit and is flanked by a woman with blond pigtails wearing Daisy Duke jean shorts, tells us that "Sambo X-15 is specifically formulated for the way America drives." The container has black-and-white checkers surrounding a black face wearing a top hat. According to the film's end credits, Sambo products were manufactured in the United States from the 1870s through the 1920s, and according to C.S.A. producer Rick Cowen, Sambo Axle Grease was an actual product manufactured in Kansas City.[37] In addition to highlighting an actual product that utilized racial imagery to sell itself, this commercial brings attention to the fact that Confederate imagery also has been used in history prime's popular culture for quite some time. The Dukes of Hazzard aired on CBS from 1979 through 1985 and in 2005 was made into a feature film, complete with Daisy Duke, the General Lee car, and its Confederate flag.

Sambo Axle Grease was not the only product that existed in both the United States and the Confederate States. The film also features an ad for Gold Dust Washing Powder, an actual product that, in history prime, included "both black children and whites in blackface [as] Goldie and Dustie" in their advertisements from the 1880s to the 1930s; Darkie toothpaste, which was sold overseas well into the 1980s; Niggerhair Tobacco, which was manufactured in Milwaukee, Wisconsin, from the 1870s to the 1950s; and Coon Chicken Inn, a chain of restaurants in Salt Lake City, Seattle, and Portland, Oregon, from the 1920s to the 1950s that featured an entrance that required patrons to walk "through the mouth of a smiling black porter." It was important for the film to feature products that were manufactured across the country because slavery in the United States and the Confederate States was a national phenomenon, not a regional one. In addition, featuring products that existed in history prime forces the viewer to ponder just how "fictional" the film really is.

The line between fictional Confederate products and products that actually existed in history prime is further blurred by the fact that the scene following the Sambo Axle Grease advertisement is not another fictional product but an actual commercial for the television series Beulah. Played by three different actresses during its three-year run (1950–1952), Ethel Waters, Hattie McDaniel, and Louise Beavers, Beulah represented "a type long present in American popular culture: the large, often dowdy, usually darker, all-knowing, all-seeing, all-hearing, all-understanding mammy figure, whose life is built around nurturing and nourishing those in the Big House."[38] By highlighting popular culture artifacts that existed in history prime, particularly one as popular as the series Beulah, the film illustrates just how thin the line really is between the history of the Confederate States and that of the United States.

Though there were far too many real-world products that used slave imagery in their advertisements, C.S.A. took things further to create fictional products that are both a natural extension of products in history prime and would comfortably fit in with Confederate States history. The first was an education offered by the Cartwright Institute for the Study of Freedom Illnesses. The institute promises to train students, in just a few short months, for a rewarding career as an overseer, paddyroller, servant monitor, or breeder. Students would explore the nature of freedom diseases such as drapetomania, rascality, and negritude. The commercial is meant to satirize local medical and technical training institutes and for-profit colleges that target people who are unemployed or underemployed. In history prime, these institutions are problematic for several reasons, not the least of which is because they promise students "a quick path to financial stability through vocational education programs. But in reality, these schools are notorious for charging exorbitant tuition without preparing students for jobs in the real world."[39] The irony of this particular ad is that, much like Sambo Axle Grease and Niggerhair Tobacco, the Cartwright Institute has its basis in history prime. In 1851, Dr. Samuel A. Cartwright, a physician from the University of Louisiana, published an article entitled "Diseases and Peculiarities of the Negro Race." He defined drapetomania as a disease that "causes Negroes to run away," and he prescribed that owners needed to treat their slaves "like children, with care, kindness, attention and humanity to prevent and cure them from running away."[40] Given the trajectory of Cartwright's research in history prime, it is not surprising that his research would be codified and expanded in the alternate history.

After C.S.A. renames the history prime television series *Beulah* as *Leave It to Beulah*, the film takes things another step by creating its own television show entitled *Runaway*. The commercial for this show looks eerily like an advertisement for the history prime television series *COPS*, which debuted on FOX in 1989. The commercial opens with an image of a black man running away from the camera; throughout the commercial, heavily armed white officers, with shirts spelling CBI on the back, find and arrest slaves. We are not told what CBI stands for, although it seems logical to suggest that it is an abbreviation for Confederate Bureau of Investigation. Since slavery is an interstate business enterprise in the Confederate States, it makes sense that there would be a federal agency in charge of the apprehension of runaway

CHAPTER FIVE

Fictional commerical

slaves. The commercial contains a song with the refrain "whatcha gonna do when we catch you," and the film's subtitle notes that the song is a "parody of the COPS theme song." Instead of the reggae styling of Inner Circle's "Bad Boys," *Runaway*'s theme song has a melody inspired by the twangy sound of country music, probably because the overwhelming majority of today's black musical styles—including blues, rock 'n' roll, jazz, hip-hop, and reggae—would exist in limited forms, if at all, within the Confederate States of America. As the commercial continues, slaves are seen hiding in the backs of trucks and in the trunks of cars; however, they are all captured and handcuffed by the white officers. Flashlights are shined in the runaways' faces while large guns are pointed at their bodies. Like COPS, *Runaway* treats the criminalization of black bodies as popular entertainment.

One Drop in the Racial Bucket

While the *Runaway* ad presents a brief glimpse into the Confederate government apparatus with the CBI, a public service announcement from the Office of Racial Standing provides a more in-depth look at the CSA's bureaucracy. The announcement begins with a white man who, while

Department of Racial Identity

driving his car on "an ordinary day," observes someone talking on the street. The viewing audience does not see who or what the driver is observing. A voice-over asks the question, "Do you know someone of questionable racial identity? A neighbor? Someone at work? Contact the Office of Racial Identity at 1–800–555–PASS. You might be eligible for a cash reward." The text on the screen tells the viewer that "sometimes you just know it" and encourages viewers to "be our extra eyes and ears." The commercial evokes a post-9/11 feeling when the nation exhibited "paranoia toward potential terrorists [and heightened] our traditional fear of too many liberties, and our deep distrust of one another."[41] The late Manning Marable discussed the immediate aftermath of 9/11 when he wrote, "People are constantly warned to carefully watch their mail, their neighbors, and one another";[42] the Office of Racial Identity commercial plays upon those same feelings of suspicion and uncertainty. In fact, the final text that appears in the commercial ("Be Our Extra Eyes and Ears") was, according to producer Rick Cowen, a direct quote from John Ashcroft, who served as attorney general in the aftermath of 9/11.[43] Instead of being suspicious of anyone who might look like a "terrorist," in the Confederate universe, citizens must beware of people passing for white. This commercial links back to the advertisement for Runaway given Willmott's reminder that black communities "have always been patrolled by other people. Not just police, but other civilians have the ability to patrol and monitor us."[44]

The Office of Racial Identity's public service announcement plays upon fears of "the Other" at the same time it highlights the fact that, in both history prime and even more strenuously in the alternate history, "the concept of whiteness was carefully protected because so much was contingent upon it. Whiteness conferred on its owners aspects of citizenship which were all the more valued because they were denied to others."[45] In the film, because whiteness means the difference between being able to own property and *being* property, the state has a vested interest in regulating white racial identity, explaining the existence of the Office of Racial Identity. This also means that people who have black ancestors but who may appear visibly white have a reason to pass because, as Cheryl Harris points out in her discussion of whiteness as property, passing "is related to the historical and continuing pattern of white racial domination and economic exploitation, which has invested passing with a certain economic logic."[46] In history prime, most mainstream credible scientists acknowledge that race is a social construct and not a biological reality; in the alternate history, race is framed as an objective feature that can be tested for on a genetic level. This idea of race existing on a genetic level sets the stage for the big reveal at the end of the film. The voice-over at the beginning of C.S.A. touts that the documentary "created a national scandal" that involved passing the racial test.

Throughout the documentary, one of the talking heads the audience hears from is Senator John Ambrose Fauntroy V, whose family has been instrumental to the perpetuation of slavery in the Confederate States. Fauntroy is running for president of the Confederate States, and because of his family's history and stature, it is assumed he will win. He is so confident in the slavocracy created by the Confederate States that he arranges for the film's British documentarians to meet with slaves because "we have nothing to hide." As the voice-over explains, "Unfortunately, the slaves we were offered had clearly received training for the interview, corrupting any natural responses to our questions and rendering their responses manufactured." The slaves are dressed in orange jumpsuits, serving as a deliberate reference to the mass incarceration of black and brown citizens taking place in history prime and currently being framed as the "New Jim Crow." For the most part, the slaves look down and refuse to speak to the documentarians, with the exception of one slave who initially shakes hands with one of the crew before being admonished by a prison guard/overseer. In an elaborate sequence of events, the audience learns that Big Sam, a presumed runaway slave, used subterfuge to get a message to the British documentarians—the slave who shook hands with the crew member managed to slip her a note during their brief physical encounter. The note, signed by John Brown, who was a thorn in the side of state-sponsored white supremacy in both history prime and the Confederate timeline, leads the documentary crew to an estate in rural Virginia, where they meet Horace, a slave who works in the Fauntroy household. Horace tells his story:

> Master Fauntroy. His family . . . and my family . . . see, a long while back, my great-great-grandmammy . . . and his great-granddaddy, they . . . you know. Me and—me and Fauntroy . . . we kin. Just 'cause he look white don't mean he *all* white. See, years ago, when all this started . . . they took the light ones into the Fauntroy family and *made* 'em white. Us dark ones got cast out . . . left for niggers. He got the jungle blood. Believe me, he got the jungle blood in 'im. And he knows it, too.

Horace is obviously referring to the systematic rape of black women during history prime's antebellum period; the resulting children increased the amount of property a slaveholder had, and as a consequence, also increased the number of mixed-race individuals in the United States. The film does not mention whether the sexual exploitation of black female bodies continues in the Confederate States, though it makes sense that it would because the practice began long before the timelines of history prime and the Confederate States diverged. In fact, the only reference to the modern domestic slave trade is during a clip highlighting the Slave Shopping Network (SSN), which features Jupiter, Prissy, and their "litter of pick-a-ninnies," who can be broken up or sold as a set to the highest bidder. If Horace's claims are accurate, then the Fauntroy family, who have occupied the highest levels of government office for decades, have been passing for white for quite some time. In a moment that parodies President Bill Clinton's press conference addressing his sexual relationship with Monica Lewinsky, John Fauntroy addresses his alleged Negro-ness by stating emphatically that "my great-granddaddy did not have sexual relations with that woman!" When asked if he will submit to a DNA test, Fauntroy quickly answers, "No." When asked whether he will appear before the House Committee on Racial Identity, he and his wife exchange concerned looks before he mutters a perfunctory, "I'll cross that bridge when I come to it," and ends the press conference.

What is interesting about the scene is not the idea of passing itself, which is, according to Cheryl Harris, "a feature of racial subordination in all societies structured on white supremacy [and] is not an obsolete phenomenon that has slipped into history."[47] Rather, the important moment comes when Fauntroy and his wife exchange glances at the thought of being subpoenaed to testify about their racial identity. Much like Clinton's initial public denial of a sexual relationship with Lewinsky—which proved to be false—the Fauntroys are aware of the history of white slave owners sexually assaulting black female slaves, so they understand that there is a possibility that Horace's story could be true. Because of the "one drop" scandal, Fauntroy loses the presidential election and later commits suicide. In some ways, Fauntroy's story unfolds as a sort of tragic mulatto trope: a stereotype in popular culture that revolves around "the plight of a fair-skinned mulatto attempting to pass for white. Usually the mulatto is made likable—even sympathetic (because of [their] white blood, no doubt)—and the audience believes that the [character's] life would have been productive and happy had [they] not been a 'victim of divided racial inheritance.'"[48] This stereotype plays itself out in films such as *Imitation of Life* (1934 and 1959), *Pinky* (1949), *Devil in a Blue Dress* (1995), and *The Human Stain* (2005). Fauntroy puts an interesting spin on the notion of passing. In his case, he spends most of his life *not* being a victim of his divided racial inheritance. On the contrary, he and his ancestors have reaped the benefits of white privilege while actively working to keep black folks enslaved. In his case, the tragic mulatto stereotype plays less like a sympathetic figure and more like a character whose metaphorical chickens have come home to roost.

During one of the news breaks prior to the audience learning about Horace's story, the anchor informs viewers that "charges may be filed following several controversial errors in the Department of Racial Identity. The watchdog group Proven White charged that DNA mistakes are commonplace and that many people don't know who they are." Fauntroy's fate, placed within the context of this news story, tells the audience that either it is possible that Fauntroy's DNA results are incorrect and he does in fact have some black ancestry in his family tree, or, as is the case in history prime, there is no genetic test to prove racial identity, and the Confederate States of America is based on a social construct, not a biological fact. If the latter theory is correct, then either the federal government does not realize that race does not have a genetic marker and therefore nullifies the point of racial testing, or else the government does understand this information and is complicit in perpetuating a lie upon Confederate citizens in an effort to preserve a white supremacist slavocracy.

Curtain Call

One of the main questions raised by C.S.A. is who really won the American Civil War. In history prime, the answer is quite obviously the Union. As historian Nell Irvin Painter points out: "The 13th, 14th, and 15th Amendments to the United States Constitution inserted the victory into federal law: emancipation, citizenship and (for men) the right to vote. A system built around a wealthy, slave-holding minority ceded place to more encompassing ideals of citizenship."[49] Painter is obviously correct in her analysis, but let us consider a reframing of the question. Willmott makes the argument that the North "won the war but we didn't win the peace."[50] With that in mind, the question we should be asking ourselves—and the question the film seeks to answer—isn't Who won the Civil War? but rather, Who won the war against white supremacy? Willmott's film, of course, maintains that the Confederacy won and continues to win the war over white supremacy. Though the Confederacy lost major ground with the Union victory during the Civil War, Confederate ideals continue to pervade history, politics, and popular culture in the United States. In her discussion of the 2013 *Shelby County v. Holder* Supreme Court decision, which dismantled critical portions of the 1965 Voting Rights Act, Painter argues: "To the extent that the right to vote remains contingent, and, therefore, subject to unwarranted restriction, Confederate ideals of limited citizenship survive."[51]

Like speculative fiction writers who hypothesized what a world with a Confederate States of America would look like, Willmott posits that the alternate history is far more destructive and less free than history prime. At the same time, his film makes the argument that the United States is far closer to a Confederate States than we would like to believe. The glorification of the Stars and Bars exists in history prime, the criminalization and exploitation of black bodies for entertainment and profit exists in history prime, and the distribution of privileges based on race exists in history prime. It is one thing to simply say that white supremacy continues to exist in the United States and that it is linked to a legacy of slavery; scholars and activists have done so for decades, without convincing everyone. It is another to point to racial disparities in education, health care, and incarceration rates, and argue that those disparities are also linked to white supremacy. Those statements can be—and are—dismissed by a fair amount of people. It is something entirely different to create a world where slavery in its rawest form continues to exist, and literally, although facetiously, highlights how our world is eerily similar to a slavocracy. In *Blazing Saddles*, Mel Brooks highlights the ridiculousness of racism and makes sure that the audience is laughing at the ignorant racists. C.S.A., in contrast, is mocking American society as a whole. Unfortunately, one of the best—and worst—things about the film is its recognition that race relations are still an issue, and so the joke continues to be on us.

6

Ladies First

Ava DuVernay and Black-Female-Centered Narratives

[My films are] infused with people of color because so often we don't see ourselves as regular people and that might sound strange hearing but for folks who love films and only see themselves as caricatures or in very broad comedies, it's nice to see and make a film that was not about heightened situations. This is about an everyday situation and this is why folks of all colors and backgrounds have appreciated it but especially the African-American community where we hear again and again the common refrain [of] thank you for showing us as we are.

Ava DuVernay, 2011

In my own work I write not only what I want to read—understanding fully and indelibly that if I don't do it no one else is so vitally interested, or capable of doing it to my satisfaction—I write all the things I should have been able to read.

Alice Walker, In Search of Our Mother's Gardens: Womanist Prose, 2011

In 2014, Ava DuVernay became the first African American woman to be nominated for a Golden Globe for Best Birector, for the film Selma.[1] That film went on to garner an Oscar nomination for Best Picture, making DuVernay the first black woman to direct a film nominated in that category. In discussing her Golden Globe– and Oscar-winning film, DuVernay spoke to political scientist Melissa Harris-Perry about her work on the film: "When I first came aboard the film the women . . . were not there at all and so it was really important to start to realign the story and gain some balance. We know historically that the women of the movement have not been bolstered, have not been amplified as much as they should be for all of the amazing work that was done, in all corners."[2] *Selma* highlights the myriad ways that black women and girls bolstered the civil rights movement. The audience sees Anna Lee Cooper (Oprah Winfrey) in her quest to register to vote; Mahalia Jackson (Ledisi Young) lifting Dr. Martin Luther King Jr.'s spirits when he "needs to hear the Lord's voice"; Diane Nash (Tessa Thompson) explaining to everyone why Selma is the next battlefield; Richie Jean Jackson (Niecy Nash) welcoming the Southern Christian Leadership Council into her kitchen; Amelia Boynton (Lorraine Toussaint) putting her body in harm's way and explaining that "we are the descendants of mighty people who gave civilization to the world"; and Coretta Scott King (Carmen Ejogo) meeting with Malcolm X during his visit to Selma to make sure that he is on the same page as everyone else. At the beginning of the film we see Anna Mae Collins, Cynthia Wesley, Carole Robertson, and Carol Denise McNair murdered during the bombing of the 16th Street Baptist Church in Birmingham. That is only a small fraction of the number of black women involved in the struggle for racial equality. The absence of black women from the mainstream narrative of the civil rights movement is puzzling when you consider law professor and activist Kathleen Neal Cleaver's recollection that "if it weren't for black women, there would have been no Montgomery Bus Boycott, few voting rights campaigns, far less marvelous educational impact—in short, the civil rights movement as we know it could not have occurred."[3] While both Cleaver and DuVernay were talking specifically about our understanding of how gender is framed in the context of the civil rights movement, the same statement could apply to women, particularly black women, in popular culture specifically and to all aspects of American life more broadly.

According to filmmaker and cultural theorist Manthia Diawara, since D. W. Griffith's 1915 film *Birth of a Nation*, "Hollywood's Blacks exist primarily for White spectators whose comfort and understanding the films must seek, whether they thematize exotic images dancing and singing on the screen, or images constructed to narrate a racial drama, or images of pimps and muggers."[4] Starting with Oscar Micheaux and continuing to the present day, black filmmakers have attempted to tell their own stories, about their own communities, to their own communities, and debunk many of the previously mentioned stereotypes by presenting black characters as fully formed human beings. While there has been and continues to be a fair number of black male directors, from Spike Lee to Ryan Coogler to Antoine Fuqua to Tyler Perry, the same cannot be said for black female directors. This is not to say that black women have never been at the center of film narratives. On the contrary, films such as Jack Hill's *Coffy* (1973), Berry Gordy's *Mahogany* (1975), Jonathan Demme's *Beloved* (1998), and Benh Zeitlin's *Beasts of the Southern Wild* (2012) feature black women or girls as the primary protagonists. For better or for worse, all of these films have been directed by men. The number of female directors working in mainstream Hollywood, let alone black female directors, has always been quite low. While Mel Brooks's *Blazing Saddles* asks the impolitic question, Where are the white women at?, no one is asking, Where are the black women at? Specifically, where are the black female directors telling stories about black women, for black women?

Black women have not been completely excluded from behind the camera, though the reality of the situation is still quite grim. In 1993, when Ed Guerrero's seminal text *Framing Blackness: The African American Image in Film* was published, the author highlighted the good news/bad news state of black films when he wrote, "Black men produced more black films in 1991 than in the entire 1980s, while black women produced no films whatsoever."[5] The mid-1990s, however, saw what can only be characterized as an explosion of black female directors telling stories about black women for the big screen. Julie Dash's *Daughters of the Dust* (1990) told the story of three generations of Gullah women on the eve of the family's migration to the North and was "the first film created by a black woman that was released in commercial distribution."[6] At that point, the metaphorical flood gates seemed to open. In 1992, Leslie Harris released *Just Another Girl on the I.R.T.*, about the life of a teenage girl in Brooklyn. Darnell Martin's *I Like It Like That* (1994) centers on a woman named Lisette and her struggle to salvage her life and marriage; it became the first major studio film written and directed by a black woman. Cheryl Dunye's *The Watermelon Woman* (1996) is a mockumentary about the search for a 1930s black film actress. Kasi Lemmons's *Eve's Bayou* (1997) focuses on ten-year-old Eve as she navigates 1962 Louisiana and the events that lead to the death of her father. Maya Angelou's *Down in the Delta* (1998) tells the story of Loretta, a drug addict, who is sent to rural Mississippi to get sober and repair the relationship with her children.

As we moved into the 2000s, the number of films directed by black women that received national releases and critical attention seemed to decrease, with the exception of Gina Prince-Bythewood's output, which included Love & Basketball (2000) and The Secret Life of Bees (2013). As discussed in the introduction, interest in black films tends to run in ten-year cycles. After black female directors and their stories had their five- to six-year run, Hollywood seemed to lose interest and the mainstream public paid little attention to the scarcity of black female directors and their stories.

The landscape changed slightly in 2010 with the release of DuVernay's I Will Follow and the establishment of the African American Film Festival Releasing Movement (AFFRM), which bypasses the studio system by negotiating directly with theaters to release black independent films. DuVernay has made no secret about the fact that her films place black women at the center of the story, and she seems to be creating what film critic Molly Haskell called "women's films," a category about which black feminist author Michele Wallace says: "A heady, ambiguous mixture of sentiment and feminist ideas, a women's film creates a universe in which women's thought and aspirations are at its center."[7] There is some evidence to suggest that Hollywood is regaining interest in telling these women's stories through films with black female directors at the helm. Spurred on by the success of black women on television, including Kerry Washington on Scandal (2010), Nicole Beharie on Sleepy Hollow (2013), Gabrielle Union on Being Mary Jane (2013), Viola Davis on How to Get Away with Murder (2014), and Taraji P. Henson on Empire (2014), there have been a handful of black-female-directed films, including Dee Rees's Pariah (2011), Victoria Mahoney's Yelling at the Sky (2011), and Gina Prince-Bythewood's Beyond the Lights (2014). This chapter analyzes DuVernay's first two feature films, I Will Follow and Middle of Nowhere (2012), as well as her other artistic endeavors, to see what messages she is sending about black women, their circumstances, and their humanity. As DuVernay stated when she accepted the 2015 Black Girls Rock Shot Callers award, "When a black woman makes a film it is not an interpretation of black womanhood; it is a reflection, and it's important to embrace it."[8] It is important to know what is it about black womanhood that is being reflected by the filmmaker and embraced by the audience.

Whether intentional or not—and there is evidence to conclude that it is—DuVernay's films advocate for a black feminist sensibility. Patricia Hill Collins notes that "clarifying Black women's experiences and ideas lies at the core of Black feminist thought."[9] Thus, by making black women the primary protagonists and by placing black women's experiences and ideas front and center in her work, DuVernay is forwarding a black feminist sensibility. Making one of a film's main protagonists a black woman is quite rare for Hollywood features; as mentioned in the introduction, of the top 100 films released in 2018, only seven featured a woman of color as the main protagonist, though that is an increase from the three films with black female protagonists in 2014.[10] One film on the 2018 list was DuVernay's version of Madeleine L'Engle's award-winning novel *A Wrinkle in Time*. This marked the first time a black female director helmed a $100 million film, and it came as no surprise to anyone that DuVernay cast a young black girl as the film's protagonist.[11] Not all films featuring black female protagonists have been directed or written by black women, and many of the roles lacked an intersectional focus; in fact, many viewed some of the portrayals as quite problematic. DuVernay has said that one of her missions is to "portray nuanced black family life,"[12] and her films create a sort of black feminist holy trinity in that they are written and directed by a black woman, place a black woman or black women at the center of the narrative, and employ roles that are intersectional in that they focus not just on race but also, either explicitly or implicitly, gender, sexual identity, and/or socioeconomic status.

Teaser Trailers

Though the bulk of the attention paid to DuVernay concentrates on her feature films, her black feminist focus is not exclusive to that portion of her storytelling. One of her earliest works was a 2010 documentary for Black Entertainment Television (BET) entitled *My Mic Sounds Nice: The Truth About Women in Hip Hop*, which, as the title explains, explored the myriad issues female emcees faced from the early days of the cultural form through the present. The documentary was conceived of as "a love letter to the art of the female emcee. It's a love letter to the women in hip-hop, whether they be DJs or emcees or graffiti artists, dancers—executives, even. It's really time that we look at these sisters and give them their due.[13] *My Mic Sounds Nice* discussed the careers of Salt-n-Pepa, MC Lyte, Missy Elliott, Lauryn Hill, Nicki Minaj, and Eve, to name a few, and looked at how these women, the overwhelming majority of whom are black, carved out spaces within a male-dominated industry. Already we see DuVernay's intersectional lens in action as her documentary tells the stories of a diverse group of women (gender) who participate in an oft-maligned musical form whose roots are in impoverished (class) black and brown communities (race). Not only that, but the documentary highlights the diversity of styles, messages, and attitudes that these black women exhibited in the music.

Three years later, DuVernay placed black women at the center of three short films. The first was a web piece that was part of *The Women's Tales*, a series of shorts sponsored by women's clothing and accessory company Miu Miu, entitled "The Door." DuVernay's short stars Gabrielle Union, Alfre Woodard, Emayatzy Corinealdi, Adepero Oduye, and Goapele. The webisode, which is ten minutes long and contains no dialogue, sees Union's character mourning the end of a relationship. Her friends attempt to ease her sadness by dressing her up and taking her out to eat, dance, and listen to music. According to DuVernay, "With each friend that comes in, these women are dressing her. So they are using clothes to evoke emotion. They are trying to choose things that are more lively and bring her out of it."[14] The short not only highlights the importance of black female friendships and how empowering those friendships can be but also the need for inclusion within the fashion industry. As the *Huffington Post*'s Julee Wilson points out, "The significance and power of a cast of black women being directed by a black woman for one of fashion's most important brands should not be lost. Even in a time when First Lady Michelle Obama serves as an example of strength and style, it's rare that we see women of color being celebrated for those qualities—especially on the covers of the top magazines and in fashion/beauty campaigns."[15] In 2013, Kerry Washington became the first black woman in almost ten years to grace the cover of *Vanity Fair*, and it was the first time ever that a black actress appeared on the magazine's cover alone. That was at the same time when "the number of black fashion models at this year's fall New York Fashion Week, for example, dropped from 8.1% to 6%."[16] "The Door" showcases the fact that black women can be fashionistas, have the physical beauty to model designer clothing, and should be more visible within the fashion industry, and highlights DuVernay's goal to "bring some luxury and beauty to the black female cinematic image."[17]

DuVernay's next project stayed within the fashion/beauty industry but moved from the Italian runways to the largest black-owned cosmetics company in the world. When Fashion Fair Cosmetics approached DuVernay about collaborating on a project, she said she was

> thrilled [because it is] a brand that has always embraced women of color, and that women of color have so often embraced. The film is a meditation on the power of "yes," illustrating what can happen when we affirm our family, our friends, ourselves. I also thought about the many ways that Fashion Fair says "yes" to us. Yes to our variance of

skin tone, yes to our different ages, yes to our body sizes, yes to the myriad of elements that we are. That's something worth celebrating.[18]

The short, entitled "Say Yes," is seven minutes long, contains no dialogue, and stars Kali Hawk as Her, a woman who arrives home to find a party in full swing. As she walks through her home, she finds each room filled with friends who invite Her to enjoy the festivities. The revelers include actors who have worked on DuVernay's feature films, such as Lorraine Toussaint, Beverly Todd, and Dijon Talton, as well as other notable black artists including *Daughters of the Dust* director Julie Dash; Issa Rae, the writer and star of the HBO series *Insecure*; *Dear White People* writer and director Justin Simien; and actress/producer Lena Waithe, who in 2017 became the first black woman to win an Emmy for comedy writing. As Her exits into her backyard, she is greeted by Him (Lance Gross), who proposes marriage, much to the delight of the party guests, who were clearly in on the surprise. As DuVernay mentioned in her quote, Fashion Fair is known for catering to the diversity among black women, and the film highlights that very point: the partygoers embody various skin tones, hair colors and textures, ages, and styles of dress. The diversity of the black community is on full display in the short, which emphasizes a black woman embracing her joy.

DuVernay's third project was also the most obviously political in focus. In 2009, ESPN developed a documentary film series entitled *30 for 30* that was initially conceived to highlight the sport stories that captured the public imagination since the network's founding. The series has analyzed a host of events and issues, including the life of baseball and football star Bo Jackson, the retirement and return of NBA Hall of Famer Michael Jordan, and the career and impact of Los Angeles Dodger pitcher Fernando Valenzuela, particularly as it pertained to the Latinx population of Southern California. With more than sixty films in the ESPN archive as of 2018, only four full-length features have highlighted female athletes: *The Price of Gold* looked at the 1994 U.S. Figure Skating Championship incident between Nancy Kerrigan and Tonya Harding, *Renée* discussed the life of transgender athlete Renée Richards, *Unmatched* looked at the friendship between tennis champions Chris Evert and Martina Navratilova, and *Marion Jones: Press Pause* looked at track star and former WNBA player Marion Jones's performance-enhancing drug use admission and her subsequent imprisonment.[19]

In 2013, in conjunction with the fortieth anniversary of Title IX, the landmark legislation signed in 1972 that "prohibits discrimination on the basis of sex in any federally funded education program or activity"[20] and is mostly associated with access to collegiate athletic opportunities, ESPN commissioned a series of documentary films that focused exclusively on female athletes and sportswriters as told by female filmmakers. The first film in the series was *Venus Vs.*, directed by DuVernay. The film chronicles tennis star Venus Williams's fight for pay equity at Wimbledon. DuVernay became involved in the project because

> Venus is a superior athlete, a legend; but she is also an activist who revolutionized her sport off the court with her fight for prize equality. I don't believe this story should be relegated to dusty history books and British newspapers. People in the United States should know of her true professional bravery and personal tenacity in making sure women athletes are regarded and rewarded on par with their male counterparts. This is my mission.[21]

Though the story was well-known in Britain, where the Wimbledon Grand Slam Tournament takes place, many in the United States were unaware of Williams's two-year fight. It was only appropriate that Williams won Wimbledon in 2007 and 2008, the first two years that the All-England Club offered equal prize money, and she collected £700,000 and £750,000 as her reward.[22]

In a similar vein as Venus Williams's fight for equality in the sports world, DuVernay has opened the door for other women, and specifically women of color, in the film industry. After finishing *Venus Vs.*, DuVernay directed an episode of the Shonda Rhimes hit series *Scandal*, marking her foray into serial television, and three years later DuVernay decided to pay it forward. In 2016, she signed on as creator, executive producer, writer, and director of the series *Queen Sugar*, airing on Oprah Winfrey's OWN Network. The series, based on Natalie Baszile's novel of the same name, follows a trio of siblings who must band together to run their family's sugarcane farm in Louisiana following the death of their father. The series is based on a book written by a black woman, follows the story of a black family, a majority of whom are women, is helmed by a black woman, and airs on a network owned by a black woman. What makes the series even more remarkable is the fact that all the episodes from the first three seasons were directed by women, some of whom had never directed television before.[23] These projects provide a small glimpse into what DuVernay seeks to reflect about black womanhood in her work. In each of these endeavors there is beauty, elegance, strength, perseverance, and diversity.

The Main Attractions

Before analyzing what images of black womanhood DuVernay is reflecting in her first two feature films, it would help to provide a brief description of each film's storylines. *I Will Follow* is a semi-autobiographical story that follows Maye (Salli Richardson-Whitfield) as she mourns the death of her aunt Amanda (Beverly Todd). The entire film takes place within a roughly twenty-four-hour period as Maye packs up her aunt's home. Throughout the film we meet an assortment of individuals including the mover, Tuliau (Tony Perez), who inadvertently damages some of Amanda's belongings; Amanda's daughter Fran (Michole White) and grandson Raven (Dijon Talton); Maye's long-distance partner Evan (Blair Underwood); and Troy (Omari Hardwick), the man who Maye had a brief affair with while she was taking care of her aunt. In his review of the film, the late Pulitzer Prize–winning film critic Roger Ebert noted that the film "doesn't tell a story so much as try to understand a woman. Through her, we can find insights into the ways we deal with death. In one way or another, every emotion in this wonderful independent film is one I've experienced myself."[24] Writing for *Shadow and Act*, a website devoted to films of the African diaspora, Tambay argues that *I Will Follow* is "a deeply personal, reflective chamber drama. Ingmar Bergman would smile."[25]

DuVernay's second feature film, *Middle of Nowhere*, follows Ruby (Emayatzy Corinealdi), a nurse who is working night shifts and has dropped out of medical school following the incarceration of her husband, Derek (Omari Hardwick). While Derek serves a seven-year sentence, Ruby tries to hold onto her family, which includes her sister, Rosie (Edwina Findley), and mother, Ruth (Lorraine Toussaint). Ruby meets and forms a connection with a bus driver named Brian (David Oyelowo), whose presence makes her already complicated life even more challenging. Rick Groen of the *Globe and Mail* remarks that the film is not "an Oprah-esque exercise in consciousness-raising. Instead, the dialogue remains taut, the choices stay hard, redemption proves elusive and blame widespread."[26] Writing for the *Toronto Star*, Peter Howell argues that the film is "remarkably true to life's haphazard rhythms."[27] For her efforts on this film, DuVernay became the first black woman to win a director's prize at the Sundance Film Festival.[28]

Throwing Down the Race Card?

For all of the discussion about how DuVernay purposely places gender in her films, *I Will Follow* is not explicit about race, and that was an intentional decision. When asked about this choice, DuVernay remarked:

> I purposely made sure there was no reference to race in the film. I wanted the actions and the beauty of the family itself to say everything that needed to be said about how black people live which is just like everybody else. Certainly I have conversations about race, probably 2–3 times a week. Not even conversations, just, something I say that's very "black girl." But for the most part, the other 90% of my day there's no reference to it at all. It's embedded in just how I walk through the world. I don't need to speak to it specifically.[29]

Though the film does not draw attention to race with neon blinking lights, race is omnipresent in the film. Even in his review, Ebert hesitantly brings up the racial issue when he writes: "Amanda's family is African-American. The neighbor and some of the visitors are white. Why do I mention race? I wasn't going to. This is a universal story about universal emotions. Maybe I mention it because this is the kind of film black filmmakers are rarely able to get made these days, offering roles for actors who remind us here of their gifts."[30] Explicit references to race may not be present in the film; however, as DuVernay mentions, race is interwoven into how these characters interact with each other and how they move through the world. In the film, we learn that Amanda was a musician who played on a multitude of hit records throughout her career. As Maye and Fran begin packing up the house, they discuss where Amanda's session tapes should reside. Maye notes that Amanda donated the tapes to the "Seattle Museum," presumably a reference to the Experience Music Project Museum; however, Fran thinks the tapes should have been donated to the "African American Museum" and notes that her mother was "always following behind some white folk." Maye reminds Fran about the special affection Amanda had for Seattle when she replies, "Come on, you know why she loved Seattle. . . . It's the one place she got flown to play, remember? Anyway, the museum specializes in music. Whatever African American museum you're advocating for, they're not going to appreciate the tapes." Fran views Amanda's choice as racially motivated and implies that her mother was a sellout; however, the opposite is the case: Amanda's decision is based on the fact that someone in Seattle respected and appreciated her and her talent, and she wanted to acknowledge and repay that respect. Acknowledgment of skill and talent is quite important; DuVernay is cognizant of the fact that black women are often pushed out of mainstream narratives of history, and because of that, Amanda's decision to reward Seattle for appreciating her work takes on a greater significance.

Later in the film Raven laments the fact that he was not able to find anything about his grandmother's work on Google, a problem that continues to plague session musicians of all races. After Maye and Fran get into a huge fight over Maye's decision to support Amanda's decision to stop chemotherapy, Raven shows Maye a YouTube video of Amanda rocking out on her drums—he Googled the studio Amanda played for and found the video on their website. Amanda's work was there, hiding in plain sight; however, people who were interested in her accomplishments had to jump through a few hoops to find her story. That same sentiment could apply to black women's accomplishments in a variety of fields. Amanda's obscurity is framed as an issue faced by session musicians as a group, and anyone who has seen the documentary *Standing in the Shadows of Motown* (2002) knows that this has always been a problem for the music industry; however, the audience is left to wonder whether her identity as a black woman pushed her even further out of the spotlight.

Of course, since Amanda was a musician, several conversations in the film are about music, and it becomes clear that her musical interests fell outside of what is stereotypically expected for black women. At one point in the film, Maye tells Raven that even though Amanda played for the likes of Barry White, Donna Summer, and the Bee Gees, if she "hadn't been born in the wrong body she would have been in a heavy metal band because they had the best solos." We do not know if the wrong body Maye refers to concerns Amanda's race, her gender, or a combination of the two. Given the overwhelming whiteness and maleness of heavy metal as a genre, it is probably safe to assume that Amanda had two strikes against her. Because of her race and gender, Amanda was deemed unacceptable as a heavy metal artist, though that is where her drummer's heart led her. Again, this is not an explicit discussion of race or gender or intersectionality; the film simply puts the statement out there and lets the audience decide how to interpret it.

Throughout the film, the audience is introduced to Amanda via flashbacks to what was probably the last good day she had before her death. We never see the scene in full: it is broken up and spread out over the course of the entire film; however, we do hear Amanda and Maye talk about music. While the topic is not clear during the first few flashbacks, it eventually becomes apparent that the women are discussing their fondness for the band U2. Amanda remarks that the band has been around for so long that they have generations of fans, and she is surprised and proud to learn that Maye's knowledge and affection for the band rivals her own—though she playfully admonishes Maye for not listing drummer Larry Mullen first when she names the band members. Again, though U2 has sold tens of millions of albums over their more than forty-year career, there are not many who would assume that these two black women would be fans—three black women if one includes DuVernay, who titled the film after a U2 song. Defying expectations of what black people in general, and black women more specifically, could and could not be was one of the film's accomplishments; as DuVernay remarked, "That's the spectrum of black people. Get over it, it's not what you think. So that's some of what I was trying to get across in the film without saying that."[31]

In *Middle of Nowhere*, DuVernay takes the same path of making race a component of the film without too many explicit references to it, while at the same time turning racial stereotypes on their heads. As far as subverting stereotypes is concerned, when Derek asks Ruby out on a date, he asks what kind of films she likes, which leads to a discussion of film genres and segregation:

> RUBY: I don't know if you like the same kind of movies I like.
> BRIAN: All right, what kind of movies do you like?
> RUBY: Indie ones. Foreign ones.
> BRIAN: Movies where a brother's got to read.
> RUBY: Yes. Those.
> BRIAN: Oh. All right. I can swing with subtitles.
> RUBY: They play on the West Side mostly. They don't even show 'em over here.
> BRIAN: It's not a problem. It's not a problem.

Again, DuVernay tosses another stereotype aside as she rebuffs the belief that black communities do not support independent or international films. Ruby laments the fact that indie and international films do not play in her neighborhood, an omission that DuVernay discusses in the film's commentary track when she states, "The movie theater business is super-segregated, you know what I mean, so if you live in a black or brown community you have to travel to the white part of town to see independent cinema, to see foreign films, and it's unfortunate."[32] In Los Angeles, black and brown film fans who are interested in these types of movies must travel to the Westside, which consists primarily of upper-middle-class, predominantly white neighborhoods such as Beverly Hills, Brentwood, and Westwood, an inconvenience that requires additional time and resources that filmgoers who do not live in those neighborhoods may not have.

Of course, race enters the film without an overt signpost that says "race is important here," primarily through Ruby's interactions with the criminal justice system. The Pew Research Center noted that in 2018, 33 percent of the sentenced prison population was black, representing a 25 percent decrease since 2009. Though millions of people in the United States deal with the prison system at some point, the racial disparities in incarceration rates show that black communities are far more likely to have such dealings. Throughout the film, the audience knows that Derek has committed some sort of nonviolent offense, but it is not until the very end of the film that we find out he was convicted on a gun smuggling charge. The focus of the film is not Derek and his time in prison; it is on how Derek's incarceration affects Ruby. Because of Derek's actions, Ruby puts her entire life on hold. According to DuVernay, Ruby is "living inside a Langston Hughes poem, in a way. She's living inside a dream deferred. A dream of what her life was meant to be, what her marriage was meant to be, what her career was meant to be. Through choices she makes, and choices made for her, nothing is happening as planned. Everything is put off. She's in a middle place."[33] The same could be said for the other women who, like Ruby, have incarcerated family members. On Ruby's bus rides to the prison, we notice that the majority of women taking that trip are women of color. Though Derek is the one who is physically in prison, in many ways Ruby and the families of incarcerated people are also imprisoned by the system. When Derek's parole is denied and Ruby decides to end their relationship, she tells Derek, "I'm not going to do another four years with you."

Having Money Isn't Everything; Not Having It Is

While discussions of race and racism are hidden in plain sight in both films, discussions of socioeconomic class are far more explicit. Toward the beginning of the *Middle of Nowhere*, Ruby is having dinner with her sister and nephew, Nickie, when she runs into Gina and her daughter, DeeDee. It turns out that DeeDee is Derek's daughter; we do not know whether Derek fathered the child before or after he married Ruby. Unfortunately, Derek is two months behind in child support, leading to a tense conversation:

CHAPTER SIX

Ruby asks for money

RUBY: We just sent school clothes last month.
GINA: She don't need school clothes. She needs money. How do you all think we're living? I depend on that money, Ruby.
RUBY: I know that, Gina. I'm trying. We're trying.

The desperation in Gina's voice is apparent. With Derek in prison, it's clear that Ruby is the one trying to provide financial support for his daughter. Shortly thereafter, the audience learns just how precarious Ruby's financial situation is when she tries to meet with Derek's lawyer after learning that Derek is eligible for early parole. Unfortunately, despite the fact that Ruby made all of the payments on time, the lawyer refuses to take the parole case unless she pays in full up front. It is clear that Ruby does not have the $2,500 the lawyer is asking for, and after a heated discussion, the lawyer agrees to a new payment plan as long as Ruby pays half of the fee in advance. That's still $1,250 that we know, based on her conversation with Gina, Ruby doesn't have. Though she does not want to, Ruby has to ask her mother for $750 to help pay the fee.

During the scene, Ruby does not look her mother in the eye until her mother tells her to "hold your head up please." Ruth begrudgingly gives Ruby the money but reminds her that the car payment is due on the fifteenth, and so Ruby must repay her before that bill is due. Though Ruth is able to come up with the money, it is clear that both women are facing financial constraints. Coming up with $750, let alone $2,500, is a huge task. Even though Ruby is ashamed of having to ask her mother for money, Ruth is adamant that there is no shame in asking for or needing financial assistance.

Going back to *I Will Follow*, even though Maye is more financially secure than Ruby and her family, money is still an issue. Though the audience does not get a full picture of Maye's life before she became her aunt's caregiver, we do have indications that she is well known. After Maye and Raven debate the intricacies of NBA stars and New York rappers, they are visited by renowned makeup artist Damone Roberts, who plays himself. Throughout their interaction, Roberts is insistent about Maye returning to work, which indicates that she is somehow linked to Hollywood and/or the cosmetic industry. When Troy comes by later to help Maye finish packing he asks her, "So, how come you never told me you were such a big deal? You're like a really important person." At the very end of the film, when Maye is finally ready to move on, she makes a YouTube video and introduces herself as "makeup artist to the stars." Clearly Maye is financially secure. Though the audience does not know the full extent of Maye's economic situation, her economic privilege is implied throughout the film. We know that Maye paused her career, moved to a new city, and devoted a year of her life to caring for her aunt, steps that required a great deal of mental, emotional, and financial resources.

Despite Maye's economic privilege, especially relative to Ruby's, the audience sees that there are still some financial issues. When the satellite repairwoman comes to remove her equipment, she looks over the long list of television programs and movies that Amanda had saved on the digital video recorder, pausing on a replay of Barack Obama's speech after winning the 2008 presidential election. On the one hand, this scene is another moment when race is once again hiding in plain sight, as we watch two black women watching a speech delivered by the first black president of the United States. At the same time, we get a deeper understanding into what is going on in Maye's mind. She laments losing all of the programs Amanda had saved and says, "I should have watched more TV with her. She'd be in here, and I'd be in my office trying to keep everything. I should have been in here." Even with Maye's economic resources, it was still a struggle to keep everything afloat, and that brief statement highlights just how precarious an economic situation black women often find themselves in. According to the 2010 report from the Insight Center for Community Economic Development, "while white women in prime working years of ages 36–49 have a median wealth of $42,000, the median wealth for women of color is only $5 [and] nearly half of all single black and Hispanic women have zero or negative wealth."[34] The report goes on to hypothesize that "the financial situations of single women of color are so precarious . . . that just one unpaid sick day or appliance repair would send about half of them into debt."³⁵ Though it is not spoken aloud, the audience understands that Maye will be okay financially and emotionally. The YouTube video signals a desire to return to her career, and she has reached an understanding with her romantic partner, Evan, which will be discussed in more detail in the next section. It may take some time to get back on her feet, but Maye is in a position of economic privilege compared to other black women specifically, and women of color more broadly. Ruby, on the other hand, is an example of exactly the type of woman that the aforementioned report is talking about. We see that coming up with $750 puts Ruby in a financially untenable situation. Thankfully, she has a support system available (Ruth) to help her; however, her mother is only in a slightly less financially precarious situation because of the risk of losing her car if Ruby does not pay her back within the prescribed time period. Here is a prime example of the diversity of black womanhood that DuVernay's work reflects. Though Maye and Ruby may face some similar experiences due to their shared race and gender backgrounds, their different socioeconomic statuses highlight the diversity among black women's experiences.

I'm Not Your Superwoman

According to Patricia Hill Collins, "Portraying African-American women as stereotypical mammies, matriarchs, welfare recipients, and hot mommas helps justify U.S. black women's oppression. Challenging these controlling images has long been a core theme in black beminist thought."³⁶ These stereotypes and controlling images have a long and varied history in popular culture. At the birth of Hollywood, and for quite some time after, "the black actress's principal function was—by contrast in language, costume, and behavior—to illuminate or aggrandize the virtue, beauty, morality, sexuality, sophistication, and other qualities embedded in the 'whiteness' of the white female actress and character."³⁷ In the twenty-first century, this otherness has been reconfigured into women who "often appear among white women as magical figures . . . [who] are capable of solving white women's personal crises without ever hinting at the depth of their own oppressive circumstance."³⁸ The iconic representation of this stereotype was Hattie McDaniel's role as Mammy in *Gone with the Wind* (1939), but we see still this character in contemporary films such as *Sex in the City* (2008) and *The Help* (2011). Black women who are not Magical Negroes are often framed as the Angry Black Woman, who is "shrill, loud, argumentative, irrationally angry, and verbally abusive."³⁹ Black feminist thought theorist Melissa Harris-Perry makes the argument that women such as Congresswoman Maxine Waters and even herself have been labeled the Angry Black Woman. There is also the jezebel or the stereotype that frames black women as "particularly promiscuous and sexually immoral."[40] *She's Gotta Have It* (1986) and *Monster's Ball* (2001) are two representations of the jezebel image. There is plenty more that can be said about these destructive and completely inaccurate ways of portraying black women in popular culture; however, the purpose here is to simply point out that none of those stereotypes exist in DuVernay's work.

Though all those stereotypes still occur in the public realm, the more recent stereotype employed to describe black women is that of the Strong Black Woman. This stereotype almost feels like a response to the previous three framings in that Strong Black Women are "motivated, hardworking breadwinners who suppress their emotional needs while anticipating those of others."[41] While the Strong Black Women feels more like an affirmation than a stereotype, it is still problematic because "when black women are expected to be super-strong, they cannot be simply human."[42] Neither Maye nor Ruby is framed as this stereotype; their characters are, for better and worse, simply human.

At first glance, it almost seems as though Maye would fit into the Strong Black Woman category. She walked away from what was by all accounts a lucrative and fulfilling career to become her aunt's primary caregiver. Throughout the film, we watch her hold everything together as she packs up their home and prepares to return to her old life. What pushes Maye outside of the Strong Black Woman stereotype, and helps frame her as a whole human being, is her vulnerability. At multiple times during the film we hear her converse with her romantic partner, Evan. There is strain in their relationship, and over the course of the film it becomes clear that Maye's decision to provide end-of-life care for Amanda is a leading cause of that strain. Evan is disappointed that Maye walked away from her life and their relationship without a second thought, and Maye is disappointed that Evan did not help and was generally unsupportive of her decision. It's clear this is an argument they have been having for the past year, but Maye finally verbalizes the real issue behind her anger:

> MAYE: So, what you gonna do when I get sick? My hair falls out and vomiting and I need to be fed and bathed and someone to pick me up off the bathroom floor?
> EVAN: That's not you.

Maye's vulnerability

MAYE: It could be, you know.
EVAN: You don't know, either.
MAYE: I know that if anything ever happened to you, as much as a scratch or a cough, I would shut it all down and be there. I wouldn't dare let anyone even think about touching you. I would take care of you because you're mine. Who's gonna take care of me?
EVAN: I am. I am now. I'll be there.

For Maye, this long-standing argument has less to do with Evan's current behavior, though that also plays a role, and more to do with the prospects of his future behavior. While the scene does connote strength, as it takes courage to speak these words, more important is how the scene highlights Maye's vulnerability. She is naked before Evan and the audience—literally, in fact, as she sits in a bathtub during the conversation, saying that she *needs* and *wants* support. As Maye states in no uncertain terms, she will be there and carry the Strong Black Woman mantle if necessary, but in return, she wants to know that Evan will take care of her in the same manner. In an interview with DuVernay, Michael Martin notes, "Maye is freed the moment she realizes that she's alone and that she can't expect Evan, or any other man, to be there at the end. . . . There are no romantic illusions left for her. Evan says 'I fucked up' and she walks out the door knowing that she can never trust him."[43] Because of that conversation, Maye's ending in the film is with an understanding that her future is not defined by their relationship.

In the hands of a less mindful writer and director, Ruby could have come across as a jezebel, since she initiates a romantic relationship with Brian while she is still married to Derek. However, Ruby's situation is far more complex than that: she initially rejects Brian's advances because of her devotion to Derek. During Derek's parole hearing, Ruby learns that Derek had sexual contact with a female officer two years prior, and it is clear that Ruby was unaware of that incident. Ruby goes out with Brian only after learning that Derek was unfaithful. Even with that knowledge, when Ruby is ready to have sex with Brian she initially refuses to do so in her own home, in the bed that she and Derek shared. When Derek's friend Rashad confronts Ruby about her relationship with Brian, Ruby is clear about the fact that she is in charge of her life and her relationships:

> RUBY: This is over when I say it's over. You don't know me. You don't know nothing about us. If you knew half of what you think you know, you wouldn't be up in my face right now.
> RASHAD: Look, you talking to my man or what?
> RUBY: I will talk to my man when I am good and damn well ready.

We can give Rashad the benefit of the doubt and argue that he does not know about Derek's infidelity; otherwise the character seems to be making the argument that male infidelity is permissible while female infidelity is not. Regardless of what Rashad does or does not know, Ruby takes ownership of her actions and her relationships, and verbalizes how complicated those relationships truly are. The audience knows that Ruby has taken several steps away from Derek, but she still refers to him as "her man" in the heated exchange.

Ruby and Derek's relationship is reminiscent of the way Michael Roemer's *Nothing But a Man* depicts the relationship between Duff and Josie. In fact, one writer titled his review of *Middle of Nowhere* with the phrase "Nothing But a Woman" and discussed the similarities between the two films when he wrote that "the central characters within each [develop]—one wanting to be acknowledged as 'nothing but man'; the other, in MON, as nothing but a woman, strong and with pride, treated with the same kind of humanity and respect that she . . . gives willingly. Nothing more; but also nothing less."[44] Both films highlight the nuances and importance of black love and how outside forces can impact relationships. Neither film sugarcoats the problems in these relationships: Duff does become verbally and physically abusive toward Josie, while Derek is guilty of a crime, spent time in prison and committed adultery. Duff had to walk away from Josie to figure out who he was, what he wanted, and what type of man he wanted to be before he could move forward and be fully vested in their relationship. In a sense, Ruby is doing the same thing. She realizes that she cannot stay tethered to Derek while he serves the rest of his prison sentence. Instead, she chooses to move on and figure out what is best for her emotional well-being. There are no recriminations, no yelling, no head-rolling or melodramatic and stereotypical responses, just a decision to do something different, signaling an understanding, as Derrick Bell argues, that

> African Americans in their relationships must struggle to achieve a level of unconditional love in a systemic context—racism—that that places conditions upon our being. Within that context, we trivialize ourselves when we attempt to define African American male/female relationships in terms of the prevailing culture: we attribute to black females mystical powers and strengths that become burdensome in their superficiality, and we attribute weakness and defeat to black males. . . . The result is that we disempower ourselves and imperil our capacity to love unconditionally and, through that love, to grow and create together.[45]

The flash-forwards at the end of the film show images of Ruby and Brian together, as well as Ruby and Derek together. Whether Ruby ends up with Brian, Derek, someone else, or no one else is immaterial; the point is that she makes a choice to reject the mystical powers and strength mentioned in the quote above and embrace her happiness.

Though Ruby is able to reach a place of acceptance in terms of her romantic relationships, the same cannot be said for her family life. Again, in the hands of a less empathetic writer and director, the conflict between Ruby, her mother, and her sister could devolve into the worst aspects of black female stereotypes. Though it is not said outright, it is implied that Ruth raised Ruby and Rosie on her own—DuVernay has said that "this is a story about [Ruby] being in a family of women."[46] Rosie has continued the cycle of single motherhood, raising a son alone by working at a restaurant called Concubines where she dresses up as a stereotypical Asian woman—an arrangement Ruby equates with working as a mammy. Ruby, by contrast, is the prodigal daughter who made it all the way to medical school but walked away from her dream because of her devotion to Derek. At a family dinner, Ruth has finally had enough and decides to confront her children:

RUTH: I know the mistakes I made, Rosie. But you don't have to make the same ones, baby.

ROSIE: Trust me, I'm not.

RUTH: Yes, you are. It's not supposed to be like this. One woman doing it alone all by yourself, trying to do everything. I used to pray that somebody would come along and help me, but there was nobody. I'm here. Why won't you let me?

ROSIE: Ma, please.

RUTH: Baby, nobody is saying anything bad about you. You hear me? Whatever it is that you have got in your mind that I say or what I think, the boy has got ears and eyes and he knows that you are struggling. Do not fool yourself to think that he doesn't know, because he does. I did that. I was too busy trying to put gas in the car to take the few extra minutes I needed to listen to you, to answer your questions, so instead you went out and got answers from all kinds of different places, and that's why you are in the situations that you are in now. [Ruth turns to Ruby] Every year is next year for you. It's always about soon—the job, the car. But soon never comes. And med school, well—nobody even brings that up anymore because you spend your entire days sitting in the dark apartment by the phone waiting for some Negro to call you from prison. Jesus, Lord. Prison!

RUBY: I'm trying my best, Ma.

RUTH: This is not your best! Your head used to be so full of all kinds of things, baby. "Ma, did you read this article?" "Did you read this poem?" "What about this book?" Now all you ever do is talk about him. What is that?

DuVernay points out that "this family of women [is] very complicated. So much of who we are as black women, as women, just trying to be family to each other comes out in this scene."[47] Despite the complications, there is still compassion in the scene along with the anger and dysfunction. Ruth does not raise her voice until the very end of the scene, when she implores Ruby to speak up for herself. It is clear that Ruth only wants what is best for Ruby and Rosie, though she cannot figure out the best way to communicate that intention. While the scene brings up images of what Daniel Patrick Moynihan described as the "tangle of pathology,"[48] it is clear that Ruth wants her daughters to do better. As DuVernay mentioned during a live tweet of the film, "Ruth is not nagging for the sake of nagging. She is desperately disappointed. She wants more for her girls."⁴⁹ It does not feel like an Angry Black Woman stereotype, nor does it feel like the film is throwing single mothers under the bus; the scene feels like a family full of black women who do not discuss their feelings finally reaching the boiling point.

Curtain Call

In the introduction to her book *Sister Citizen: Shame, Stereotypes, and Black Women in America*, Melissa Harris-Perry talks about Zora Neale Hurston's seminal text *Their Eyes Were Watching God* when she writes: "It does not seem like an overtly political text, but in many ways it is emblematic of the racial and gender politics that we observe in contemporary American politics. . . . Janie's journey is a political one because it is motivated by her refusal to accept this role [as de mule uh de world]."⁵⁰ In that same fashion, Ava DuVernay's work thus far has been political not only because it rejects the controlling images of black women that popular culture continues to reproduce, but also because, as a black female artist, her work, as mentioned earlier, is not "an interpretation of black womanhood; it is a reflection." What DuVernay reflects in her work are images of black women that are rare in the mainstream popular culture landscape. Even in the works that do not contain a syllable of dialogue, the black women in DuVernay's oeuvre are diverse in terms of looks and style. Her subjects are smart, complicated, fully realized human beings who fight for what they want and yet are vulnerable enough to seek love and to be loved in return.

While the simple act of placing a black woman at the center of a narrative is still a rare and big step, DuVernay shows us that that is not always enough. Through her characters we see that it is possible to go beyond the caricatures that typically grace the big and small screens, and we see some of the possibilities that can occur when black women control their own stories.

Who's the Hero of the Piece?
Hollywood's Representation of Jackie Robinson's Legacy

> We are wondering to whom you are referring to when you say we must be patient. It is easy for those who haven't felt the evils of a prejudiced society to urge it, but for us who as Americans have patiently waited all these years for the rights supposedly guaranteed us under our Constitution, it is not an easy task. Nevertheless, we have done it.
> — Michael G. Long, *First Class Citizenship: The Civil Rights Letters of Jackie Robinson*, 2007

> America holds up Robinson as its hero to justify its claims that this nation is no longer racist and that whatever racism used to exist was a vestige of slavery peculiar to the South, not a prejudice common to all white Americans.
> — Doug Battema, "Jackie Robinson as Media's Mythological Black Hero," 1997

According to the late baseball historian Jules Tygiel, "The Jackie Robinson story is to Americans what the Passover story is to the Jews: it must be told to every generation so that we must never forget."[1] What is it about Robinson's story that we should not forget? Since his major league debut with the Brooklyn Dodgers in 1947, there have been three cinematic accounts of Robinson's story. The first generation told Robinson's story in the 1950 film *The Jackie Robinson Story*, which followed Robinson from childhood through his first few years with the Dodgers. The next generation retold his story with Arnold Rampersad's 1997 book *Jackie Robinson: A Biography*, which followed Robinson from cradle to grave, and a 1990 made-for-TV film, entitled *The Court-Martial of Jackie Robinson*, which told Robinson's story to the more visual learners. Then, it took only another twenty-three years for the current generation to retell Robinson's story in visual form with the 2013 film *42*, which focused on Robinson's time with the minor-league Montreal Royals and his first season in Brooklyn. Like any other art form, films are a product of the environment and times in which they are produced. While these three films span over sixty years, this chapter will focus on the most recent incarnation and analyze what messages *42* sends about Robinson, racism, and society as a whole.[2]

The Jackie Robinson Story

Much has already been written about how *The Jackie Robinson Story* fits into the framing of race relations in the 1950s, as well as Robinson's overall narrative. Rob Edelman makes the argument that *The Jackie Robinson Story* is very much a product of its era in that "as it highlights Robinson's struggle, the film acknowledges the reality of racism in America. But the scenario stresses that, in due course, fairness will prevail."[3] This ideal comes through at the end of the film as the omnipotent voice-over maintains: "Yes, this is the Jackie Robinson story, but it is not his story alone, not his victory alone; it is one that each of us shares. A story, a victory that can only happen in a country that is truly free. A country where every child has the opportunity to become president or play baseball for the Brooklyn Dodgers." The film acknowledges the fact that Robinson, though a superior athlete, was initially denied the opportunity to coach and play at the highest levels because of his race; however, as the voice-over reminds us, Robinson was eventually given the opportunity to prove himself because America is a free country where equal opportunities are available to all. In retrospect, the voice-over is ironic given that, almost seventy years after the film's release, racial disparities in education, health care, mortality, arrests, incarcerations, and wealth show that equal opportunity, even in a country that is free, is still elusive for some.

As mentioned in the chapter on *Nothing But a Man*, the 1960s ushered in an age of "significant films" in which black characters arrived on the screen in greater numbers than ever before and were attempting to address the racial tensions bubbling to the surface all across the nation.[4] This change in how Hollywood portrayed black characters actually began slowly in the 1950s, as the film industry grappled with how television was changing the entertainment landscape, and people in the burgeoning civil rights movement

Patriotic Robinson at the House Un-American Activities Committee hearings, 1949

were learning how to use public spectacle to push the country toward instituting social change. Because creating fully formed black characters was a relatively new phenomenon, the portrayals were uneven. This lack of knowledge and lack of interest in portraying nuanced black characters allowed Story to frame Robinson's journey as a white savior trope. The film, which is viewed by some as the "prototypical white savior film . . . lauds [Robinson's] accomplishments while making it clear that his success was dependent upon a string of white, paternalistic characters: the white boys who gave him his first baseball glove on the sandlot; UCLA football coach Bill Spaulding; and Branch Rickey, President and General Manager of the Brooklyn Dodgers."[5] Though white savior films such as To Kill a Mockingbird (1962) became more ubiquitous in the decade following, Story helped define a formula that can tell the story of a black person without necessarily placing that black person at the center of the narrative. Due in part to the way Robinson's story is told in the film, and in part to the period when it was released, The Jackie Robinson Story feels less tied to the civil rights movement and more tied to the Cold War.

Alessandra Raengo argues that constraints of the biopic genre, as well as Cold War considerations, led *The Jackie Robinson Story* to "showcase America's fulfillment of its democratic ideals [because the] film contains a number of strategic omissions deliberately concealing systemic racism."[6] The Cold War rhetoric is highlighted by the fact that the film ends with Robinson's testimony in front of the House Un-American Activities Committee (HUAC).

With an instrumental version of "America the Beautiful" playing in the background, Robinson's image dissolves into a picture of the Statue of Liberty as he states, "I do know that democracy works for those who are willing to fight for it, and I'm sure it's worth defending. I can't speak for any 50 million people—no one person can—but I'm certain that I and other Americans of many races and faiths have too much invested in our country's welfare to throw it away or let it be taken from us." HUAC testimony, and the associated protocol of blacklisting those who were suspected to be Communist sympathizers, are certainly recognizable symbols of Cold War politics and hysteria, so the inclusion of Robinson's statement fits with Raengo's analysis. The fact that Robinson's remarks are severely edited in the film suggests that systemic racism had no place in *Story*'s narrative. As Aaron Baker notes, the film "individualizes Robinson's experience of racism to imply the appropriateness of his unique opportunity and self-sufficient responses to its roadblocks."[7] The film focuses on the portion of Robinson's testimony that reassures the powers-that-be that young black men would fight for the United States if the Cold War with the Soviet Union turned into a hot war, a sentiment challenged by remarks made by activist/artist/athlete Paul Robeson, who was quoted saying that African Americans would refuse to fight in "an imperialist war,"[8] and underscores the fact that black people believed in democracy even when the tenets of democracy were being denied to them. What the film neglects to include is the portion of Robinson's testimony that rebukes systemic racism: "White people must realize that the more a Negro hates communism because it opposes democracy, the more he is going to hate any other influence that kills off democracy in this country—and that goes for racial discrimination in the Army, and segregation on trains and buses, and job discrimination because of religious beliefs or color or place of birth. . . . The fact that it is a Communist who denounces injustice in the courts, police brutality, and lynching when it happens doesn't change the truth of these charges."[9] Highlighting this portion of Robinson's testimony, which reads as quite frustrated and angry, would not have been in line with the stoic version of Robinson portrayed in the film;

it would have complicated the us-versus-them Cold War rhetoric that was prevalent at the time and would have run counter to the "individual acts of discrimination" definition of racism the film projects. The minimization of systemic racism and the emphasis on democratic ideals and individual achievement overcoming prejudice that *The Jackie Robinson Story* highlights are right in line with 1950s mainstream white popular culture thinking.

The Court-Martial of Jackie Robinson

Though many baseball scholars have discussed *The Jackie Robinson Story* from a multitude of angles, the same cannot be said for *The Court-Martial of Jackie Robinson*. The 1990 made-for-TV film aired on TNT and starred Andre Braugher as Robinson. Many things had changed between 1950 and 1990: the Cold War was officially over, instances of de jure Jim and Jane Crow were less overt, and professional baseball had a multitude of black and brown players.

While *The Jackie Robinson Story* primarily focuses on individual acts of discrimination, *Court-Martial* moves in a very different direction. The opening credits scroll against a backdrop of photographs that highlight Jim and Jane Crow. One photo shows a black man walking past a movie theater that has a "Colored Balcony" sign, while another photograph depicts several white police officers beating and restraining a black man. The final image of the opening credits is the infamous photograph of Thomas Shipp and Abram Smith's lynching—an image that provided the inspiration for the song "Strange Fruit" sung by Billie Holiday in 1939. According to Angela Y. Davis, the song, which is based on the poem written by Abel Meeropol, "had urgent and far-reaching social implications—[it is] a song about the hate, indignities, and eruptions of violence that threatened black people in the United States, a song that was able to awaken from their apolitical slumber vast numbers of people from diverse racial backgrounds."[10] Even before a single line of dialogue is spoken, it is clear that *Court-Martial* will be a more visceral film than *The Jackie Robinson Story*.

While self-sufficiency is key to *The Jackie Robinson Story*, the Jackie Robinson in *Court-Martial* continuously relies on outside advice and support. Toward the beginning of the film we see *Pittsburgh Courier* journalist Wendell Smith, played by J. A. Preston, discussing black players with two white scouts; Smith makes it clear that everyone knows that the reintegration of professional baseball is coming. The narrative of baseball's reintegration presented in *Court-Martial* is more in line with actual historical events than *Story*'s version. When the Dodgers' general manager, Branch Rickey, signed Robinson, sportswriters such as Smith, Sam Lacy, and Lester Rodney had been publicly advocating for the erasure of baseball's color line for quite some time. There had been demonstrations and calls for legal action against teams that did not sign black players, and that collective action led then–New York City mayor Fiorello La Guardia to create "a Committee on Baseball to push the Yankees, Giants, and Dodgers to sign black players."[11] *Court-Martial* advocates for the idea that racial progress was not just the result of top-down edicts; it was also the product of bottom-up grassroots agitating.

In *Court-Martial*, Robinson turns to Smith when he is facing military charges, and the film shows the journalist writing columns on Robinson's behalf. In his autobiography *I Never Had It Made*, Robinson recounts that it was not he who reached out to Smith; it was "some of my black brother officers [who] were determined to help me beat the attempted injustice in my case. They wrote letters to the black press. The *Pittsburgh Courier*, then one of the country's most powerful weeklies, gave the matter important publicity. The Army, sensitive to this kind of spotlight, knew that if I was unfairly treated, it would not be a secret."[12] Though there is no byline attached, an article from the *Pittsburgh Courier* dated August 5, 1944, has the headline "Lt. Jackie Robinson Faces Court-Martial." It is likely that Smith wrote the piece. In reality, instead of turning to Smith, Robinson asked the NAACP for assistance by writing, "I feel I am being unfairly punished because I wouldn't be pushed around by the driver of the bus."[13] Though he did not hear back from the NAACP until the day after the trial began, it is telling that Robinson went outside military channels for assistance.[14] Again, this film does not embrace the "pull yourself up by the bootstraps" method of empowerment; Robinson received support from his fellow black soldiers, from Smith, and from boxer Joe Louis, who is featured prominently in the film advising Robinson on how to navigate the army's racist environment.

In addition to moving from self-sufficiency to collective action, *Court-Martial* moves the entire Robinson family from passive characters to people actively engaged with each other and with the world around them. Two characters in particular, Jackie's wife, Rachel Robinson, and his mother, Mallie Robinson, are significantly more forceful in the second film. When *The Jackie Robinson Story* was released in 1950, the second wave of the feminist movement was approximately ten years in the future, and female characters in films were not usually framed as fully formed protagonists. Forty years later, when *Court-Martial* was filmed, though the roles were still small, the portrayals of both Rachel and Mallie Robinson had significantly changed.

Both films include a scene in which Robinson contemplates dropping out of UCLA. In Story, Mallie Robinson, played by Louise Beavers, is somber and resigned. Jackie questions the utility of a college degree, arguing that his brother Mack graduated from college and the only job he could find was as a street sweeper. Mack appears resigned to his fate and simply states that at least it is a steady job. In Court-Martial, Mallie, played by Ruby Dee, is livid at the idea that Jackie would leave school. This time it is Mack who reminds everyone that his college degree and his Olympic medal were not enough to secure him a coaching job, and that he is not at all pleased with his circumstances. Mallie Robinson reads them the riot act, and the only thing that ends her monologue is a radio newscast announcing the attack on Pearl Harbor. Court-Martial also portrays Rachel Robinson as having a more active role in Jackie Robinson's life. Ruby Dee, who played Rachel in The Jackie Robinson Story, remarked that, "The moment I talked with [Rachel] I had the feeling I wasn't doing her justice.... She was a stronger woman than I portrayed."[15] In Court-Martial, Kasi Lemmons plays Rachel as an independent, outgoing woman. This is a tribute to the expanding role of women in film writ large as well as a testament to how Court-Martial emphasizes Jackie Robinson's personal support system. When he initially contemplates leaving college, it is Rachel who tries to deter him. In one scene, Rachel informs Jackie that she has joined the Naval Cadet Corps. Jackie does not agree with her decision and demands that she quit. Instead of acquiescing, Rachel returns his ring and promptly ends their engagement. When Mallie Robinson hears about the end of the engagement, she admonishes her son, saying, "Oh, I understand all right. You're being a man and you're saying, 'Oh Rae, you can't do this and don't do that.' Well, Rae's not the sort of woman who will take that and I'm not either." It is clear that Rachel intends to chart her own path with or without Jackie, a decision that he eventually respects.

Just as Mallie and Rachel Robinson are more forceful in Court-Martial than in Story, Robinson himself undergoes a similar transformation. In Story, while "Robinson's dialogue was minimal [and] the basic narrative tended to emphasize the need for passive composure," Court-Martial portrays Robinson as "very assertive, skeptical, and independent, avoiding the charges of 'Uncle Tom-ism' that had occasionally been leveled at him in the 1960s."[16] Part of that change has to do with the changing times, and part of it has to do with the fact that Robinson did not have any formal acting training, which would have been useful even if he was playing himself. Braugher, in comparison, studied theater at Stanford University and the Juilliard School,

Robinson promises consequences

and therefore had the training and experience to portray a wider range of emotions. In *Court-Martial*, when a colonel refuses to advance his application to Officer Candidate School, Robinson first requests to go over his head and then enlists Joe Louis's help to attain his goal. When a white officer defends segregated seating in the commissary during a phone conversation, Robinson meets with the officer in person to express his displeasure with the seating arrangements and to make sure that the officer knows that Robinson is black. Robinson is framed as a man who knows his rights, knows military policy, and knows segregation was wrong as well as one who actively works to make things better for the black soldiers under his command. Robinson demands the respect his humanity and rank deserve, and because of that he is labeled a troublemaker and shipped to Texas, a move that leads to his eventual court-martial. When Robinson refuses to move to the back of a military transport bus, a request that he knows violates military policy, he forcefully argues his case even as the military police (MP) continually refer to him as "the nigger lieutenant." After enduring a barrage of racial epithets, Robinson makes it clear that there will be consequences if the MP calls him that name again. At that point, the camera moves to a close-up of

Robinson's face, which conveys the emotional toll the language has taken on him, as well as the rage it has produced. In Hollywood in the 1950s, the primary responses blacks could give to racism were disappointment and resignation. By 1990, black characters were allowed to show anger about their treatment as second-class citizens.

In addition to presenting more emotive characters, *Court-Martial* gives the audience a slightly better understanding of systemic racism than *Story* provides. For example, the made-for-TV film shows that there was legislation in place that prevented racial integration. Mandated segregated buses, which instigated Robinson's court-martial, was not a policy put in place by a single individual; these were company policies and city and/or state laws that demanded the separation of the races. *Court-Martial* also makes it clear that the armed forces as an institution was racist, and that the racism was not solely based upon discriminatory acts by individuals, since the racially segregated units and facilities were part of the fabric of military operations. A coda at the end of the film reassures the audience that the systemic racism illustrated in the film is no longer a problem since "President Harry S. Truman signed an Executive Order on July 26, 1948, prohibiting racial segregation in the Armed Forces. Today, the Army is considered one of the most integrated organizations in the United States." While *Court-Martial* acknowledges that systemic racism existed, it presents it only in forms that have been successfully eradicated for the most part. Much of this shift can be attributed to the general change in attitudes regarding race and racism in the years between *Story* and *Court-Martial*; however, another possible explanation lies with the increased discussions on race and racism that were occurring at the time the film was being written and produced. In June 1989, Spike Lee's controversial opus on race relations, *Do the Right Thing*, opened in theaters and sparked a national conversation on race relations. The film deals with "police profiling and brutality; urban, ethnic conflict; [and] the crisis in black families and relationships" and challenges the audience "to grapple with the dynamics of race, class, power, mobility and privilege in ways too few films have done since."[17] The racial conversation was intensified two months later when a group of white teenagers attacked and killed sixteen-year-old Yusef Hawkins in Bensonhurst, New York.[18] *Court-Martial* can be read as not just a tribute to Jackie Robinson but also as a contribution to a public discussion of racism that was already in progress.

Finally, *Court-Martial* shifts the importance of Robinson's legacy away from the baseball diamond. The film ends with Robinson playing for the Kansas City Monarchs, and the scout who spoke with Wendell Smith earlier in the film assuring Robinson that the offer to sign him to the Dodgers is not a joke. Aside from some brief clips of Robinson playing baseball, basketball, and football in college, the film spends very little time engaging with Robinson as an athlete. Instead, it portrays him as an outspoken advocate for civil rights. In fact, the film's coda reads in part: "In 1947, Jack Roosevelt Robinson became the first black man to play major league baseball, and in 1962 was inducted into the Baseball Hall of Fame. He devoted the rest of his life to the civil rights movement and the quality of all men." The statement highlights the idea that Robinson was talented enough to earn induction into the Hall of Fame; however, it also underscores that his contributions to society were not limited to his role as an athlete.

A Big-Budget After-School Special

The same year Rampersad's Robinson biography was released, 42 writer-director Brian Helgeland won an Oscar for writing the screenplay for the film L.A. Confidential. He would be nominated again for the 2004 film Mystic River. His feature film directorial debut was for the Mel Gibson film Payback (1999), and he went on to direct the films A Knight's Tale (2001) and The Order (2003).

Rachel Robinson had been trying for fifteen years to get a film about her late husband's life to the big screen. Shortly after the release of Malcolm X in 1992, Spike Lee was tapped to direct a biopic of Jackie Robinson after Rachel expressed a preference for a black filmmaker. She is quoted as saying: "I really felt, and I still feel, that a black man can understand another black man and all the nuances of his life better than anyone else can."[19] Unfortunately, according to Lee, the project fell through for a variety of reasons, the primary one being financing, and the rights to Robinson's story went to ESPN and Academy Award–winning actor, director, and producer Robert Redford.[20] That project was to star Redford as Branch Rickey and focus on the relationship between Robinson and Rickey.[21] Redford later backed out of the project, and Helgeland was eventually brought on board with a $40 million budget. The emphasis on the Robinson/Rickey relationship remained.

When 42 opened in the summer of 2013, it grossed $27 million during its opening weekend and managed an overall gross of $95 million.[22] Critics responded favorably; however, a lot of the praise was full of caveats. The

Guardian's Mark Kermode wrote that 42 was "inspirational fare, although such a remarkable story perhaps deserves a more remarkable movie."[23] Richard Roeper of the *Chicago Sun-Times* wrote that the film "is competent, occasionally rousing and historically respectful—but it rarely rises above standard, old-fashioned biography fare. It's a mostly unexceptional film about an exceptional man," and Scott Foundas of *Variety* wrote that 42 "is a relentlessly formulaic biopic [whose] cumulative effect is to render its subject markedly smaller and more ordinary than he actually was."[24] The *New York Times* called the film "a hero-worshiping [fable] suitable for fourth-grade classrooms," while Wesley Morris from Grantland remarked that the film "has been made with such reverence for Robinson's importance that Robinson is barely there."[25]

Though *Court-Martial* championed community efforts and grassroots advocacy in its narrative, 42 goes back to the narrative advanced by *Story*. 42 frames baseball's reintegration as a top-down endeavor that assumes that significant historical events are the results of the machinations of powerful (white) men at the top of the political, social, or economic food chain. The audience sees this at the beginning of the film when Branch Rickey, played by Harrison Ford, casually lays out his intention to sign a black player to the Dodgers. While Rickey's underlings react with shock and horror and point out all the ways Rickey will suffer for making this decision, the audience is left with the impression that Rickey, being a moral and courageous man, sees an inequity and decides to correct it. This view is tempered somewhat throughout the film as Robinson, played by Chadwick Boseman, repeatedly asks Rickey why he signed him and Rickey gives no less than three different answers to that question—all of them true to a certain extent. Like *Story*, this narrative completely erases the massive efforts by Lester Rodney, Sam Lacy, and Wendell Smith to force MLB teams to desegregate in the early 1940s. The film actually has Smith and Robinson meeting for the first time *after* Robinson signs with the Dodgers organization. After the Robinsons are bumped from their flight due in large part to Rachel's defiance of segregation laws, the couple takes a long bus trip from Louisiana to Florida. Smith is waiting when they get off the bus:

SMITH: Jackie Robinson. Wendell Smith. *Pittsburgh Courier*.
ROBINSON: A reporter?
SMITH: [chuckles] Mr. Rickey sent me to meet you. I'm gonna be your Boswell.

SMITH: My who?
SMITH: Your chronicler. Your advance man. Hell, even your chauffeur.

Besides unintentionally making the case that someone really needs to write a definitive biography of Wendell Smith, 42 ignores the fact that in real life, Robinson and Smith met months earlier. There was already a grassroots movement aimed at desegregating all aspects of American life, including baseball, prior to Robinson's signing. In addition to protests and threats of legal retaliation, several sportswriters arranged tryouts for black players with MLB teams. In 1945, Smith arranged a tryout for Robinson, Sam Jethroe, and Marvin Williams with the Boston Red Sox, which, needless to say, was unsuccessful.[26] It is clear that Smith helped make the arrangements and that the *Courier* paid the players' travel expenses, and, according to Ken Burns's 2016 documentary on Robinson, Smith did attend the tryout.[27] Even if we ignore that for a moment, the scene is still highly problematic because as ESPN sportswriter Howard Bryant points out, "Robinson . . . acts as though he's never heard of the *Pittsburgh Courier*. In black America at that time, the *Chicago Defender*, *Pittsburgh Courier* and *Baltimore Afro-American* were the leading black newspapers, shipped across the country. An athlete of Robinson's stature, especially one raised amid the segregated and parallel structures of American life, would have known of the *Courier* the way most people today have heard of *Time* magazine."[28] Indeed, Robinson had not only heard of Smith and the *Courier* at this point, but credited their activism with assisting him with his court-martial.

42 also returns to a reliance on self-sufficient responses to racism. Though Smith is present at the games, Robinson must carry his burden alone: there is no mention of Dan Bankhead, who roomed with Robinson during the events depicted in the film, and no mention of future Hall of Famer Larry Doby, who signed with Cleveland two months after Robinson arrived in Brooklyn. In many ways, 42 represents a step backward in popular culture's imagining of racism and Robinson. This most recent incarnation of Robinson's story is both more conservative, with a small c, than the previous films in that it spans a much shorter period of time than *Story* or *Court-Martial*, and more Conservative, with a capital C, in its framing of racism than *Court-Martial*. After the election of Barack Obama in 2008, the mainstream white storyline that followed argued that the United States had finally become a postracial society. Many understood that this was not the case. The *Atlantic*'s Ta-Nehisi Coates makes the argument that Obama's election actually "demonstrated

The Robinsons meet Smith

integration's great limitation—that acceptance depends not just on being twice as good but on being half as black," and the common meme that blacks must be twice as good to succeed "holds that African Americans—enslaved, tortured, raped, discriminated against, and subjected to the most lethal homegrown terrorist movement in American history—feel no anger toward their tormentors."[29] 42 appears to embrace the thought process Coates describes, as Robinson shows little to no anger about the racism he is subjected to or his inability to fight it.

Court-Martial presents a Jackie Robinson who is angry about racism and segregation, is not afraid to express that anger, and knows how to use that anger to push back against white supremacy. 42 presents a more subdued Robinson, with only two instances showing Robinson either actively defying white supremacy or expressing anger toward the racism he experiences. Early in the film, a scene shows Robinson barnstorming with the Kansas City Monarchs. The team pulls up to a gas station to fill up, and, when Robinson walks toward the bathroom, the attendant tells him, "Come on, boy, you know you can't go in there." Robinson walks back toward the bus, looking annoyed, and calmly tells the attendant, "Take that hose out of the tank. . . . We'll get our ninety-nine gallons of gas someplace else." The attendant, realizing the amount of money he will lose by clinging to his racism, allows the players to use the facilities. Much later in the film, when Robinson is now with the Brooklyn Dodgers, Philadelphia Phillies manager Ben Chapman engages in a three-minute long tirade replete with racist language and insults, after which Robinson retreats to the hall between the dugout and locker room, where he screams, cries, and beats his bat against the wall until it finally breaks. When Rickey comes up to him, Robinson yells, "No! The next white son of a bitch that opens his mouth—I'll bash his goddamn teeth in." Of course, Rickey reminds Robinson that he cannot respond to Chapman's racism. It is also telling that the most visceral expressions of racism in 42 are individual acts—the gas station attendant and Chapman—not systemic or institutional. The only instances of institutional racism depicted in the film occur when the Dodgers are refused service at a hotel due to Robinson's presence. Upon learning that not only will Robinson not be allowed at the hotel, which was standard operating procedure wherever the Dodgers went, but that the entire team must leave, one of Robinson's teammates blames him for their inconvenience and wants an apology—a request that does not go over well with Robinson. The only instance of systemic racism in the film occurs during a game in Leland, Florida, when a sheriff throws Robinson off the field for violating the state's segregation laws. After Robinson is banished from the field, the next scene tempers the moment as Jackie and Rachel are approached by an unknown white man who tells them that he is "pulling for you to make good. A lot of folks around here feel the same way. If a man's got the goods, he deserves a fair chance, that's all." Racism is framed as the bad acts of a few individuals instead of a systemic problem.

The most important departure of 42 from *Court-Martial* is that the more recent film lacks historical context, and, in doing so, manages to diminish Robinson's impact. Early in the film, when Robinson arrives in Sanford, Florida, for spring training, he meets a man named Mr. Brock, who houses Robinson and Smith until they are run out of town, and the two have the following conversation:

> MR. BROCK: My wife asked me, What do you serve when a hero's coming to dinner?
> ROBINSON: Mr. Brock, I'm just a ballplayer.
> MR. BROCK: Oh no, no, you tell that to all the little colored boys playing baseball in Florida today. To them, you're a hero.

Though the dialogue specifically rejects the notion that Robinson was "just a ballplayer," the film itself portrays the opposite message. The reason Robinson is revered by so many people is because his life and influence were about so much more than baseball, as evidenced by the coda at the end of *Court-Martial*. Since 42 only shows Robinson as a ballplayer, the audience does not get the sense that he accomplished anything significant outside of sports, or that his actions—or restraint, depending on the point of view—had any effect outside the arena of baseball. Neither *The Jackie Robinson Story* nor *42* shows Robinson's interaction with any of the larger civil rights forces at work during the time. *42* ends by fast-forwarding to the present day and providing the coda that reads: "Every year in April, all MLB players wear the number 42 as a reminder of Jackie's accomplishments on and off the field." *Story* places Robinson within the context of the Cold War by ending with his HUAC testimony, and *Court-Martial* connects Robinson to World War II and the black press. Since *42* does not show any of Robinson's off-the-field accomplishments or connect him to larger historical forces, the film limits Robinson's impact to the baseball diamond.

Show, Don't Tell

In addition to the film's historical and political shortcomings, *42* is problematic on a filmic level. Throughout the film, Helgeland forgets the first rule of film storytelling: show, don't tell. Film is a visual medium, and therefore it is important to engage the audience by showing them what you want them to know instead of telling them. In a few key instances, the film relies on exposition instead of action. We see this clearly in the scene where Rickey and his minions choose Robinson to reintegrate professional baseball. Rickey tells us that Robinson was a four-sport athlete at UCLA who played on integrated teams; he also tells us that Robinson was court-martialed for defying a segregation order, though the film does not actually mention that Robinson won his case. Helgeland commits this film transgression again later, when Pee Wee Reese, a white player who supported Robinson, receives a piece of hate mail that Rickey reads aloud:

> RICKEY: "Nigger lover. Watch yourself. We'll get you, carpetbagger." Pretty typical stuff.
> REESE: Well, it's not typical to me, sir.
> RICKEY: [chuckles] How many of those letters have you gotten, Pee Wee?
> REESE: Just the one. Ain't that enough? [Rickey drops three full file folders onto a desk.] What are those?
> RICKEY: Well, I'll tell you what they aren't. They aren't letters from the Jackie Robinson fan club.
> REESE: [Reading the letters] "Get out of baseball or your baby boy will die." "Quit baseball or your nigger wife . . ." "Get out of the game or be killed." Does Jackie know?
> RICKEY: Well, of course he does. And the FBI. They're taking the threat in

Cincinnati pretty seriously. So excuse me if I don't get too upset about you getting called a carpetbagger. You should be proud.
REESE: Well, I'd just like to play ball, sir. That's all.
RICKEY: Oh, I understand. I bet Jackie just wants to play ball. I bet he wishes he wasn't leading the league in hit-by-pitch. I bet he wishes people didn't want to kill him.

It's a telling scene, though given the stoic nature of the characters, there is not much emotion attached. As it stands, in most of these tell-don't-show instances, Robinson's actions and emotions are mediated through white characters. We do not see Robinson's collegiate athletic achievements; we hear Rickey's assistants read about them. We do not see Robinson's court-martial; we hear Rickey discuss it. We do not see the Robinson family read the hate mail and death threats; we hear Pee Wee Reese read them. A scene actually showing Jackie or Rachel reading the racist hate mail they constantly received would have taken the same amount of time and been a far more effective device. It would have given the audience an idea about the toll that Jackie suppressing his emotions took on the Robinson family. As it stands, there is only one scene in the film that shows the effect this great experiment had on Robinson's emotional and psychological health—his breakdown in the hallway. We know from Robinson's autobiography and Rampersad's book that holding his emotions in check had a physical effect on Robinson as well, causing everything from hair loss to ulcers, but this is not mentioned in the film at all.

Of course, it is easy to play the role of Monday-morning quarterback on any film, and it is typically regarded as poor film criticism to do so; however, it is important in this case not only to note the ways in which the film is deficient, but also to point out the simple ways that it could have worked better and to push back against the arguments used to defend the conservative choices made in the film. The most frequent defense of leaving large swaths of pertinent information on the cutting room floor is time constraints. There is only so much information a director and editor can cram into a two-hour film, and that could help explain why 42 focuses on such a small portion of Robinson's career and life. While that is certainly true, other biopics made in recent years have managed to convey a lot of information in a small amount of time. *Notorious*, the 2009 biopic of rapper Christopher Wallace, a.k.a. Notorious B.I.G., is five minutes shorter than 42 but manages to span almost two decades of Wallace's short but influential life. Clint Eastwood's *J. Edgar* (2011) was fewer than ten minutes longer than 42 but covered seven decades. *Mandela: A Long Walk to Freedom* (2013) was thirteen minutes longer than 42 and covered over five decades. *The Jackie Robinson Story* comes in at a brisk seventy-six minutes and chronicles approximately fifteen years of Robinson's life. Clearly there are ways to tell expansive stories in short amounts of time. The primary argument in favor of shorter films is that they can be shown more frequently in theaters and therefore make more money. In 2013, however, eleven films that had higher grosses than 42 had longer running times, showing that a shorter running time does not always lead to higher grosses.[30]

Whose Movie Is This Anyway?

As mentioned earlier, after Spike Lee's Robinson project fell through, the focus of the proposed film shifted from Robinson himself to the relationship between Rickey and Robinson. This change in focus moved 42 far closer in content and tone to *The Jackie Robinson Story* than *The Court-Martial of Jackie Robinson*. As such, 42 feels like it belongs in the white savior film genre, like its fifty-year-old predecessor. It is telling that white savior films enjoyed a resurgence during President Obama's time in office, with films such as *Gran Torino* (2008), *Avatar* (2009), *The Blind Side* (2009), *The Help* (2011), *Django Unchained* (2012), and *Elysium* (2013). According to Matthew Hughey, "White savior films emerge as powerful cultural devices that attract, seduce, and command the U.S. public in a time of unsettled understandings of race, racism, and racial identity. In a climate in which many whites believe they are unfairly victimized and losing dominance, many people are exhausted with talking about race."[31] Of course, because films like 42, *Dangerous Minds* (1995), *Glory* (1989), *Glory Road* (2006), *Race* (2015), and *Green Book* (2018) are based upon actual people and events, it is easier for filmmakers to defend their choices to focus on white characters' involvement in black and brown people's lives. At the same time, this focus on white savior films can cause one to wonder why "Hollywood seems to hold greater interest in the narratives of heroic Whites saving people of color than in the stories about people of color helping their own communities or resisting the racist status quo."[32] All three Robinson films discussed here are based on actual events; however, they are told from three different perspectives, and only one completely bypasses the traditional white savior narrative. Interestingly, it was the film made for television, where the financial stakes are not as high, that managed to break the mold.

To be fair, Branch Rickey's actions in the film differ slightly from those traditionally found in white savior films, where the savior in question moves in and around black and brown spaces in an effort to "save" people of color from their circumstances. The underlying premise of the white characters' actions is rooted in the bootstraps mentality: if these people work hard and have the assistance of well-meaning white folks, then they can overcome the effects of racism. At the same time, Rickey is not the white leader Derrick Bell asks for, in that Rickey does not "reject loyalty to whiteness in favor of loyalty to humanity," nor does he "recognize and reject the privileges of whiteness," although he most certainly recognizes that racism, particularly in baseball, "is not a black but a white problem."[33] Instead of rejecting his privilege, Rickey uses it to browbeat fellow owners into accepting Robinson on the field and eventually sign black and brown players to their own teams. We see this less-than-gentle persuasion when Rickey has a phone conversation with the Phillies general manager, Herb Pennock:

> PENNOCK: Branch, how long have we known each other?
> RICKEY: Oh, twenty years, maybe more.
> PENNOCK: That's right. Been over some solid road together. So, um, you can trust me when I tell you Brooklyn's due here tomorrow, but you cannot bring that nigger down here with the rest of your team.
> RICKEY: Why's that, Herb? His name is Jackie Robinson, by the way.
> PENNOCK: Yeah, Branch, I understand he's got a name, but we're just not ready for that sort of thing here in Philadelphia. Now, I'm afraid that we're not gonna be able to take the field against your team if that boy's in uniform.
> RICKEY: Well, what you do with your team is your decision, Herb. But my team's gonna be in Philadelphia tomorrow with Robinson. And if we have to claim the game as a forfeit, so be it. That's nine-zero in case you forgot.

Pennock does field a team against the Dodgers, though it must be pointed out that this was the series during which the Dodgers were refused hotel lodgings and Ben Chapman went on his racist tirade. All in all, the Philadelphia series may not have been great for Robinson, but the phone conversation between the general managers allows the audience to see Rickey standing up for Robinson and facing direct pressure for his role in reintegration. It may be harsh to argue that Rickey's role in the film is as a white savior, and instead more accurate to place him somewhere between the white savior and a race traitor.

Well, At Least There's That

While the discussion of racism and the focus on a white savior makes *42* more conservative than *Court-Martial* and *Story* in some ways, the one space where the most recent film is more progressive than its predecessors is in the portrayal of Rachel Robinson. In *Story*, the Robinson family as a whole is framed as meek and somewhat resigned to being treated as second-class citizens. *Court-Martial* gives Mallie and Rachel Robinson more to do, in addition to making the whole family more forceful in their words and actions. While *42* neither includes nor mentions Mallie or Mack Robinson, Rachel is framed as Jackie's equal partner in the quest to survive reintegration. Whether this change is due to Rachel Robinson's involvement with the project, or a general change in how female protagonists are portrayed on screen, is unknown. When the Robinsons are on their way to Florida, they have a layover in New Orleans. While at the airport, Rachel spots a "Whites Only" bathroom and remarks that she has never seen one in person. Rachel's response is to enter the bathroom, which causes the airline attendant to bump them from their flight to Florida. Much like her portrayal in *Court-Martial*, in this version Rachel Robinson does not suffer fools or foolishness lightly. When Rachel and Wendell Smith attend their first game, the two hear the racial vitriol being hurled by fans:

> RACHEL: Jack's got a thick skin. He'll be okay.
> WENDELL: Well, how about you?
> RACHEL: I better get one in a hurry.

Whenever Jackie scores a run, he looks for Rachel in the stands and the two share a moment. After Ben Chapman hurls insults at Robinson in Philadelphia, it is clear that Robinson is close to losing his temper. Rachel Robinson repeats to herself, "Look at me, baby," and almost wills her husband to remain calm.

Rachel Robinson does not simply exist in this film to provide emotional support; she also knows the game of baseball. At one point, it is implied that Jackie has slipped into a hitting slump. As he heads into a long road trip, she imparts some wise advice:

> RACHEL: Try not to lunge at the plate.
> JACKIE: You serious?
> RACHEL: That's why they're throwing the fastballs inside. Fight those inside fastballs off. . . . Sooner or later they won't be able to help but throw a curve.

JACKIE: And what'll happen then, coach?
RACHEL: [Imitates ball being hit and cheering crowd.]

In 42, Rachel and Jackie Robinson are portrayed as being true partners on and off the field. For all of its faults in terms of portraying Jackie Robinson's contribution to society, the film does provide a glimpse into the romance between Rachel and Jackie and the ways in which the two supported each other during a tumultuous period. Like *Nothing But a Man* seemed to suggest, 42 makes the argument that the black family is the answer to having the strength to combat racism.

Curtain Call

In assessing the importance of Robinson's story, Jules Tygiel makes the argument that Robinson's story "must be told to every generation so that we must never forget," so what is it about Robinson's story that we should not forget? We should not forget that Robinson publicly supported John Carlos and Tommy Smith's 1968 Olympic protest, and was the only player who testified in support of Curt Flood's lawsuit against MLB's reserve clause, but you wouldn't know that by watching any of the screen adaptations of Robinson's story.[34] Also missing are how white sportswriters turned against him when his gag order was lifted; the fact that MLB would not employ him after he retired as a player; and the choice words he had about baseball's hiring practices shortly before his death. Nor is there anything regarding his business dealings or his political machinations with Nelson Rockefeller and Richard Nixon. The two big-screen adaptations, *The Jackie Robinson Story* and 42, fall into the trap that snares many Hollywood films when it comes to telling America's history of white supremacy: they frame racism as the words and actions of bad people. If racism were just about individual acts of discrimination, it would be eradicated by now. The message seems to be that if people of color just wait patiently, all the bad people will either see the error of their ways or simply die off, and our problems will be solved. It's not just about the racist language Robinson endured, or the hotels that wouldn't house Robinson, or the next generation of black and brown MLB players; it's the fact that white supremacy is ingrained in our institutions, including MLB, which was segregated, integrated, and resegregated over the course of its history prior to Robinson's arrival.

The voice-over at the very beginning of 42 states: "In 1946, there were sixteen Major League Baseball teams with a total of four hundred players on their rosters. Every one of the four hundred players were white. But when opening day came in 1947, that number dropped to three hundred ninety-nine." That opening makes it seem like it was an anomaly that baseball was segregated in 1946, and not the result of deliberate and concerted efforts. In his detailed critique of the film, Dave Zirin wrote:

> 42 rests on the classical Hollywood formula of "Heroic individual sees obstacle. Obstacle is overcome. The End." That works for *Die Hard* or *American Pie*. It doesn't work for a story about an individual deeply immersed and affected by the grand social movements and events of his time.... This is particularly ironic since Jackie Robinson spent the last years of his life in a grueling fight against his own mythos. He hated that his tribulations from the 1940s were used to sell a story about an individualistic, Booker T. Washington approach to fighting racism.... This was a man tortured by the fact that his own experience was used as a cudgel against building a public, fighting movement against racial injustice. He wanted to shift the discussion of his own narrative from one of individual achievement to the stubborn continuance of institutionalized racism in the United States. The film, however, is a celebration of the individual and if you know how that pained Mr. Robinson, that is indeed a bitter pill.[35]

Zirin's analysis of Robinson is correct. In 1969, Robinson was interested in writing a biography about his life. He contacted Random House about the project, and, according to the editor, future Pulitzer Prize–winner Toni Morrison, Robinson "wanted his book to be about more than baseball. He wanted it to be about the larger picture, about society and the times he had lived through."[36] The biography, *I Never Had It Made*, was eventually published elsewhere, as Random House deemed the project to be too political. The biography devotes 96 pages to his baseball career and 164 pages to his life outside of baseball. In the biography's epilogue, Robinson discusses the title and the world around him when he writes:

> This is why I have devoted and dedicated my life to service. I don't like to be in debt. I still owe. Some of my friends tell me I've paid the note a thousandfold. But I still feel I owe—'till every man can rent and lease and buy according to his money and his desires; until every child can have an equal opportunity in youth and manhood; until hunger is

not only immoral but illegal; until hatred is recognized as a disease, a scourge, an epidemic, and treated as such; until racism and sexism and narcotics are conquered and until every man can vote and any man can be elected if he qualifies—until that day Jackie Robinson and no one else can say that he has it made.[37]

It is safe to say that Robinson understood not only how he influenced the world around him but, equally important, how the world around him impacted his life. 42 and *The Jackie Robinson Story* disregard that side of Jackie Robinson, while the made-for-TV *Court-Martial* comes closest to portraying a full picture of Robinson.

Institutional racism within the film industry itself, and de jure segregation within American society as a whole during the 1950s, help explain the limited view *The Jackie Robinson Story* had of Robinson's life. At the same time, because the film was made at the beginning of his career, many of the events he participated in, and issues he advocated for and against, had not taken place yet. By the 1990s, a more complete picture of Robinson was available, and, given the conversations about race that were occurring at the time, *The Court-Martial of Jackie Robinson* could and did expand upon Robinson's life and present a more nuanced account of the kinds of racism Robinson endured and fought against. The "postracial" ideology and the conservative backlash against President Obama, and any discussions of systemic racism, informed the safe version of Robinson and racism portrayed in 42. No film can be everything to everyone, and no film can cover the entirety of an individual's life; however, it is incumbent on filmmakers to fully understand the subject they are bringing to the screen. The problems with *The Jackie Robinson Story* and 42 seem to stem from the erroneous notion that Jackie Robinson's impact on history and culture is primarily due to his status as a ballplayer. It is certainly true that we know who Robinson was because he helped reintegrate professional baseball, but some filmmakers make the mistake of thinking Robinson's legacy ends there. That does a huge disservice to the audience and to Robinson himself. Unfortunately, the things we should not forget about Robinson's story have yet to be adequately portrayed in popular film.

8

Are We Allowed to Be Children?
Black Teen Films, Trauma, and the Race to Adulthood

> It's hard to remember the last good black coming-of-age film that was not a mere exploration of human misery.... There is joy in being young and black, though evidence of this in American cinema is difficult to find.
>
> Adam Serwer, "Film Review: 'Pariah' and the Untold Stories in Black Cinema," 2011

> Like my white friends, I learned how to be a proper teenager through these movies—except most of the films I watched didn't have many black characters. When they did, it was most often the "token black friend," a girl who existed to support the white characters and to act as representative of an entire race.
>
> Vanessa Willoughby, "What I Learned from Token Black Characters in Teen Movies," 2015

In a 2014 op-ed for the *Washington Post* discussing the high-profile killings of seventeen-year-old Trayvon Martin, eighteen-year-old Michael Brown, and twelve-year-old Tamir Rice, reporter Stacey Patton laments the fact that "Black America has again been reminded that its children are not seen as worthy of being alive—in part because they are not seen as children at all, but as menacing threats to white lives. America does not extend the fundamental elements of childhood to black boys and girls."[1] bell hooks echoes this sentiment in her discussion with Melissa Harris-Perry regarding the 2014 film *Beasts of the Southern Wild*, a film both women found disturbing due in large part because the film features "an abused black child being represented as entertaining. . . . I'm hurting because we can't get past the construction of black children as little mini-adults whose innocence we don't have to protect."[2] The inability to see black children as children can literally mean the difference between life and death in the real world. In the cinematic world, this misrecognition manifests itself in the dearth of black adolescents from the traditional teen film genre, and when black teens *are* represented in film, their characters are framed in ways that their white counterparts are not.

Films featuring and marketed toward teenagers began in the 1950s, with titles such as *Rebel Without a Cause* (1955), *I Was a Teenage Werewolf* (1957), and *Gidget* (1959). The decade most associated with teen films is the 1980s, when director John Hughes ushered in a teen film renaissance by directing *Sixteen Candles* (1984), *The Breakfast Club* (1985), and *Ferris Bueller's Day Off* (1986). Hughes's films, and the majority of other teen films of the era, allowed their characters to engage in relatively benign activities such as playing hooky from school, serving out detention for minor offenses, worrying over dating options, and stressing over college plans. In the overwhelming majority of these films, there were few, if any, people of color. The most memorable character of color from these eighties teen films is Long Duk Dong from *Sixteen Candles*, who has been described as "the socially inept mute, the lecherous but sexually inept loser; one part harmless Charlie Chan, one part mustachioed villain Fu Manchu"—in other words, a walking caricature of Asian masculinity.[3] If black characters existed at all in these universes, it was to provide background flavor (as in *Ferris Bueller's Day Off*) or to help establish a white character's street cred (as in *Adventures in Babysitting*). These films usually took place in suburban enclaves that have few if any people of color living in them. For black teenagers growing up in the 1980s, there was little representation on the big screen.

When black teenage characters began to populate the big screen in the 1990s, it was in the gangsta pictures discussed in Chapter 4. Films such as *Boyz n the Hood* (1991), *Juice* (1992), and *Menace II Society* (1993) framed black teenagers as violent mini-adults whose sociopathic behavior needed to be policed at all costs.

In these films, teenagers who are not directly involved in the violence are still affected by it in many traumatic ways. According to these narratives, while black teenagers may contemplate college like their white counterparts, they do their homework to the sounds of gunshots. Even if they are not involved in criminal activity, they can still be gunned down in the streets. In other words, black teenagers do not have the luxury of simply being teenagers. Even the quintessential black teen film, *Cooley High* (1975), features characters who get caught up in the criminal justice system.

In what is frequently dubbed as the black version of George Lucas's 1973 film *American Graffiti*, *Cooley High* features a group of high school friends growing up in Chicago housing projects in 1964. Preach (Glynn Turman), Cochise (Lawrence Hilton Jacobs), and their friends engage in typical filmic teenage behavior: skipping class, going to parties, smoking weed, drinking, and joyriding. Aside from hustling money from a couple of local sex workers, the young men are not framed as dangerous, even if they do get into an occasional fight. Cochise is headed for college on an athletic scholarship, and Preach is framed as exceptionally bright but unfocused. Unfortunately, Cochise is beaten to death, and though his death serves as the catalyst for Preach to get his life together, the fact that tragedy is necessary shows that even in a film that is often heralded as *the* black teen film, the teens are not immune from trauma and are not allowed to be innocent.

In 2016, *Slate* magazine assembled a group of film critics, scholars, and filmmakers to compile a list of the top fifty greatest films by black directors. The list included the aforementioned *Cooley High*, *Boyz n the Hood*, and *Juice*, as well as teen films such as Reginald Hudlin's *House Party* (1990), Gina Prince-Bythewood's *Love & Basketball* (2000), and Dee Rees's *Pariah* (2011). Unlike previous films featuring black teenagers, these later three subject their main characters to far less physical trauma, and are more in line with teen films featuring white protagonists. This chapter will discuss *House Party*, *Love & Basketball*, and *Pariah* to see what messages about black teens they are transmitting to audiences, and will look at how the portrayal of black teenage life has evolved from the 1990s to the 2010s. These films highlight the fact that viewers take for granted that the low-stakes tropes associated with mainstream teen films are universal; however, even in the care of black writers and directors who want to normalize the experiences of black teens, when those tropes are superimposed onto the black experience, we see that black teenagers, by virtue of growing up under a system of heteronormative patriarchal white supremacy, are not allowed to simply *be* teenagers.

Can I Kick It?

Based on Reginald Hudlin's senior thesis, *House Party* relies on a teen comedy staple: when your parents are out of town, a party must ensue.

Christopher Martin plays the unsupervised party-thrower, Play, who also has a laser-like focus on attracting women. Christopher Reid plays Kid, who, because he was involved in a school fight, is grounded by his father, played by Robin Harris. Despite being grounded, Kid sneaks out of the house to attend the party. The partygoers include the DJ, Bilal (Martin Lawrence), the much sought-after young ladies Sidney (Tisha Campbell) and Sharane (A. J. Johnson), and the neighborhood bullies Stab (Paul Anthony), Pee-Wee (Bowlegged Lou), and Zilla (B-Fine). A night of dancing, rapping, and evading various authority figures follows. The very beginning of the film sets the stage as Kid dreams about attending a house party. Everyone is dancing in slow motion while the bass booms large through the speakers. Right before Kid wakes up, the roof of the house literally flies off into space, showing just how awesome that party/dream must be. While most films in general, and teen films in particular, segregate characters based on their socioeconomic status, *House Party* shows Sidney, whose parents own a couple of grocery stores, hanging out with her best friend Sharane, who lives in a housing project. Likewise, Play's middle-class status is quite different from Kid's working-class world, but they are still best friends, and everyone comes together for the party without much drama.

Like many black films of the 1990s, *House Party* has strong ties to hip-hop music and culture. The two main characters are played by hip-hop artists Kid 'n Play, whose 1988 album *2 Hype* went gold and helped them secure the starring roles in this film; two of its sequels; a 1992 film entitled *Class Act*; and, in a rare feat for any recording artist, a self-titled Saturday-morning cartoon that aired during the 1990–1991 season. According to Hudlin, wanting to use rappers as the lead actors made sense because "the talents required in rapping lend themselves to acting, in terms of a kind of charisma, a kind of mental and verbal agility, a strong sense of presence. That's what rap is about, constructing who you are, making yourself a star."[4] This rationale helps explain why so many hip-hop artists, including LL Cool J, Ice Cube, Ice-T, Common, Queen Latifah, and Will Smith, have been so successful as actors; the latter two have even garnered Academy Award nominations for their performances.

So Fresh and So Clean

As the review of *House Party* for the *Slate* list remarks, "Black teenage movie characters were finally allowed to be as freewheeling and mischievous—without things ever getting too heavy—as their white counterparts had been in high school romps for decades."⁵ For the most part, that is exactly what the film delivers. When it was released, many critics agreed with *Slate*'s assessment, as the film has a 96 percent fresh rating on Rotten Tomatoes, higher than many of the white teen films from the same era. Roger Ebert's review of the film noted:

> We hardly ever see black teenagers at all in films, and when we do they're painted in images that are either negative and threatening, or impossibly clean-cut. His teenagers are neither: They're normal, average kids with the universal desire to go to a party and dance.... It was refreshing for a change to see a story about young blacks that didn't revolve around social problems, thriller elements, drugs or any particular form of seriousness. "House Party" is silly and high-spirited and not particularly significant, and that is just as it should be.⁶

Entertainment Weekly's Owen Gleiberman remarked that "*House Party* revives what's best in that tradition: It turns rebellion into fun, and vice versa. Here, at last, is a shrewd and sassy pop entertainment about black life," and Desson Howe of the *Washington Post* observed that *House Party* "is fast-moving, never dull, extremely funny, and manages to touch, with light-hearted (and R-rated) profundity on almost every youthful issue you can imagine," and even managed to reassure white audiences about how safe the film is by writing: "But don't worry, concerned citizens, ain't no pizza restaurant gonna burn down,"⁷ a not-so-subtle knock on Spike Lee's *Do the Right Thing*, which was released eight months prior. Not every critic raved about the film. Alfred Bruce criticized the film in *Cineaste* when he opined: "There is no sight of teenage pregnancy, single mothers, or people down on their luck.... Not only is there no drug use, there is no temptation, not even a reason to 'Just Say No.' There is sexual abstinence. There are family values. But there is no attempt to craft a picture complete with everyday situations that black teenagers must face."⁸ This is not a critique lobbed at teen films featuring white characters, despite the fact that white teenagers deal with teen pregnancy and drug use in the real world as well. A film featuring black teenagers who do not do drugs, will not engage in unsafe sex, and who berate the one person in the film who drinks alcohol to excess is seen as too unrealistic for Bruce. There is an expectation that white teenagers can have moments when they are not expected to contend with every serious issue facing society at large; however, black teenagers must always be shown bearing the weight of the world on their shoulders. *House Party* rejects this notion and shows that black teenagers can have mindless fun. That being said, Bruce's critique misses the part in *House Party* where teen pregnancy is addressed: Pop tells Kid he wants him to stay in school because he does not want Kid making the same mistakes he did. Pop was a teen parent and is now a single father due to his wife's death, and he makes it clear that Kid cannot and will not follow in his footsteps.

Either despite or because of the film's light-hearted focus, the critical reviews and star power helped propel *House Party* to box-office success. Hudlin made the film for $2.5 million, and it grossed over $26 million.[9] It won two major awards at the Sundance Film Festival, for cinematography as well as the Filmmakers Trophy, in addition to being nominated for the Grand Jury Prize.[10] Much like the discussion in the chapter on *Harlem Nights*, twenty-five years after its release, *House Party* continues to be framed as a cult classic; however, the film is beloved not just with black audiences but with multiracial audiences all over the world. In 2015, to celebrate its twenty-fifth anniversary, the film was screened at the Houston Cinema Arts Festival, the Museum of the Moving Image New York, the Everything Is Festival in Portland, Oregon, and the Tabernacle in London.[11]

Here We Go Again

Unfortunately, *House Party* does not completely ignore the larger issues black teenagers face in the United States. One of the throughlines of the film is harassment from two white police officers. Kid first encounters the officers when he sneaks out of his house to attend the party. As he walks down the street, the officers pull up in their car, shine a bright light in his face, call him "eraser head," and ask him where he's going. They start to check his ID, but when Officer Wanarski[12] notices that they are out of doughnuts, they instead leave the scene with the warning, "Watch yourself, you understand, because we are." Kid does not take the encounter too seriously, and insults the officer's masculinity when he replies, "Thank you, Cagney and Lacey" after the officers are out of earshot. Kid encounters the police five minutes later after he crashes an upscale backyard party in an effort to evade the school bullies. Prior to the cops' arrival, Kid converses with the party's DJ, played by music legend George Clinton, and it is implied that they have a prior relationship, so Kid's presence is not completely unwelcome. In an effort to escape the bullies, Kid accidentally knocks down a partygoer, but unfortunately, his getaway is unsuccessful and everyone is detained by the police. The camera pans across the faces and torsos of the bullies and Kid

Kid is warned

as they are kneeling on the ground with their fingers interlaced behind their heads. The shot ends with Officer Boyd pointing a gun at the teenagers, who, as the audience and the cops know, are clearly unarmed and not dangerous.

The partygoers, who are all black, explain to the officers that they do not want to press charges because Kid's actions were accidental, and because the teens "need discipline, not solitary confinement." The officers insist that the teens had "been in a few incidents this evening," which is clearly not the case—unless the unprovoked stop counts as an incident. Officer Wanarski then misrepresents the adults' concerns by saying that they were "too scared to make a statement," which clearly isn't the case. The officers address the teens as "perpetrators" and then force them to repeat the phrase "I am somebody" before allowing them to leave. The partygoers are appalled at the officers' behavior. Toward the end of the film, the audience learns that the man Kid knocked down is Sidney's father, who stands by his decision not to press charges because of "those fascist cops."

The officers' contempt is not limited to the teens. When Pop discovers that Kid has snuck out of the house, he sets out to find his son and instead encounters the officers. In a replay of the earlier scene with Kid, the cops shine a light in Pop's eyes and order him to stop walking. Pop is not here for the cops' harassment. When they ask where he is going, Pop replies, "I'm going to mind my own fucking business; that's where I'm going. Do you have a problem with that, Officer?" When he goes to put his hands in his pockets, both officers draw their weapons and yell "Freeze!" As the cops engage in an unjustified stop-and-frisk, Pop launches into a heated response, stating: "I know why you stopped me. I know why. Cause I'm a po' black man, in a black neighborhood, on a black block, and y'all just want to bust my black ass." Harris does not play the encounter as though Pop is afraid of the cops; the character is clearly more annoyed that he is being harassed and is far more concerned about finding his son than with appeasing the cops' feelings. The officers try to justify their stop by saying that Pop looks suspicious and they are responding to a disturbance, and that Pop could be coming from that disturbance. Again, Pop is not having any of it as he replies: "The only disturbance here is you fuckin' with me." He then proceeds to read their names off the badges and says he won't hesitate to file a complaint. When the encounter ends with the cops telling him to go home, Pop emphatically replies, "Fuck you."

In the wake of the Black Lives Matter movement calling attention to police harassment and multiple extrajudicial killings of unarmed black folks, this scene feels more serious in retrospect than the filmmakers probably intended. In the real world, even at the time the film was made, Pop's encounter could have and probably would have ended very differently. Viewers can frame this scene as a fantasy, an enactment of how they wish they could behave when they are stopped by law enforcement in the real world. At the same time, much like *The Glass Shield*, *House Party* counteracts the "stock story about the criminality of men of color. The [film] shows an alternative view that deconstructs the image of the violent, menacing thug."[13] Neither Kid nor Pop poses any sort of threat to the police officers or the audience, though arguably, Pop poses a very real threat to Kid, for wholly understandable reasons.

The police show up once more during the film, and this time their presence is actually useful from a law enforcement standpoint. After being denied entry to Play's party, Stab prepares to set Play's house on fire in retaliation. Pee-Wee and Zilla discourage these actions while the teen partygoers inside the house chant the familiar refrain: "The roof, the roof, the roof is on fire. We don't need no water; let the muthafucker burn." The officers catch the bullies in the act and detain them. Unfortunately, the officers take things too far when instead of taking them to jail, the officers decide to "take [the teens] to the docks, [where] nobody can hear them scream." We see Stab, Pee-Wee, and Zilla later in the film as they complain about the beatdown the cops gave them, though we do not see any physical evidence of serious injury. They lament the fact that they are "tired of getting beat down by punk-ass cops," so this clearly is not the first occurrence. Hudlin argues that this interaction between the bullies and the officers highlights the relationship many black communities have with law enforcement because: "On the one hand, blacks appreciate the importance of protection and someone to restore order, but, at the same time, the people in that position abuse that right because they don't respect the people they're protecting."[14]

The cops receive their comeuppance in a post-credits sequence. As mentioned earlier, the film begins with a dream sequence showing the roof of a house literally being blown away. At the end of the credits, we see the police officers walking in a parking lot when that roof lands on their heads. Like Pop's incident with the police, which plays as a fantasy for how many viewers would like to behave when they encounter law enforcement, the roof treating the cops to a fate similar to that of the Wicked Witch of the East provides viewers with a sense of closure.

I Ain't No Joke

Gina Prince-Bythewood's directorial debut, *Love & Basketball*, is usually framed as a love story and/or a sports film; however, it is also useful to frame it as a coming-of-age story. The film spans twelve years in the lives of Monica (Sanaa Lathan) and Quincy (Omar Epps), beginning when they are twelve years old, and follows the pair as they negotiate friendship, romance, and their love of basketball into adulthood. The film opens with three young boys playing basketball in the backyard of Quincy's home, and his new neighbor expresses a desire to play. Monica is wearing jeans, a T-shirt, and a baseball cap that covers her hair. At first, the boys do not realize that Monica is a girl; when she removes her cap and they figure it out, they lament that "girls can't play no ball." Monica promptly schools them by making the first basket and proudly declaring, "I'm gonna be the first girl in the NBA." Unlike the majority of black coming-of-age films and sports films in general, *Love & Basketball* features a female protagonist: it follows Monica's journey as she struggles to prove herself to everyone from the boys on the court to the basketball scouts and finally to her coaches.

The film does not shy away from the various double standards Monica faces because she is a female athlete. At home, her mother, Camille (Alfre Woodard), bemoans the fact that Monica is a tomboy and tries to impose a level of femininity on her that Monica clearly does not approve of. As Camille is unpacking, she finds a bright yellow dress that she wants Monica to wear on her first day of school. Monica is visibly disdainful of her mother's clothing selection as Camille laments the fact that Monica's dresses were packed in a box underneath a bunch of rags—Monica was clearly trying to hide them. Later in the film, Monica tells her family that she is a lesbian because "that's what you think anyway." Though Monica is kidding, her mother hopes she will grow out of "this tomboy phase" and says Monica "would be pretty if [she] would do something with her hair." Camille's gender policing follows a long history of attempts to contain black women's sexuality, particularly in the athletic realm. Because basketball is framed as a masculine sport, women who play it are often policed in terms of looking feminine and projecting heterosexuality. Monica understands this policing perfectly, which is why she "comes out" as a lesbian at the dinner table—she knows that heterosexism and specific ideals regarding black femininity are at the heart of her mother's attempts to dispel the tomboy image. One only has to Google Don Imus's framing of the Rutgers University women's basketball team as "nappy-headed hos," or pretty much any article on tennis great Serena Williams, to see this racial and gender policing in action. Monica is not here for anyone's nonsense: she embraces her athleticism and will not let anyone deter her from how she projects her black womanhood.

Next door, Quincy's parents are involved in a different sort of gender policing. Although his mother warns him about bringing girls home after she finds an earring in his room, the discussion is less about his sexual escapades and more about how some women will try to trap him since he is on his way to a lucrative NBA career. Women are referred to as "tricks" and "hos" by Quincy, and neither his mother Nona (Debbi Morgan) nor his father Zeke (Dennis Haysbert) bothers to correct him.

The gender disparities continue throughout the film as the crowd at the women's high school basketball game is almost nonexistent, while the men's game is packed to the rafters, complete with cheerleaders for both teams, professional photographers, and journalists. Since Monica's team is playing for the championship, the disparity is not a matter of quality: both teams are good; it is a lack of respect, as well as prevailing attitudes and stereotypes about female athletes, that limit the women's exposure. As David Berri pointed out in a 2015 *Time* magazine piece on women's sports, "In the sports media, women only create about 10% of the content. A recent study found that ESPN's Sportscenter persistently devotes less than 5% of its highlight program to women's sports."[15] One year later, Jessica Learish found that out of the 209 games played during the previous WNBA season,

Monica isolated in Spain

only 14 were nationally televised."[16] Of course, it is not surprising that women's sports are not given their due by sportswriters when Andy Benoit of *Sports Illustrated* tweets that "'women's sports in general (are) not worth watching.'"[17] If that is how sportswriters feel about women's sports, then the lack of coverage is to be expected.

However, in order for women's professional sports to be ignored by sports media, opportunities for women to actually play professional sports in the United States first have to exist. In 1993, when the latter part of the film takes place, Monica must move to Spain to pursue her dream of playing professional basketball because there are no opportunities in the United States. When the team is in the locker room, Monica is sitting in a corner by herself, taping her ankle, while the coach gives an impassioned pep talk in Spanish. It is clear that Monica is isolated from her teammates physically, given how the shot is composed, as well as linguistically—she has to ask one of her teammates to translate what the coach said. Quincy does not have this issue; we see him playing for the Los Angeles Lakers before he suffers a season-ending injury during a game.

Other aspects of gender disparity come up in the first high school game we see Monica play in, when the referee gives her a technical foul for unsportsmanlike conduct: Monica blocks a shot and gives her opponent the side-eye. This is not behavior that would have warranted a technical foul in the men's game. Monica struggles to get recruited because of her "attitude"; Quincy holds a press conference to tell the world where he is going to attend college. She verbalizes the double standard when she tells Quincy, "You jump in some guy's face, you talk smack, and you get a pat on your ass, but because I'm a female, I get told to calm down and act like a lady. I'm a ballplayer, okay?" Quincy does not rebut Monica's argument but still encourages her to check her attitude. Either Quincy is ignoring Monica's insight, or he recognizes the double standard and simply does not want Monica to be held back by it. While several white teen films focus on the female protagonist's appearance, those characters are rarely shown dealing with the level of sexism Monica does.

Unlike *House Party*, in which the threat of racialized police violence is present, *Love & Basketball* is focused primarily on gender inequity. Throughout their primary and secondary school years, Monica and Quincy exist in all-black spaces. The same is true for *House Party*, with the exception of the high school principal who cannot distinguish between a ho and a hoe. *Pariah* also takes place in all-black spaces and focuses more on the boundaries between and within sexual orientations. The difference between the films is the socioeconomic background of the community where the film's action takes place. This difference proved to be a problem when Prince-Bythewood was shopping the film. In one interview discussing the fact that the film was initially turned down by every studio, she states:

> I wanted to put it out in the world that these two characters travel the same way that anybody else travels both in career and in love.... When I went out with this film, this got turned down by everybody. I kept getting a repetitive refrain that it was soft. That was the note and why people didn't want to do it. I didn't understand. How is it soft? Because no one's getting chased by a knife or no one's been shot? How do you address that?[18]

This film straddled a very interesting line. On the one hand, Prince-Bythewood centered her narrative in the same type of middle-class, racially homogenous communities that most white teen films had been taking place in for two decades. At the same time, when *Love & Basketball* was released in 2000, Hollywood was still caught up in the black gangsta motif of the 1990s, which helps explain the reaction that the film was "too soft." Studio executives still did not have a frame of reference for middle-class black communities and black teenagers who engaged in the same nonthreatening activities as white teenagers. Dee Rees had similar issues making *Pariah*; she noted that "fundraising was incredibly difficult. People loved the script but would call it 'too small' and 'too specific,' which was basically code for 'too black' and 'too gay.'"[19]

Films like Boyz n the Hood and Menace II Society were the default frame of reference studio executives had for black teenagers, and films that did not show black teenagers struggling with or against criminality, and films that did not focus specifically on black males, were deemed inauthentic. It is worth noting that filmmaker Spike Lee served as executive producer for both Love & Basketball and Pariah, which supports the theory that if black folks were in a position to greenlight films, then not only would more black films be made and released but those films would reflect a wider variety of black experiences. The unfortunate reality of the situation is that the two films that focused on black female protagonists and had black women directors had to be cosigned by a black male producer in order to make it to the screen. That says a lot about Lee's ability to see talent, his attempt to expand Hollywood's representation of black communities, and Hollywood's sexism. All three of the films discussed in this chapter were made by first-time directors, but the films focused on and directed by women required the extra push.

In House Party, the characters come from various socioeconomic backgrounds, and Pop zeroes in on the notion that the police harass him because he is a poor black man in a poor black neighborhood. In Love & Basketball, Zeke is a former professional basketball player and Monica's father, Nathan (Henry Lennix), is a banker, putting them in a very different tax bracket than Pop. The father in Pariah is a police officer and the mother works in a doctor's office, which places the family in the middle-class tax bracket, although Arthur (Charles Parnell), and his wife, Audrey (Kim Wayans), discuss finances and the necessity of overtime in much the same way that Pop does. While financial security cannot protect against police misconduct, it can lessen the number of encounters a person has with law enforcement, which in turn produces fewer opportunities for those encounters to become violent.

I Need Love

Before both Monica and Quincy end up at the University of Southern California, a powerhouse for women's and men's basketball, they are allowed to engage in typical teenage behavior to a certain extent. Monica's focus is squarely on the basketball court, so we see her on the court and at home talking about the game. Quincy's experiences are a bit more diverse; we see him hanging out with friends, albeit at Monica's basketball game, and dating. Both characters attend a school dance where everyone is shown dancing and enjoying themselves. While in *House Party*, Kid and Sidney abstain from sex because the condom they have is way past its expiration date, Monica and Quincy do have sex with each other, as they have access to functional contraceptives. Their romantic relationship is not without its issues, however; as one writer points out, "When Q and Monica finally do get together, toward the end of high school, he's so dumb, he has to see her in a skintight white dress to get it."[20] Monica has to embody the ideals of mainstream heterosexual femininity for young men to notice her.

The sexual relationship between Monica and Quincy rubbed the studio and the MPAA the wrong way as well. Prince-Bythewood notes that despite the fact that *Love & Basketball* was her first film, she was given remarkable freedom except for the sex scene, noting that "the only note that I ever got from the studio during the filmmaking process was that when I shot that scene, they looked at the dailies and they said, they didn't think she was enjoying it enough. And my argument was, it's the first time and despite what the male fantasy might be, it's not that great."[21] The scene also initially caused the film to receive an R rating because, Prince-Bythewood was told, "You did too good a job and it feels too real. And you can tell it's the girl's first time."[22] Despite the fact that there were films released at the time with PG-13 ratings that featured more explicit sex scenes, Prince-Bythewood reedited the scene to receive the desired rating because she wanted young girls to see the film. The MPAA's double standard when it comes to showing male sexuality and female sexuality on screen is well documented, and one has to wonder whether or not the character's race also played a role in how the scene was received.[23] Because Monica was not a jezebel and did not display stereotypical hypersexual characteristics, studio executives and MPAA members did not know what to do with her sexuality.

Me, Myself, and I

Though *Love & Basketball* does not contain any encounters with law enforcement, there is one aspect of life that Quincy has to deal with that his white counterparts in teen films do not. As previously mentioned, much lip service is given to the fact that women are framed as impediments to success for male professional athletes. While Quincy is in college, Zeke informs him that he (Zeke) is facing a paternity suit. Quincy asks his father point-blank whether the allegation is true, and Zeke emphatically denies it. Father and son are discussing the matter at a bar when their conversation is interrupted by a fan wanting Quincy's autograph. Later that evening, Quincy talks to his mother and defends his father, saying, "This is only about money." He also asks, "How many times have you yourself told me to watch those hos out there?" and "You're going to take the word of some trick over Pop?" After a lifetime of allowing Quincy to believe that women are untrustworthy, it is no surprise he reacts this way. Unfortunately for Quincy, his mother hired a private detective and has pictures of Zeke with the other woman. What began as a loving father-son relationship is destroyed.

It is interesting that both *House Party* and *Love & Basketball* feature strong father-son bonds, and that *Pariah* features a strong father-daughter bond. In *House Party*, Pop shows his love at the beginning of the film when he wakes Kid up and admonishes him to eat breakfast before school. It is clear that Pop has been working all night—he literally falls asleep with his clothes and shoes on, and Kid lovingly removes his father's shoes before heading to the kitchen. Because it's clear that Pop is exhausted, one would expect that he had prepared a small breakfast of some cereal and toast. Nope, the table is full of hash browns, toast, scrambled eggs, pancakes, bacon, orange juice, and milk. Kid grabs a piece of toast and is about to head out the door when his father yells, "Chris, finish your breakfast, boy." In *Love & Basketball*, the relationship between Zeke and Quincy is exemplified by the fact that Zeke hugs and kisses his son at the end of every scene they have together. According to Prince-Bythewood, that was a choice Haysbert brought to the character because it was that relationship that attracted the actor to the part.[24] Like Pop, Zeke tries to get Quincy to focus on academics, asking him to consider Princeton as opposed to Zeke's alma mater, USC, but because Quincy does not believe an Ivy League school's basketball team is worthy of his athletic talents, he rejects his father's wisdom. When Quincy confronts Zeke about the affair and, more importantly, the lie, Quincy is heartbroken at his father's betrayal. The scene ends with Quincy sitting on the couch, beginning to sob. Lastly, in *Pariah*, it is the father who supports his daughter Alike (Adepero Oduye) by playing basketball with her, teaching her how to drive, and defending her against people, both within the family and external to it, who disrespect her because of her sexual orientation.

The fact that his family is breaking up, and more importantly, the fact that his father lied to his face, takes a toll on Quincy. During his next game we see him make multiple mistakes: turning over the ball, committing fouls, hogging the ball, and missing shots. His team loses, and the fans mercilessly boo him. Quincy continues to lash out when he engages in underage drinking at a party, behavior that is almost standard operating procedure for college students, and then breaks up with Monica. While many young people have to deal with divorce and sometimes lash out as a way to cope, there are not too many people who are forced to deal with these issues in such a public manner. Because Quincy is a top-level recruit who is projected to be a one-and-done, he has to deal with his personal issues in front of over ten thousand fans in the arena and millions of fans watching the games on television. The fact that Quincy cannot grieve privately, and the fact that Monica has to travel several thousand miles to pursue her career, have less to do with their race and more to do with their status as ballplayers. Of course, the characters do earn their happily-ever-after ending: Monica and Quincy marry and have a child, and Monica fulfills her dream of playing professional basketball at home—she plays for the newly formed Los Angeles Sparks.

Parents Just Don't Understand

The gender policing Monica endures in *Love & Basketball* is ratcheted up to a new level for Alike in Dee Rees's *Pariah*. Whereas Monica invokes being a lesbian to embarrass her parents, Alike really is a lesbian, but that is not a conversation her parents are ready to have. While Monica is not interested in conforming to anyone else's ideas of how she should project her authentic self, Alike goes through the motions to avoid confrontation. At the very beginning of the film we see Alike and her best friend, Laura (Pernell Walker), hanging out at a bar/strip club. Alike is having fun but seems out of her element and has to push Laura to leave because it is past curfew. As they ride the bus home, Laura wants to make sure that Alike arrives home safely, but Alike is adamant that Laura not miss her bus stop. The reason is revealed once Laura exits the bus: Alike "undresses" on the bus so she can conform to her parents' ideal of who she should be. She puts on earrings, and removes her baseball cap, hair stocking, and T-shirt, revealing a glittery, girly shirt underneath. As Adam Serwer writes in his review of the film, Alike "literally puts her closet back on as she rides the bus home from the club."[25] When Alike arrives home, her mother, Audrey, is concerned that curfew has been violated, but lets Alike off the hook because, "At least you look cute." The audience realizes the next day that this is not a one-time event, since Alike leaves home wearing one outfit but, after arriving at school, makes an immediate beeline for the bathroom so she can change into more comfortable clothes.

Once again, it is the mother who engages in the gender policing. Alike's father, Arthur, is far more accepting of who Alike is, though it is clear he is

Alike comes out

in denial about her sexual orientation. When Audrey forces Alike to wear a frilly sweater and skirt to church instead of the button-down shirt and khaki pants Alike has chosen, Arthur says that Alike looks fine as she is. Like Camille in *Love & Basketball*, Audrey is "tired of the tomboy thing" and wishes Alike would dress in a more feminine manner and take better care of her hair. It is interesting to note that the mothers in both films feel isolated in one form or another. Camille is a stay-at-home mom who gave up her dream of starting a catering business so that she could run the household. Audrey is employed at a doctor's office; however, we see her eating separately from her coworkers, who stop talking when Audrey enters the room. It could be that these mothers simply want their daughters to be more like them and/or have bought into the sexist, heterosexist, and narrow definitions of how black women should look and behave. This seems to be the case with Camille, who is surprised, but not hostile, when Monica "comes out" as a lesbian. In contrast, Audrey reacts violently at the end of the film when Alike comes out to her parents. Audrey calls Alike a "nasty-ass dyke" and punches her before Arthur can restrain her. For Audrey, the gender policing stems from a conservative religious notion that homosexuality is bad or unnatural, and she believes that by forcing femininity onto Alike that she can control or change her daughter's sexual orientation. However, Audrey's efforts are ultimately futile because, as Jessica Zach notes, "Unlike in many teen coming-out dramas, the *Pariah* main character, Alike, is refreshingly self-assured about her sexual orientation. The film's central drama instead emphasizes her uncertainty about how to express her newfound identity in the world."[26]

Just a Friend

The films discussed here deal with the main characters choosing whether or not to engage in sexual activity. In *House Party*, Kid and Sidney decide to abstain because they do not want to engage in unsafe sexual practices—the condom in Kid's wallet is gross. Their discussion about contraception makes it clear that neither of them has had sex before. When Monica and Quincy do have sex in *Love & Basketball*, it is clear that Monica has never had sex before, and it is implied that Quincy has.

Alike finds herself in a similar situation to the female characters in the other films. Alike's mother introduces her daughter to Bina (Aasha Davis), whose mother is one of Audrey's coworkers. Audrey pushes Alike to walk to school and to hang out with Bina arguably because Bina projects the ideal of femininity that Audrey wants Alike to embody. Alike is suspicious of anyone her mother likes and initially brushes Bina off; however, the two do have common interests that lead to a friendship. Bina then escalates the friendship by kissing Alike—a move that makes Alike quite uncomfortable. In the first place, Bina mentions she has a boyfriend and Alike has not read Bina as a lesbian or as bisexual. Secondly, this was Alike's first kiss, so she has no frame of reference for how to react to it. Shortly after the kiss, Bina invites Alike over to hang out, and they have sex. The next morning, Alike is able to enjoy a moment or two of happiness before Bina yanks the rug out from under her: Bina is cold and abrupt, frames the encounter as them "just playing around," and reminds Alike that no one can know what happened. Alike is devastated and runs home in tears. On the one hand, this chain of events seems like a cruel way to punish Alike for having sex with another woman. On the other hand, disastrous postcoital experiences have been a staple of teen stories ranging from Spike Lee's *School Daze* (1998) to Joss Whedon's *Buffy the Vampire Slayer* episode "Innocence" (1998) to *Cruel Intentions* (1999). Being a lesbian does not insulate one from this particular story trope.

Stop, Look, Listen

The fact that *Pariah*'s protagonist is a black lesbian puts the film in a unique category. As mentioned earlier, mainstream teen films, particularly in the 1980s, rarely had black characters; it was equally rare for those films to feature LGBTQ characters. In the 1990s and the 2000s, it was not unusual for the main protagonist of a mainstream teen film to have a black or LGBTQ friend, but still, it was rare for a teen of color or an LGBTQ teen to be the central protagonist. Given that history, it goes without saying that LGBTQ teens of color rarely, if ever, saw themselves on the big screen.

Black LGBTQ characters in general have not had an abundance of representation in Hollywood. The most notable characters include Celie Johnson and Shug Avery from *The Color Purple* (1985), directed by Steven Spielberg, and it is telling that the relationship between the two women was toned down significantly from Alice Walker's book on which the film was based. Jennie Livingston's 1991 documentary *Paris Is Burning* follows the lives of "African American and Hispanic gay men, drag queens and transgender women as they compete in simultaneously fierce and fun competitions involving fashion runways and vogue dancing battles"[27] and continues to be criticized by many. bell hooks argues that the film is a form of cultural appropriation, that the white lesbian filmmaker did nothing to interrogate her own subject position, and that "the whiteness celebrated in *Paris Is Burning* is not just any old brand of whiteness but rather that brutal imperial ruling-class capitalist patriarchal whiteness that presents itself—its way of life—as the only meaningful life there is."[28] Despite hooks's condemnation of the film, *Paris Is Burning* served as the visual reference for *Pariah*, according to an interview with the film's director of photography, Bradford Young.[29] The year 2016 saw the release of Barry Jenkins's sophomore effort, *Moonlight*. In his review of the film, A. O. Scott remarks, "To describe *Moonlight* . . . as a movie about growing up poor, black and gay would be accurate enough. It would also not be wrong to call it a movie about drug abuse, mass incarceration and school violence. But those classifications are also inadequate, so much as to be downright misleading."[30] Based on Tarell Alvin McCraney's stage play, *Moonlight* follows Chiron at three different points in his life, spanning roughly a twenty-year period. We meet him as a nine-year-old who is being bullied by his classmates and mentored by a kind-hearted drug dealer; we see him again in high school with his best friend Kevin, with whom he shares both an intimate experience and a violent experience; and we meet Chiron and Kevin again as adults when they reconnect and bond over the roads not taken. The film was a critical success and hopefully will lead to more films that deal with the intersection of race and sexual orientation: *Moonlight* became the first LGBTQ film to win an Oscar for Best Picture. Still, films about the intersection of race, sexual orientation, and sexual identity are rare.

Most of the films that feature black LGBTQ characters have been independent features, such as Lizzie Borden's *Born in Flames* (1983), Cheryl Dunye's *The Watermelon Woman* (1996), Patrik Ian-Polk's *The Skinny* (2012) and *Blackbird* (2014), and Sean Baker's *Tangerine* (2015). In addition, no discussion of the representation of black LGBTQ communities is complete without mentioning Marlon Riggs's *Tongues Untied* (1989) and *Black Is...Black Ain't* (1994), which were released for PBS. Larger Hollywood films, and independent films that received wide release, that feature black LGBTQ characters are even more rare, but they do exist: Beeban Kidron's *To Wong Foo, Thanks for Everything! Julie Newmar* (1995) featured Wesley Snipes as a cross-dresser on a road trip with John Leguizamo and Patrick Swayze; F. Gary Gray's *Set It Off* (1996) told the story of four female bank robbers, one of whom, Cleo (Queen Latifah), is a lesbian; Spike Lee's *She Hate Me* (2004) stars Anthony Mackie as an unemployed businessman who helps impregnate lesbian couples, including his former girlfriend, played by Kerry Washington. Justin Simien's *Dear White People* (2014) looks at the lives of black college students at a predominately white university; one of those students is Lionel Higgins (Tyler James Williams), an introverted black gay journalism student who does his best to navigate the intersections of race and sexual orientation.

Given the paltry amount of representation LGBTQ characters have received thus far, *Pariah* serves an additional narrative purpose than those of *House Party* or *Love & Basketball*. According to a study released by the Black Youth Project, "43 percent of African-American gay youths have thought about or attempted suicide, and 26 percent reported being the target of anti-gay bullying. Additional research found that 84.9 percent of LGBT youths reported hearing homophobic remarks from their peers, and 56.9 percent said that their teachers or other school staff used similar anti-gay slurs."[31] Thankfully, this is not Alike's reality. Although she seems alienated from her peers, there is no indication that her isolation is because of her sexual orientation. In fact, Alike overhears her female classmates saying positive things about her, and she is seen having lunch with her A.P. English teacher, indicating an adult support system at school. The isolation we see Alike experience at school is more than likely the result of the fact that she is more introverted than her peers. The Black Youth Project also found that "more than 90 percent of black gay youths listed 'family acceptance' as the main factor that could actually make their lives more bearable," and this is where Alike's experience tracks with the data.[32] Though her story does not end with her mother accepting her, it is made abundantly clear that her father, sister, and best friend love and support her. Arthur asks her to come home after the fight; her sister, Sharonda, tells her, "I hope you know it doesn't matter to me" as the two listen to their parents argue about Alike; and her friend Laura gives her a safe place to stay in a gesture reminiscent of when Laura's mother threw her out and she had to live with her sister. In the end, Alike enrolls in an early-college program at Berkeley and emphatically tells her father, "I'm not running, I'm choosing." In the poem she reads at the end of the film, Alike describes her state of mind and state of being:

> Heartbreak opens onto the sunrise for even breaking is opening and I am broken, I am open. Broken into the new life without pushing in, open to the possibilities within, pushing out. See the love shine in through my cracks? See the light shine out through me? I am broken, I am open, I am broken open. See the love light shining through me, shining through my cracks, through the gaps. My spirit takes journey, my spirit takes flight, could not have risen otherwise and I am not running, I am choosing. Running is not a choice from the breaking. Breaking is freeing, broken is freedom. I am not broken, I am free.

These are the words of a person who has experienced trauma, has learned from her ordeal, and is moving forward. While it would be great to have a film with black LGBTQ teens doing all of the normal teen stuff that their cisgender, heterosexual peers do, the societal oppression heaped upon the LGBTQ community and the lack of representation of LGBTQ youths in film makes that frame difficult. Until films show more black LGBTQ teens, and black LGBTQ characters overall, it is equally important to show these characters thriving in hostile environments and/or liberating themselves from those environments.

Curtain Call

In his review of *Pariah*, David Leonard argues that the film "expand[s] the definition of what it means to be black in the twenty-first century."[33] Cultural critic Nelson George agrees, describing the film as "the most visible example of the mini-movement of young black filmmakers telling stories that complicate assumptions about what "black film" can be by embracing thorny issues of identity, alienation and sexuality."[34]

All three of the films discussed in this chapter expand the ways in which we think about teen films and how black teenagers are portrayed on the big screen. As noted in Chapter 4, in the 1990s black teens were framed as budding sociopaths, incorrigible criminals, or traumatized victims who sometimes had to flee black communities in order to survive and thrive. More than twenty years of these types of portrayals have had real-world consequences; one study from the *Journal of Personality and Social Psychology* "linked the higher use of force by police on black youth to the common perception that, by age 10, they are less innocent. The study also cited U.S. Department of Education data that said black students are far more likely to be harshly disciplined at school than students of other races who commit the same infractions."[35] Being seen as and treated as a young person can literally mean the difference between life and death for black children.

The title of this chapter asks whether black children are allowed to be children, and the three films discussed here provide an answer: yes and no. At times the main characters are allowed to have fun, study, date, and figure out who they are and how they want to exist in the world. Other times, they are faced with police harassment, gender inequality, and hetersexism that impact how they navigate everyday life. These experiences range from the innocuous and humorous police encounters in *House Party* to the horrific family fight in *Pariah*. Audiences looking for black teen films free of systemic inequalities will have a hard time finding any. It is worth noting that all the main characters make it to the end of the films having achieved some sort of satisfaction—though to be fair, the butt-whupping Kid receives from Pop over the end credits may not feel like a satisfactory ending, but we do know he survives the experience to appear in the sequel. Because the black children and teens in these films have to deal with racism, sexism, and heterosexism at such a young age, they sometimes struggle to simply be teenagers. Until society at large recognizes black children as children, there is no way that filmmakers cannot present the reality that black teens face. For now, filmmakers are at least trying to show black teens as the multifaceted human beings that they really are.

Post-Credit Sequence

> We live in a box of space and time, Movies are windows in its walls. They allow us to enter other minds, not simply in the sense of identifying with the characters, although that is an important part of it, but by seeing the world as another person sees it.
>
> — Alison Nastasi, "25 Delightful Roger Ebert Quotes About Movies," 2014

> In our never-ending conversation—or argument—about which films deserve to be remembered, which films are cultural touchstones, which films defined and advanced the art form, we habitually overlook stories by and about black people.
>
> — Aisha Harris and Dan Kois, "The Black Film Canon," 2016

In Spike Lee's 1989 seminal film, *Do the Right Thing*, Buggin' Out protests Sal's Famous Pizzeria because black and brown folks lack representation on Sal's Wall of Fame. Buggin' Out raises the argument that because members of these communities are the sole customers of the establishment, they deserve a place on the wall. More than ten years later, when the American Film Institute released its list of the 100 best American films, not a single film with a black director or a predominately black cast was included on the list. As Dennis Sullivan and Fred Boehrer point out, "The list is the AFI's centennial wall of fame, if you will, so again how ironic that a movie that speaks so poignantly about inclusion for all on life's wall of fame finds itself looking from the outside in, its nose pressed flat against the window glass."[1] In 2007, when the AFI revisited its list, *Do the Right Thing* was included and was the sole entry by a black director. Of course, it is easy to brush off the importance of such accolades by saying they don't matter—or, as Sal argued, if you want pictures on the wall, open your own restaurant. Unfortunately, it is not that simple with film. In 2016, when *Slate* created its list of the top fifty films directed by black filmmakers, a list that was in response to the multitude of top-film lists that ignore or reject black films and black filmmakers, Aisha Harris and Dan Kois argue, "These lists are important: They affect the types of movies that self-proclaimed cinephiles and casual viewers alike seek out and watch, and they help define our ideas about whose perspectives matter. The exclusion of blackness from these film canons shapes our expectations about what constitutes greatness in film. And it helps cement the expectation that whiteness is somehow as 'universal' in art as so many believe it to be in life."[2]

If black films are not recognized as historically and/or culturally significant, it also makes it easier for the powers-that-be to not fund them. As mentioned in the introduction, Hollywood typically has one to two years when black films are in vogue, but shortly thereafter, an eight- to ten-year drought occurs. While the hashtag #OscarsSoWhite focused attention on the lack of recognition black films receive from the Academy, the larger problem was a lack of quality black films in the pipeline. The 2010s seemed to break from the established pattern. The last several years have seen the release of multiple black films, many of which received box-office success and critical acclaim. The culmination occurred in 2017, when no less than 18 black folks were nominated for Academy Awards and four of them walked away with statues. The year 2017 saw the release of Amma Asante's *A United Kingdom*, Jordan Peele's *Get Out*, J. D. Dillard's *Sleight*, Benny Boom's *All Eyez on Me*, Malcolm D. Lee's *Girl Trip*, and Reginald Hudlin's *Marshall*. The next year, 2018, began with the release of Ryan Coogler's *Black Panther* and Ava DuVernay's *A Wrinkle in Time*, and ended with Steve McQueen's *Widows*, Steven Caple Jr.'s *Creed 2*, Barry Jenkins's *If Beale Street Could Talk*, and Peter Ramsay's *Spider-Man: Into the Spider-Verse*. It remains to be seen if Hollywood responds to this seeming explosion of black films by providing even more opportunities for black filmmakers to tell stories, or by shutting them out for ten years.

Fighting for inclusion on the metaphorical walls of fame should not focus solely on critics, awards, and "best of" lists; there must also be a push to have film scholars recognize the importance of black films. While there are some black films and filmmakers who have received critical attention over the years, a plethora of titles remain ignored for one reason or another. This book is an attempt to move the conversation forward, to show that black films can be analyzed from various points of view, and to highlight the fact that even the films that look trivial on the surface can be read in profound ways. As the quote from Roger Ebert at the beginning of this chapter highlights, black films are a way for audiences to identify with black characters and to see the world as black folks see it. These films also give audiences a glimpse into how black folks were perceived and what conversations black communities were having at the time the films were released.

As the civil rights movement was reaching its apex, black films like *Nothing But a Man* focused on exposing the realities of white supremacy and the effect racism had on black folks. Michael Roemer's film highlights the racial divisions between blacks and whites, as well as the intraracial divisions within black communities along the lines of socioeconomic class, gender, and generation. Duff's experiences show the audience how racism is intimately connected to economic opportunity, and what can happen to a person when that opportunity is constricted. The 1970s ushered in the Blaxploitation movement, which gave writers and directors more freedom to create empowered characters; the success of these films reflected an acknowledgment of black communities as film consumers. *Blazing Saddles* straddles multiple fences by showcasing a black hero who represents Blaxploitation sensibilities while still dealing with overt racism, which was the touchstone of black films of the 1960s. At the same time, by moving from the serious race film to the racial satire, the film forces audiences to understand that Bart is the smartest person in the film, and that the white racists that surround him deserve to be mocked at every turn.

While there have always been a handful of "woke" white directors who made meaningful black films, the 1980s expanded opportunities for some black directors to tell their own stories. That decade also saw the rise of the black superstar, and some, like Eddie Murphy, took full advantage of their newfound status. *Harlem Nights* probably will not go down in history as Murphy's finest film; however, its inclusion of three generations of black comedians has made the film popular within black communities. The film critiques and rejects a toxic definition of black hypermasculinity, and it comments on women and sex work without judging or degrading the women or the profession. Murphy also took the heist, a staple genre in Hollywood for decades, adds black protagonists, and turned *Nights* into a financially successful cult classic.

The 1990s was the decade of the black gangsta films, which makes Charles

Burnett's decision to focus *The Glass Shield* on a black law enforcement officer intriguing. The film was not a box-office success when it was originally released, but in hindsight, and in the era of Black Lives Matter, the film's discussion of police maleficence and the workings of the "thin blue line" make the film wholly relevant to contemporary political discussions.

The 2000s brought satire back into the frame, and Kevin Willmott's *Confederate States of America* takes modern-day popular culture artifacts to tell an alternative history of the United States. The film shows us what a contemporary slavocracy would look like, and, unfortunately, it looks eerily similar to the real world.

While *Nothing But a Man* and *Harlem Nights* feature interesting female protagonists, Ava DuVernay's work places black women and black feminist sensibilities at the core of her narratives. Her characters do not reproduce the controlling narratives usually associated with black female characters; instead, DuVernay's subjects are smart, complicated, fully realized human beings who fight for what they want and yet are vulnerable enough to seek love and to be loved in return.

The ways in which Hollywood has framed Jackie Robinson's legacy constitute a perfect encapsulation of racial progress in the United States and a prime example of how Hollywood has and has not grappled with white supremacy. In the 1950s, with *The Jackie Robinson Story*, institutional racism within the film industry itself and de jure segregation within American society as a whole help explain the limited view of Robinson's life. To add insult to injury, a white savior takes up a substantial portion of *Story*'s narrative space. By the 1990s, a more complete picture of Robinson was available, and given the conversations about race that were occurring at the time, *The Court-Martial of Jackie Robinson* is able to expand upon Robinson's life. The film also presents a more nuanced account of the kinds of racism Robinson endured and fought against during his life. The "postracial" ideology and the conservative backlash against President Obama, as well as any discussions of systemic racism, informs the safe version of Robinson and racism portrayed in 42. For good measure, the white savior is added back into the narrative. Audiences and historians still are left with the question of what a film about Jackie Robinson would look like if it was written and directed by a black filmmaker.

Finally, a seemingly innocuous genre, the teen film, is forced to grapple with systems of privilege and oppression when the genre focuses on black protagonists. A simple tale of sneaking out to a party is hampered by police harassment and abuse; a devotion to sports runs headfirst into sexism and a lack of opportunity and respect for female athletes; and creating a sense of self is dampened by the intersections of race, homophobia, and heteronormativity. Even with the best of intentions, black teenagers do not have the freedom to simply be teenagers in life or on the big screen.

So what does all of this mean? At first glance, this book looks like a collection of unrelated essays on black films. Taken as a whole, it shows an evolution in the ways in which black characters have progressed and regressed over time; it shows the increasing number of black filmmakers who are telling stories; and it shows the multiple intersecting identities that can be analyzed within black films—race may be a unifying common denominator, but it is not the only identity these films discuss. The book shows that critical race theory and black feminist thought are useful theoretical paradigms for analyzing black film and argues that if scholars are interested in good old-fashioned content analysis, then there are a multitude of black films just waiting to be discussed.

NOTES

Coming Attractions

1. Ramin Setoodeh, "Spike Lee on 'Da Sweet Blood of Jesus' and Hollywood's Diversity Problem," *Variety*, June 23, 2014, variety.com/2014/film/markets-festivals/spike-lee-da-sweet-blood-of-jesus-hollywood-diversity-problem-1201243416/.

2. "Sundance 2012: Ava DuVernay Becomes First Black Woman to Win Best Director Prize for *Middle of Nowhere* (VIDEO)," "Black Voices," *Huffington Post.com*, January 30, 2012, updated March 31, 2012, www.huffingtonpost.com/2012/01/30/ava-duvernay-sundance_n_1241286.html.

3. Kevin Fallon, "Chris Rock's Brutal Oscars Monologue Was Legendary. But It Wasn't Perfect," *TheDailyBeast.com*, February 28, 2016, www.thedailybeast.com/articles/2016/02/28/chris-rocks-brutal-oscars-monologue-was-legendary-but-it-wasn-t-perfect.html.

4. Chris Rock, "Chris Rock Pens Blistering Essay on Hollywood's Race Problem: 'It's a White Industry,'" *Hollywood Reporter*, December 3, 2014, www.hollywoodreporter.com/news/top-five-filmmaker-chris-rock-753223.

5. Beretta E. Smith-Shomade, Racquel Gates, and Miriam J. Perry, "When and Where We Enter," *Cinema Journal* 53, no. 4 (2014): 123.

6. Ibid.

7. Stuart Hall, "What Is This 'Black' in Black Popular Culture?" *Social Justice* 20, no. 1/2 (Spring-Summer 1993): 105.

8. James W. Loewen, *Lies My Teacher Told Me: Everything Your American History Textbook Got Wrong* (New York: Simon & Schuster, 2007), 136.

9. Junot Díaz, "The Junot Díaz Episode," *FanBrosShow*, November 18, 2013, podcast, 48:45, https://forallnerds.com/junot-diaz-episode/.

10. Scott Mendelson, "*Black Panther* Shatters Stereotypes, Breaks Box Office Records with $400M+ Debut," *Forbes*, February 18, 2018, www.forbes.com/sites/scottmendelson/2018/02/18/black-panther-crushes-conventional-wisdom-with-record-218m-debut/#4dcf195f64c7.

11. Mia Mask, *Contemporary Black American Cinema: Race, Gender and Sexuality at the Movies* (New York: Routledge, 2012), 5.

12. Lisa Doris Alexander, *When Baseball Isn't White, Straight and Male: The Media and Difference in the National Pastime* (Jefferson, NC: McFarland, 2012), 7.

13. Patricia Hill Collins, *Black Sexual Politics: African Americans, Gender, and the New Racism* (New York: Routledge, 2004), 350; Patricia Hill Collins, *Black Feminist Thought: Knowledge, Consciousness, and the Politics of Empowerment*, 10th ed. (New York: Routledge, 2000), 69.

14. Kimberlé Crenshaw, "Mapping the Margins: Intersectionality, Identity Politics, and Violence Against Women of Color," in *Critical Race Theory: The Key Writings That Formed the Movement*, ed. Kimberlé Crenshaw et al. (New York: New Press, 1995), 358.

15. Stacy L. Smith, Marc Choueiti, and Katherine Pieper, *Inequality in 800 Popular Films: Examining Portrayals of Gender, Race/Ethnicity, LGBT, and Disability from 2007–2015*, Annenberg School for Communication and Journalism, University of Southern California (Los Angeles: September 2016), 2, annenberg.usc.edu/pages/ffi/media/MDSCI/Dr%20Stacy%20L%20Smith%20Inequality%20in%20800%20Films%20FINAL.ashx.

16. Ibid.

17. Cornel West, "Foreword," in *Critical Race Theory: The Key Writings That Formed the Movement*, ed. Kimberlé Crenshaw et al. (New York: New Press, 1995), xi.

18. Derrick Bell, "Who's Afraid of Critical Race Theory?" *University of Illinois Law Review* 1995, no. 4 (1995): 899.

19. Ibid., 901.

20. Ibid.

21. Mark A. Reid, *Black Lenses, Black Voices: African American Film Now* (Lanham, MD: Rowman & Littlefield, 2005), 33.

22. Rock, "Chris Rock Pens Blistering Essay on Hollywood's Race Problem: 'It's a White Industry.'"

23. Paula Young Lee, "A White Buddy for Miles Davis: Don Cheadle's Struggle to Get *Miles Ahead* Financed Is Absurd—and Not Surprising," *Salon.com*, April 13, 2016, www.salon.com/2016/02/19/a_white_buddy_for_miles_davis_don_cheadles_struggle_to_get_miles_ahead_financed_is_absurd_and_not_surprising/.

24. Christian Blauvelt, "*Red Tails* DVD: George Lucas Talks About His 'Real Dogfight Movie.'" *Entertainment Weekly*, May 22, 2012, www.ew.com/article/2012/05/22/red-tails-dvd-george-lucas-rick-mccallum.

25. Emily Rabbitt, "This New Movie Is a Landmark Victory for Race—So What's the Problem?" *Groundswell.com*, April 7, 2015, www.groundswell.org/dreamworks_home_diversity/.

26. Ben Child, "Italian Posters for *12 Years a Slave* Herald Brad Pitt over Chiwetel Ejiofor," *The Guardian*, December 24, 2013, www.theguardian.com/film/2013/dec/24/12-years-slave-italy-posters-pitt-ejiofor.

27. Stacy L. Smith et al., *Inequality in 700 Popular Films: Examining Portrayals of Gender, Race, & LGBT Status from 2007–2014*, Annenberg School for Communication and Journalism, University of Southern California (Los Angeles: August 2015), 20.

28. John Singleton, "Can a White Director Make a Great Black Movie?" *Hollywood Reporter*, September 19, 2013, https://www.hollywoodreporter.com/news/john-singleton-can-a-white-630127.

29. Terri Francis, "Whose "Black Film" Is This? The Pragmatics and Pathos of Black Film Scholarship," *Cinema Journal* 53, no. 4 (Summer 2014): 147.

30. Andre Seewood, "Towards Defining the Black Film: the Genuine, the Compromised, and the Token," *Shadow andAct.com*, March 2, 2015, accessed on *IndieWire.com*, https://www.indiewire.com/2015/03/towards-defining-the-black-film-the-genuine-the-compromised-and-the-token-155411/.

Chapter 1. I Ain't Fit to Live with No More: *Nothing But a Man* Revisited

1. Christopher Sieving, *Soul Searching: Black-Themed Cinema from the March on Washington to the Rise of Blaxploitation*

(Middletown, CT: Wesleyan University Press, 2011), 10.

2. Rick Worland, *Searching for New Frontiers: Hollywood Films in the 1960s* (Hoboken, NJ: Wiley Blackwell, 2018), 83.

3. Andre Seewood, "Towards Defining the Black Film: The Genuine, The Compromised, and The Token," *Shadow andAct.com*, March 2, 2015, acccessed on *IndieWire.com*, https://www.indiewire.com/2015/03/towards-defining-the-black-film-the-genuine-the-compromised-and-the-token-155411/.

4. "Nothing But a Man," *Wikipedia.com*, accessed March 4, 2019, https://en.wikipedia.org/w/index.php?title=Nothing_But_a_Man&oldid=83975 1667.

5. Rick Harrison, "Nothing But a Man," *Independent Film & Video Monthly* 27, no. 6 (2004): 10, ProQuest.

6. Michael T. Martin and David C. Wall, "Cinematic Principles and Practice at Work in Nothing But a Man: A Conversation with Robert Young," in *The Politics and Poetics of Black Film: Nothing But a Man*, ed. David C. Wall and Michael T. Martin, Studies in the Cinema of the Black Diaspora (Bloomington: Indiana University Press, 2015), 171.

7. Robert Young, "Filmmakers' Statements: Robert Young," in *The Politics and Poetics of Black Film: Nothing But a Man*, ed. David C. Wall and Michael T. Martin, Studies in the Cinema of the Black Diaspora (Bloomington: Indiana University Press, 2015), 40.

8. Emma Brockes, "Director Michael Roemer on His Seminal 60s Drama Nothing But a Man," *The Guardian*, April 5, 2013, www.theguardian.com/film/2013/oct/01/director-michael-roemer-nothing-but.

9. Jennine Lanouette, "Nothing But a Good Tale," *Village Voice* 38, no. 9 (1993): 56, ProQuest.

10. Hal Hinson, "When Injustice Gets Under the Skin," *Washington Post*, July 10, 1993, D1, ProQuest.

11. "Richard Chew," IMDb.com, accessed March 4, 2019, https://www.imdb.com/news/ni30459520.

12. Sachs, Ira, "Interview: Director Ira Sachs Reminds Us 'Love Is Strange,'" by Patrick McDonald, HollywoodChicago.com, August 27, 2014, www.hollywoodchicago.com/news/24449/interview-director-ira-sachs-reminds-us-love-is-strange.

13. William Julius Wilson, *The Declining Significance of Race: Blacks and Changing American Institutions* (Chicago: University of Chicago Press, 1978), 1.

14. Patricia Hill Collins, *Black Sexual Politics: African Americans, Gender, and the New Racism* (New York: Routledge, 2004), 122.

15. Judith E. Smith, "Civil Rights, Labor, and Sexual Politics in Nothing But a Man," in *The Politics and Poetics of Black Film: Nothing But a Man*, ed. David C. Wall and Michael T. Martin (Bloomington: Indiana University Press, 2015), 116.

16. Zach Lewis, "Without Theatres: Nothing But a Man Is Unapologetically Political and Deeply Humanistic" (Review), *PopOptiq.com*, accessed March 4, 2019, https://www.popoptiq.com/nothing-but-a-man-review/.

17. United States Department of Labor Office of Policy Planning and Research, "The Negro Family: The Case for National Action," by Daniel Patrick Moynihan, 1965, https://www.dol.gov/general/aboutdol/history/webid-moynihan.

18. Patricia Hill Collins, *Black Feminist*

Thought: Knowledge, Consciousness, and the Politics of Empowerment, 10th ed. (New York: Routledge, 2000), 75.

19. John Nickel, "Disabling African American Men: Liberalism and Race Message Films," Cinema Journal 44, no. 1 (Autumn 2004): 35.

20. "(Mis)representation of the Black Female on Film: the Celluloid Sister; Part II," Michigan Citizen, August 7, 1999, n.p., ProQuest.

21. Albert Johnson, "The Negro in American Films: Some Recent Works," Film Quarterly 18, no. 4 (Summer 1965): 25.

22. Chris Norton, "Black Independent Cinema and the Influence of Neo-Realism: Futility, Struggle and Hope in the Face of Reality," Images: A Journal of Film and Popular Culture, no. 5 (1997): n.p., www.imagesjournal.com/issue05/features/black3.htm.

23. Martin Luther King Jr., "I've Been to the Mountaintop," speech, Memphis, April 3, 1968, AmericanRhetoric.com, http://www.americanrhetoric.com/speeches/mlkivebeentothemountaintop.htm.

24. Malcolm X, "The Ballot or the Bullet," speech, Detroit, April 12, 1964, American RadioWorks.com, http://americanradioworks.publicradio.org/features/blackspeech/mx.html.

25. Norton, "Black Independent Cinema and the Influence of Neo-Realism: Futility, Struggle and Hope in the Face of Reality," n.p.; Michael T. Martin and Adele Stephenson, "Close-Up Gallery: Nothing But a Man," Black Camera, an International Film Journal 3, no. 2 (Spring 2012): 197.

26. Smith, "Civil Rights, Labor, and Sexual Politics in Nothing But a Man," 114.

27. George Butte, "Suture and the Narration of Subjectivity in Film," Poetics Today 29, no. 2 (2008): 302, ProQuest.

28. Ibid, 303.

29. Derrick Bell, "White Superiority in America: Its Legal Legacy, Its Economic Costs," Villanova Law Review 33, no. 5 (1988): 767.

30. Charles R. Lawrence III, "If He Hollers Let Him Go: Regulating Racist Speech on Campus," in Words that Wound: Critical Race Theory, Assaultive Speech, and the First Amendment, ed. Mari J. Matsuda et al. (Boulder, CO: Westview Press, 1993), 452.

31. Ibid., 453.

32. Smith, "Civil Rights, Labor, and Sexual Politics in Nothing But a Man," 120.

33. Noel Carroll, Interpreting the Moving Image (Cambridge: Cambridge University Press, 1998), 204.

34. Derald Wing Sue, "Racial Microaggressions in Everyday Life," Psychology Today, October 5, 2010, www.psychologytoday.com/blog/microaggressions-in-everyday-life/201010/racial-microaggressions-in-everyday-life.

35. Amy Taubin, "The South and the Fury," Village Voice, February 23, 1993, 54, ProQuest; Harrison, "Nothing But a Man"; Donald Bogle, Toms, Coons, Mulattoes, Mammies & Bucks: An Interpretive History of Blacks in American Films, 4th ed. (New York: Continuum, 2001), 302.

36. "(Mis)representation."

37. Collins, Black Sexual Politics, 122.

38. Roger Ebert, "Nothing But a Man" (Review), RogerEbert.com, June 4, 1993, www.rogerebert.com/reviews/nothing-but-a-man-1993.

39. Melissa V. Harris-Perry, Sister Citizen: Shame, Stereotypes, and Black Women in America (New Haven, CT: Yale University Press, 2011), Kindle edition, 21.

40. Ibid., 215.

41. "(Mis)representation."

42. "Meet the 2012 Sundance Filmmakers #24: Ava DuVernay, *Middle of Nowhere*," IndieWire.com, January 10, 2012, www.indiewire.com/article/meet-the-2012–sundance-filmmakers-24–ava-duvernay-middle-of-nowhere.

43. Sergio, "Why Sidney Poitier's *A Warm December* Is No 'Click [sic] Flick,'" *IndieWire.com*, August 18, 2014, https://www.indiewire.com/2013/08/why-sidney-poitiers-a-warm-december-is-no-click-flick-165700/.

44. Johnson, "The Negro in American Films: Some Recent Works," 25.

45. Martin and Wall, "Cinematic Principles and Practice at Work in *Nothing But a Man*: A Conversation with Robert Young," 172.

46. Nickel, "Disabling African American Men: Liberalism and Race Message Films," 35.

47. Hoyt W. Fuller, "*Nothing But a Man* Reconsidered," *Negro Digest* 14, no. 7 (May 1965): 49, https://books.google.com/books?id=7zkDAAAAMBAJ&pg=PA3&lr=&source=gbs_toc&cad=2#v=onepage&q&f=false.

48. Martin and Wall, "Cinematic Principles and Practice at Work in *Nothing But a Man*: A Conversation with Robert Young," 187.

49. Smith, "Civil Rights, Labor, and Sexual Politics in *Nothing But a Man*," 127.

50. Fuller, "*Nothing But a Man* Reconsidered," 39.

51. Smith, "Civil Rights, Labor, and Sexual Politics in *Nothing But a Man*," 136.

52. Ibid., 127.

53. Bogle, *Toms, Coons, Mulattoes, Mammies & Bucks*, 195.

54. Michael T. Martin and David C. Wall, "Historicity and Possibility in *Nothing But a Man*: A Conversation with Khalil Muhammad," in *The Politics and Poetics of Black Film: Nothing But a Man*, ed. David C. Wall and Michael T. Martin, Studies in the Cinema of the Black Diaspora (Bloomington: Indiana University Press, 2015), 147.

55. Carroll, *Interpreting the Moving Image*, 207.

56. Smith, "Civil Rights, Labor, and Sexual Politics in *Nothing But a Man*," 116.

Chapter 2. "Hey, Where Are the White Women At?": The Presentation of Racism and Resistance in *Blazing Saddles*

1. "Race Relations on Campus," *The Journal of Blacks in Higher Education* 62 (2008): 101.

2. Roger Ebert, "Blazing Saddles" (Review), RogerEbert.com, February 7, 1974, https://www.rogerebert.com/reviews/blazing-saddles-1974.

3. Linda Wertheimer, "Blazing Saddles Makes National Film Registry" (Transcript), NPR, December 30, 2006, https://www.npr.org/templates/story/story.php?storyId=6700144.

4. Novotny Lawrence, *Blaxploitation Films of the 1970s: Blackness and Genre* (New York: Routledge, 2008), 19–20.

5. Donald Bogle, *Toms, Coons, Mulattoes, Mammies, & Bucks: An Interpretive History of Blacks in American Films*, 4th ed. (New York: Continuum, 2001), 242.

6. Vincent Canby, "Blazing Saddles" (Review), *New York Times*, February 8, 1974, https://www.nytimes.com/1974/02/08/archives/screen-blazing-saddles-a-western-in-burlesque.html; Nadya Faulx, "Blazing Saddles, the Best

Interracial Buddy Comedy, Turns 40," NPR, February 7, 2014, https://www.npr.org/sections/codeswitch/2014/02/07/272452677/blazing-saddles-the-best-interracial-buddy-comedy-turns-40.

7. John Podhoretz, "Saddles Revisited," *Weekly Standard*, June 16, 2014, 43.

8. Andre Seewood, "Towards Defining the Black Film: The Genuine, the Compromised, and the Token," *ShadowandAct.com*, March 2, 2015, accessed on *IndieWire.com*, https://www.indiewire.com/2015/03/towards-defining-the-black-film-the-genuine-the-compro mised-and-the-token-155411/.

9. Ibid.

10. John W. Roberts, *From Trickster to Badman: The Black Folk Hero in Slavery and Freedom* (Philadelphia: University of Pennsylvania Press, 1989), 23.

11. Ibid.

12. Trudier Harris, "The Trickster in African American Literature," (Teacher Serve: National Humanities Center, 2010), http://nationalhumanitiescenter.org/tserve/freedom/1865-1917/essays/trickster.htm.

13. *Back in the Saddle*, directed by Wes Rubinstein and Mike Ruiz, *Blazing Saddles* (1974) (Burbank, CA: Warner Home Video, 2001), Blu-Ray.

14. Ibid.

15. Harris, "The Trickster in African American Literature."

16. Michael V. Tueth, *Reeling with Laughter: American Film Comedies: From Anarchy to Mockumentary* (Lanham, MD: Scarecrow Press, 2012), 105.

17. Pat Dowell, "The Mythology of the Western: Hollywood Perspectives on Race and Gender in the Nineties," *Cineaste* 21.1/2 (1995): 8.

18. Tueth, *Reeling with Laughter: American Film Comedies: From Anarchy to Mockumentary*, 88.

19. Wes D. Gehring, *Parody as Film Genre: "Never Give a Saga an Even Break"* (Westport, CT: Greenwood Press, 1999), 5.

20. Faulx, "Blazing Saddles, the Best Interracial Buddy Comedy, Turns 40."

21. Charles R. Lawrence III, "If He Hollers Let Him Go: Regulating Racist Speech on Campus," *Words That Wound: Critical Race Theory, Assaultive Speech, and the First Amendment*, eds. Mari J. Matsuda, Charles R. Lawrence III, Richard Delgado, and Kimberlé Williams Crenshaw (Boulder, CO: Westview Press, 1993), 67.

22. Patricia Hill Collins, *Fighting Words: Black Women and the Search for Justice* (Minneapolis: University of Minnesota Press, 1998), 85.

23. Richard Delgado and Jean Stefancic, eds., *The Derrick Bell Reader* (New York: New York University Press, 2005), 35.

24. Ibid., 36–37.

25. Ronald Takaki, *A Different Mirror: A History of Multicultural America* (Boston: Back Bay Books, 2008), 150.

26. Ibid.

27. Bogle, *Toms, Coons, Mulattoes, Mammies & Bucks*, 13–14.

28. Lawrence, *Blaxploitation Films of the 1970s: Blackness and Genre*, 20.

29. A. Van Jordan, "Blazing Saddles," *Virginia Quarterly Review* 88, no. 2 (2012): 198.

30. Gehring, *Parody as Film Genre*.

31. John G. Cawelti, "The Gunfighter and the Hard-Boiled Dick: Some Ruminations on American Fantasies of Heroism," *American Studies* 16, no. 2 (1975).

32. Frederick Jackson Turner,

Rereading Frederick Jackson Turner (New Haven, CT: Yale University Press, 1998), 32.

33. Kareem Abdul-Jabbar and Alan Steinberg, Black Profiles in Courage: A Legacy of African-American Achievement (New York: William Morrow, 1996), 120.

34. Brian W. Dippie, "The Winning of the West Reconsidered," Wilson Quarterly 14, no. 3 (1990): 72.

35. Dowell, "The Mythology of the Western: Hollywood Perspectives on Race and Gender in the Nineties," 6.

36. Back in the Saddle.

37. Ibid.

38. Walter Metz, "From Harlem to Hollywood: The 1970s Renaissance and Blaxploitation," Beyond Blaxploitation, eds. Novotny Lawrence and Gerald Butters (Detroit: Wayne State University Press, 2016), 239.

Chapter 3. *Harlem Nights*, Awkward Framing, and Complicated Gender Politics

1. Roger Ebert, "Harlem Nights" (Review), RogerEbert.com, April 18, 1989, www.rogerebert.com/reviews/harlem-nights-1989.

2. Desson Howe, "Harlem Nights" (Review), Washington Post, November 24, 1989, www.washingtonpost.com/wp-srv/style/longterm/movies/videos/harlemnightshowe.htm.

3. Hal Hinson, "Harlem Nights" (Review), Washington Post, November 17, 1989, www.washingtonpost.com/wp-srv/style/longterm/movies/videos/harlemnights.htm.

4. Susan Stark, "Is This Racist, Sexist Garbage, or Simply Entertainment?" Detroit Free Press, December 1, 1998.

5. "Harlem Nights," RottenTomatoes.com, accessed June 27, 2016, www.rottentomatoes.com/m/harlem_nights/reviews/?type=user.

6. Joel G. Robertson, "FFR—Harlem Nights (1989)," Forgotten Flix Remembers, podcast, September 5, 2015, https://forgottenflix.com/ffr021/.

7. William Kleinknecht, "Murphy Film Canceled After Shooting Wounds 3 Outside Michigan Theater," Austin American-Statesman, November 19, 1989, A7. ProQuest. Web, March 1, 2019. Veronica Wells, "Bet You Didn't Know: Secrets Behind the Making of Harlem Nights," MadameNoire.com, November 26, 2012, madamenoire.com/236653/bet-you-didnt-know-secrets-behind-the-making-of-harlem-nights/.

8. "Violence Darkens the Bright Opening of Eddie Murphy's Plush, Flush Harlem Nights," People, December 4, 1989, www.people.com/people/archive/article/0,,20116112,00.html.

9. Robertson, Forgotten Flix Remembers.

10. In July 2012, there was mass shooting at an Aurora, Colorado, theater during a screening of *The Dark Knight Rises*. Twelve people were killed and seventy people were injured. No mainstream commentators or government officials blamed the film for the violence.

11. Wells, "Bet You Didn't Know: Secrets Behind the Making of Harlem Nights."

12. Racquel J. Gates, Double Negative: The Black Image and Popular Culture (Durham, NC: Duke University Press, 2018), 240.

13. Patricia Hill Collins, Black Sexual Politics: African Americans, Gender, and the New Racism (New York: Routledge, 2004), 166.

14. Ibid., 168.

15. Ed Guerrero, *Framing Blackness: The African American Image in Film* (Philadelphia: Temple University Press, 1993), 126.

16. Martin Brest, director, "Commentary Track," *Beverly Hills Cop* (1984) (Los Angeles: Paramount Home Entertainment, 2002), Blu-Ray.

17. Donald Bogle, *Toms, Coons, Mulattoes, Mammies & Bucks: An Interpretive History of Blacks in American Films*, 4th ed. (New York: Continuum, 2001), 284, 285.

18. Philippa Gates, "Always a Partner in Crime: Black Masculinity in the Hollywood Detective Film," *Journal of Popular Film and Television* 32, no. 1 (2004): 21, https://doi.org/10.3200/JPFT.32.1.20–30.

19. "A Brief History of the DPOA," Detroit Police Officers Association, accessed June 20, 2016, www.detroitpoa.com/dpoa_history.php.

20. I want to thank Melba Joyce Boyd and David Goldberg for their oral history of Detroit, their thoughts on the history of the Detroit Police Department, and their thoughts on *Beverly Hills Cop*.

21. "1984 Domestic Gross," Box OfficeMojo.com, accessed July 22, 2016, www.boxofficemojo.com/yearly/chart/?yr=1984&p=.htm.

22. "Harlem Nights," IMDb.com, accessed March 1, 2019, https://www.imdb.com/title/tt0097481/?ref_=nv_sr_1; "Harlem Nights," The-Numbers.com, accessed July 11, 2016, www.the-numbers.com/movie/Harlem-Nights#tab=summary.

23. "Harlem Nights," BoxOfficeMojo.com, accessed May 16, 2016, www.boxofficemojo.com/movies/?id=harlemnights.htm; Ibid.

24. "*Harlem Nights* Beats the Daylights Out of Rivals," *Globe and Mail*, November 22, 1989, ProQuest; "*Harlem Nights* Near Record of Fall Box Office Openings," *Ottawa (Ontario) Citizen*, November 22, 1989, ProQuest.

25. Robertson, *Forgotten Flix Remembers*.

26. Ebert, "Harlem Nights" (Review).

27. Vincent Canby, "Review/Film; Of Murphy, By Murphy, And Starring . . . Murphy," *New York Times*, November 17, 1989, www.nytimes.com/movie/review?res=950DE7D7133DF934A25752C1A96F948260.

28. William Thomas, "*Harlem Nights* Review," *Empire*, October 14, 2015, www.empireonline.com/movies/harlem-nights/review/.

29. Cary D. Wintz, ed. *The Emergence of the Harlem Renaissance* (New York: Garland, 1996), x.

30. Steven Watson, *The Harlem Renaissance: Hub of African-American Culture, 1920–1930*, Circles of the Twentieth Century (New York: Pantheon Books, 1995), 8–9.

31. Timothy Greenfield-Sanders, director, *The Black List: Intimate Portraits of Black America* (New York: HBO, 2008).

32. Wells, "Bet You Didn't Know: Secrets Behind the Making of *Harlem Nights*."

33. Jenkins as a character is arguably the most problematic in the film. Shaw portrays Jenkins as a man with a high-pitched voice and a stutter. The timbre of Jenkins's voice was meant as a nod to Mike Tyson, but the stutter does not have an obvious reference point. Using a disability as a comedic element is the height of ableism. The main characters seem to be laughing with the character when he explains how he's going to win his next fight and Sugar Ray replies that

"It took me awhile but I got it," or when Sugar Ray hails Jenkins a taxi when it's clear that his stutter is impeding his efforts. The antagonists in the film mock Jenkins—such as when Cantone imitates Jenkins's stutter—and overall the portrayal feels mean-spirited as opposed to one that highlights diversity within black communities.

34. Bogle, *Toms, Coons, Mulattoes, Mammies & Bucks*, 318.

35. Collins, *Black Sexual Politics*, 123.

36. Ibid., 125.

37. Eddie Murphy, "Eddie! An Exclusive Interview with Eddie Murphy by Spike Lee," *Spin*, 1990, 34, books.google.com/books?id=hV6_z7r2zQMC&lpg=PA5&lr&pg=PA98#v=onepage&q&f=true.

38. Della Reese, "The Christmas Angel: An Interview with Della Reese," by Jennifer Sikora, 5MinutesForMom.com, November 24, 2012, www.5minutesformom.com/68235/the-christmas-angel-an-interview-with-della-reese/.

39. *Misogynoir* refers to the specific ways that black women are pathologized in popular culture. The term was created by Moya Bailey. The full discussion of the term can be found here: http://moyazb.tumblr.com/post/84048113369/more-on-the-origin-of-misogynoir.

40. Sharon Harley, "'Working for Nothing but for a Living': Black Women in the Underground Economy," in *Sister Circle: Black Women and Work*, ed. Sharon Harley and the Black Women and Work Collective (New Brunswick, NJ: Rutgers University Press, 2002), 51–52.

41. bell hooks and Isaac Julien, "States of Desire," *Transition* 53 (1991): 178.

42. Kamala Kempadoo, "Women of Color and the Global Sex Trade: Transnational Feminist Perspectives," *Meridians* 1, no. 2 (Spring 2001): 40.

43. Harley, "'Working for Nothing but for a Living': Black Women in the Underground Economy."

44. Kempadoo, "Women of Color and the Global Sex Trade: Transnational Feminist Perspectives," 44.

45. Stark, "Is This Racist, Sexist Garbage, or Simply Entertainment?"

46. Harley, "'Working for Nothing but for a Living': Black Women in the Underground Economy," 51.

Chapter 4. Who's the Real Gangsta?: *The Glass Shield* and the Politics of Black Communities and Police Relations

1. "About Black Lives Matter," Black Lives Matter, accessed March 4, 2019, blacklivesmatter.com/about/.

2. Ibid.

3. Alex Altman, "Person of the Year: The Short List No. 4: Black Lives Matter," *Time*, December 10, 2015, time.com/time-person-of-the-year-2015-runner-up-black-lives-matter/?iid=toc_121015.

4. Robert E Kapsis, *Charles Burnett: Interviews* (Jackson: University Press of Mississippi, 2011), 123.

5. Cliff Thompson, "The Devil Beats His Wife: Small Moments and Big Statements in the Films of Charles Burnett," *Cineaste* 23, no. 2 (1997), www.jstor.org/stable/41689017.

6. Nicole Smith Futrell, "Vulnerable, Not Voiceless: Outsider Narrative in Advocacy Against Discriminatory Policing," *North Carolina Law Review* 93, no. 5 (June 2015): 1599.

7. Racquel J. Gates, *Double Negative: The Black Image and Popular Culture* (Durham, NC: Duke University Press, 2018), 84.

8. Katharine Bausch, "Superflies Into Superkillers: Black Masculinity in Film from Blaxploitation to New Black Realism," *Journal of Popular Culture* 46, no. 2 (2013): 267.

9. Justin P. Brooks, "Will Boys Just be *Boyz n the Hood*—African American Directors Portray a Crumbling Justice System in Urban America," *Oklahoma City University Law Review* 22, no. 1 (1997): 4; Grant Farred, "*Menace II Society*: No Way Out for the Boys in the Hood," *Michigan Quarterly Review* 35, no. 3 (1995): 476, hdl.handle.net/2027/spo.act2080.0035.003:13.

10. Mark A. Reid, *Black Lenses, Black Voices: African American Film Now* (Lanham, MD: Rowman & Littlefield, 2005), 56.

11. Shawn Cohen and Bob Fredericks, "NYPD as Diverse as New York City Itself: Study," *New York Post*, September 8, 2014, nypost.com/2014/09/08/nypd-is-as-diverse-as-new-york-city-itself/.

12. Futrell, "Vulnerable, Not Voiceless: Outsider Narrative in Advocacy Against Discriminatory Policing," 1601.

13. Jeremy Ashkenas and Haeyoun Park, "The Race Gap in America's Police Departments," *New York Times*, April 8, 2015, www.nytimes.com/interactive/2014/09/03/us/the-race-gap-in-americas-police-departments.html.

14. Paul Butler, "Stop and Frisk and Torture-Lite: Police Terror of Minority Communities," *Ohio State Journal of Criminal Law* 12, no. 57 (2014–2015): 68.

15. Eduardo Bonilla-Silva, *White Supremacy and Racism in the Post-Civil Rights Era* (Boulder, CO: Lynne Rienner, 2001), 108.

16. Paula Massood, "Film Reviews: Menace II Society," *Cineaste* 20, no. 2 (1993): 44.

17. According to IMDb.com, *New Jack City* had an estimated budget of $8.5 million and grossed approximately $47 million; *Boyz n the Hood* had an estimated budget of $6 million and grossed $57 million; *Menace II Society* had an estimated budget of $3.5 million and grossed $27.9 million; *Set It Off* had an estimated budget of $9 million and grossed $36 million; and *Juice* had an estimated budget of $5 million and grossed $20 million.

18. Kenneth Chan, "The Construction of Black Male Identity in Black Action Films of the Nineties," *Cinema Journal* 37, no. 2 (1998): 35–36.

19. Kapsis, *Charles Burnett: Interviews*, 101.

20. Radley Balko, "Mass Shooting Hysteria and the Death of John Crawford," *Washington Post*, September 25, 2014, www.washingtonpost.com/news/the-watch/wp/2014/09/25/mass-shooting-hysteria-and-the-death-of-john-crawford/.

21. Ibid.

22. Judd Legum, "Everything the Police Said About Walter Scott's Death Before a Video Showed What Really Happened," April 8, 2015, thinkprogress.org/justice/2015/04/07/3644189/everything-police-said-walter-scotts-death-video-showed-really-happened/.

23. Ibid.

24. Brandon Ellington Patterson, "10 Things You Should Know About the Killing of Laquan McDonald by Police," *Mother Jones*, December 1, 2015, www.motherjones.com/politics/2015/11/laquan-mcdonald-chicago-police-shooting-video-explainer.

25. Jay Hathaway, "Video of Sam DuBose's Death Drastically Different From the Police Report," *Gawker.com*, July 29,

2015, gawker.com/video-of-sam-du boses-death-drastically-different-from-t-1720896658.

26. Julia Simon-Kerr, "Systemic Lying," *William & Mary Law Review* 56, no. 6 (2015): 2178.

27. Joseph Goldstein, "'Testilying' by Police: A Stubborn Problem," *New York Times*, March 18, 2018, www.nytimes.com/2018/03/18/nyregion/testilying-police-perjury-new-york.html.

28. Futrell, "Vulnerable, Not Voiceless: Outsider Narrative in Advocacy Against Discriminatory Policing," 1599.

29. Hari Ziyad, "Empathy Won't Save Us In the Fight Against Oppression. Here's Why," BlackGirlDangerous.org, August 11, 2015, www.blackgirldangerous.org/2015/08/empathy-wont-save-us-in-the-fight-against-oppression-heres-why/.

30. Futrell, "Vulnerable, Not Voiceless: Outsider Narrative in Advocacy Against Discriminatory Policing," 1627.

31. Chan, "The Construction of Black Male Identity in Black Action Films of the Nineties," 35–36.

32. Celeste A. Fisher, *Black on Black: Urban Youth Films and the Multicultural Audience* (Lanham, MD: Scarecrow Press, 2006), xiv.

33. "*The Glass Shield*" (1994), IMDb.com, accessed December 13, 2015, www.imdb.com/title/tt0109906/?ref_=rvi_tt.

34. Gene Siskel and Roger Ebert, "Congo, The Glass Shield, Pocahontas, Fluke" (Review), SiskelEbert.org, December 13, 1995, https://siskelebert.org/?p=3485.

35. Jonathan Rosenbaum, "The World According to Harvey and Bob," *Chicago Reader*, June 16, 1995, www.jonathanrosenbaum.net/1995/06/the-world-according-to-harvey-and-bob/; Kapsis, *Charles Burnett: Interviews*, xx.

36. Siskel and Ebert, "Congo, The Glass Shield, Pocahontas, Fluke" (Review).

37. "Weekend Box Office June 2–4, 1995," BoxOfficeMojo.com, https://www.boxofficemojo.com/weekend/chart/?yr=1995&wknd=22&p=.htm.

38. Ibid.

39. Charles Burnett, "Charles Burnett: The Glass Shield Q&A at Lincoln Center 9/10/2016," Reelblack, September 14, 2016, www.youtube.com/watch?v=v2E9eLQ1KJE.

Chapter 5. "If You're Going to Tell People the Truth ... Make Them Laugh": *C.S.A.: The Confederate States of America* **as Mockumentary and Truth-Telling**

1. The phrase *history prime* is derived from the television series *Sliders*, which aired on Fox and the science fiction channel SyFy from 1995 to 2000. The series followed a group of people who traveled to different parallel universes where history had been altered in some way: in one world the Soviet Union won the Cold War; in another, dinosaurs still roamed; in yet another, World War II did not occur. The Earth where the travelers originated from is referred to as Earth Prime.

2. Kevin Willmott, "Playing with History: A *Black Camera* Interview with Kevin Willmott," by Derrais Carter, *Black Camera, an International Film Journal* 6, no. 2 (Spring 2015): 46.

3. Ibid.

4. Mick LaSalle, "What If the South Had Won the Civil War?" SFGate.com (*San Francisco Chronicle*), February 24, 2006, www.sfgate.com/movies/article

/What-if-the-South-had-won-the-Civil-War-2503771.php.

5. Ann Hornaday, "C.S.A.: A Bitter State of the Union" (Review), *Washington Post*, March 31, 2006, www.washingtonpost.com/wp-dyn/content/article/2006/03/30/AR2006033000818.html.

6. Cynthia Fuchs, "*C.S.A.: Confederate States of America (2004)*" (Review), *Pop Matters.com*, March 30, 2006, www.popmatters.com/review/csa_confederate_states_of_america_2004/.

7. Esther Iverem, *We Gotta Have It: Twenty Years of Seeing Black at the Movies, 1986–2006* (New York: Thunder's Mouth Press, 2007), 564.

8. Ty Burr, "'CSA' raises real questions with a bogus documentary," *Boston Globe* (Boston.com), February 24, 2006, www.boston.com/ae/movies/articles/2006/02/24/csa_raises_real_questions_with_a_bogus_documentary/.

9. Hilary Lewis, "NYC's Dalton School Apologizes for Showing Movie Satirizing Slavery," *Hollywood Reporter*, January 31, 2014, www.hollywoodreporter.com/news/nycs-dalton-school-apologizes-showing-676218.

10. Ward Moore, "Bring the Jubilee," in *The Best Alternate History Stories of the 20th Century*, eds. Harry Turtledove and Martin H. Greenberg (New York: Del Rey/Ballantine, 2001), 165.

11. Ibid., 172.

12. MacKinlay Kantor, *If the South Had Won the Civil War* (New York: Tom Doherty Associates, 1960), 88, 89.

13. Ibid., 93.

14. Harry Turtledove, *How Few Remain* (New York: Ballantine Books, 1997), 14.

15. Winston Churchill, "If Lee Had Not Won the Battle of Gettysburg," *Wisconsin Magazine of History* 44, no. 4 (Summer 1961): 244.

16. Ibid., 245.

17. Ibid., 251.

18. Roxane Gay, "I Don't Want to Watch Slavery Fan Fiction," *New York Times*, July 25, 2017, www.nytimes.com/2017/07/25/opinion/hbo-confederate-slavery-civil-war.html.

19. Ta Nehisi-Coates, "The Lost Cause Rides Again," *The Atlantic*, August 4, 2017, www.theatlantic.com/entertainment/archive/2017/08/no-confederate/535512/.

20. Alexandra Juhasz and Jesse Lerner, eds., *F Is for Phony: Fake Documentary and Truth's Undoing* (Minneapolis: University of Minnesota Press, 2006), 2.

21. Cynthia J. Miller, *Too Bold for the Box Office: the Mockumentary from Big Screen to Small* (Lanham, MD: Scarecrow Press, 2012), 9.

22. Thomas Doherty, "The Sincerest Form of Flattery: A Brief History of the Mockumentary," *Cineaste* 28, no. 4 (Fall 2003): 22.

23. Malcolm Gladwell, "Malcolm Gladwell on Pioneers, Tokens, and 'The Satire Paradox,'" interview by Larry Wilmore, *Larry Wilmore Black on the Air*, July 20, 2017, podcast, 1:06:27, https://www.theringer.com/2017/7/20/16077718/malcolm-gladwell-larry-wilmore-golf-black-on-the-air-podcast-d10d7b45a79c.

24. Thomas Prasch, "Between What Is and What If: Kevin Willmott's CSA," in *Too Bold for the Box Office: The Mockumentary from Big Screen to Small*, ed. Cynthia J. Miller (Lanham, MD: Scarecrow Press, 2012), 191.

25. Lewis MacLeod, "'A Documentary-Style Film': Borat and the Fiction/Nonfiction Question," *Narrative* 19, no. 1 (January 2011): 115.

26. Derrick Bell, *Faces at the Bottom of*

the Well: The Permanence of Racism (New York: Basic Books, 1992) ix.

27. Derrick Bell, "Who's Afraid of Critical Race Theory?" University of Illinois Law Review 1995, no. 4 (1995): 899.

28. Bell, Faces at the Bottom of the Well, 194.

29. Jerome McCristal Culp Jr., "The Michael Jackson Pill: Equality, Race, and Culture," Michigan Law Review 92, no. 8 (August 1994): 438–439.

30. Kevin Willmott and Rick Cowen, "CSA: The Confederate States of America" (Transcript), by Greg Allen, Day to Day, NPR, October 28, 2005, www.npr.org/templates/story/story.php?storyId=4979746.

31. James M. McPherson, Battle Cry of Freedom: The Civil War Era, ed. C. Vann Woodward, the Oxford History of the United States (New York: Oxford University Press, 1988), 387.

32. Ibid.

33. Ken Burns, director, "Forever Free" (Episode 3), The Civil War, PBS, September 24, 1990.

34. Robert E. May, The Southern Dream of a Caribbean Empire 1854–1861 (Baton Rouge: Louisiana State University Press, 1973), 10–11.

35. Ibid., 229.

36. Frank Lawrence Owsley, King Cotton Diplomacy: Foreign Relations of the Confederate States of America, 2nd ed. (Chicago: University of Chicago Press, 1931), 104.

37. Willmott and Cowen, interview.

38. Donald Bogle, Prime Time Blues: African Americans on Network Television (New York: Farrar, Straus and Giroux, 2001), 22.

39. Whitney Barkley, "How For-Profit Colleges Rip Off Students," CNN, October 31, 2014, www.cnn.com/2014/08/28/opinion/barkley-corinthian-for-profit-colleges/index.html.

40. Samuel A. Cartwright, "Diseases and Peculiarities of the Negro Race," De Bow's Review (New Orleans, 1851), retrieved from Africans in America, PBS, www.pbs.org/wgbh/aia/part4/4h3106t.html.

41. Cornel West, Democracy Matters: Winning the Fight Against Imperialism (New York: Penguin Books, 2004), 6.

42. Manning Marable, The Great Wells of Democracy: The Meaning of Race in American Life (New York: BasicCivitas Books, 2002), 306.

43. Willmott and Cowen, interview.

44. Carter, Derrais, "Playing with History: A Black Camera Interview with Kevin Willmott," 48.

45. Cheryl I. Harris, "Whiteness as Property," Harvard Law Review 106, no. 8 (June 1993): 1744.

46. Ibid., 1713.

47. Ibid., 1712.

48. Donald Bogle, Toms, Coons, Mulattoes, Mammies & Bucks: An Interpretive History of Blacks in American Films, 4th ed. (New York: Continuum, 2001), 9.

49. Nell Irvin Painter, "After the Civil War, Memory Took Time to Desegregate," New York Times, July 2, 2013, www.nytimes.com/roomfordebate/2013/07/02/who-won-the-civil-war/after-the-civil-war-memory-took-time-to-desegregate.

50. Carter, Derrais, "Playing with History: A Black Camera Interview with Kevin Willmott Willmott," 46.

51. Painter, "After the Civil War, Memory Took Time to Desegregate."

Chapter 6. Ladies First: Ava DuVernay and Black-Female-Centered Narratives

1. Rebecca Ford, "Golden Globes: Selma's Ava DuVernay Becomes First Black

Woman to Receive Director Nomination," *Hollywood Reporter*, December 11, 2014, www.hollywoodreporter.com/news/golden-globes-selmas-ava-duvernay-756511.

2. Ava DuVernay, "Selma Director DuVernay Joins 'MHP' for Extensive Interview," by Melissa Harris-Perry, January 13, 2015, www.msnbc.com/melissa-harris-perry/selma-director-duvernay-joins-mhp-extensive-interview.

3. Kathleen Neal Cleaver, "Racism, Civil Rights, and Feminism," in *Critical Race Feminism: A Reader*, ed. Adrien Katherine Wing (New York: New York University Press, 1997), 48.

4. Manthia Diawara, "Black American Cinema: The New Realism," in *Black American Cinema*, ed. Manthia Diawara (New York: Routledge, 1993), 3.

5. Ed Guerrero, *Framing Blackness: The African American Image in Film* (Philadelphia: Temple University Press, 1993), 175.

6. Jacqueline Bobo, *Black Women as Cultural Readers* (New York: Columbia University Press, 1995), 6.

7. Michele Wallace, "Why Women Won't Relate to 'Justice': Losing Her Voice," in *Dark Designs and Visual Culture* (Durham, NC: Duke University Press, 2004), 147.

8. "Black Girls Rock 2015," directed by Joe DeMaio, BET, April 5, 2015, television.

9. Patricia Hill Collins, *Black Feminist Thought: Knowledge, Consciousness, and the Politics of Empowerment*, 10th ed. (New York: Routledge, 2000), 16.

10. Stacy L. Smith et al., *Inequality in 700 Popular Films: Examining Portrayals of Gender, Race & LBGT Status from 2007–2014* (Los Angeles: Annenberg School for Communication and Journalism, University of Southern California, 2015), 20.

11. Yohana Desta, "Ava DuVernay and *Queen Sugar* Look Like the Future of Television," *Vanity Fair*, September 13, 2016, www.vanityfair.com/hollywood/2016/09/ava-duvernay-queen-sugar-interview.

12. Ava Duvernay, "Conversations with Ava DuVernay: A Call to Action: Organizing Principles of an Activist Cinematic Practice," by Michael T. Martin, *Black Camera, an International Film Journal* 6, no. 1 (Fall 2014): 76.

13. Ava DuVernay and MC Lyte, "Female Emcees Say My Mic Sounds Nice," interview by Allison Keyes, NPR News, August 30, 2010, www.npr.org/template/story/story.php?storyId=129530573.

14. Ava DuVernay, "Q&A: Director Ava Marie DuVernay on Her Glam New Video for Miu Miu," by Araceli Cruz, *Rolling Stone*, February 8, 2013, www.rollingstone.com/culture/news/q-a-director-ava-marie-duvernay-on-her-glam-new-video-for-miu-miu-20130208.

15. Julee Wilson, "Miu Miu Debuts Stunning New Short Film 'The Door' Starring Gabrielle Union and Alfre Woodard (VIDEO)," *HuffingtonPost.com*, February 11, 2013, www.huffingtonpost.com/2013/02/11/gabrielle-union-miu-miu-the-door_n_2664312.html.

16. Frank Hagler, "Kerry Washington's *Vanity Fair* Cover Is Smokin'—But White People Still Might Not Notice It," *Mic.com*, August 14, 2013, mic.com/articles/59293/kerry-washington-s-vanity-fair-cover-is-smokin-but-white-people-still-might-not-notice-it.

17. Duvernay, "Conversations with Ava DuVernay: A Call to Action:

Organizing Principles of an Activist Cinematic Practice," 65.

18. Veronica Wells, "Simply Beautiful: Ava DuVernay & Fashion Fair Create Short Film 'Say Yes,'" MadameNoire.com, August 15 2013, madamenoire.com/291382/simply-beautiful-ava-duvernay-fashion-fair-create-short-film-say-yes/.

19. ESPN Films: 30 for 30, ESPN, accessed March 29, 2015, espn.go.com/30for30/.

20. "Title IX of the Education Amendments of 1972," The United States Department of Justice, updated December 31, 2014, www.justice.gov/crt/about/cor/coord/titleix.php.

21. "Nine for IX: *Venus Vs.*," ESPNW, June 26, 2013, espn.go.com/espnw/w-in-action/nine-for-ix/article/8948839/nine-ix-film-summary-director-venus-vs.

22. "Prize Money and Finance," Wimbledon.com, 2014, accessed March 31, 2015, https://www.wimbledon.com/en_GB/aboutwimbledon/prize_money_and_finance.html.

23. Bethonie Butler, "Why Ava DuVernay Hired Only Female Directors for Her New TV Show *Queen Sugar*," *Washington Post*, September 15, 2016, www.washingtonpost.com/news/arts-and-entertainment/wp/2016/09/15/why-ava-duvernay-hired-only-female-directors-for-her-new-tv-show-queen-sugar/.

24. Roger Ebert, "*I Will Follow*" (Review), RogerEbert.com, March 8, 2011, www.rogerebert.com/reviews/i-will-follow-2011.

25. Tambay A. Obenson, "DVD Review—*I Will Follow* (A Deeply Personal, Reflective Chamber Drama) + Interviews Galore," *IndieWire.com*, August 23, 2011, https://www.indiewire.com/2011/08/dvd-review-i-will-follow-a-deeply-personal-reflective-chamber-drama-interviews-galore.

26. Rick Groen, "*Middle of Nowhere* Is a Taut Study of a Woman Marooned" (Review), *Globe and Mail*, February 8, 2013, www.theglobeandmail.com/arts/film/film-reviews/middle-of-nowhere-is-a-taut-study-of-a-woman-marooned/article8341882/.

27. Peter Howell, "*Middle of Nowhere*" Review: The Ring that Binds, the Bars that Divide," *Toronto Star*, February 7, 2013, www.thestar.com/entertainment/movies/2013/02/07/middle_of_nowhere_review_the_ring_that_binds_the_bars_that_divide.html.

28. "Sundance 2012: Ava DuVernay Becomes First Black Woman to Win Best Director Prize for *Middle of Nowhere* (Video)," "Black Voices," *HuffingtonPost.com*, January 30, 2012, updated March 31, 2012, www.huffingtonpost.com/2012/01/30/ava-duvernay-sundance_n_1241286.html.

29. "Filmmaker Interview: Ava DuVernay Talks About *I Will Follow*," Film Independent.org, updated August 23, 2011, accessed September 14, 2014.

30. Ebert, "*I Will Follow*."

31. "Filmmaker Interview: Ava DuVernay Talks About *I Will Follow*."

32. Ava DuVernay and Emayatzy Corinealdi, "Commentary Track," *Middle of Nowhere* (2012) (Santa Monica, CA: Lionsgate Home Entertainment, 2015), DVD.

33. Ava DuVernay, "Four Questions with *Middle of Nowhere* Director Ava DuVernay," by Dan Schoenbrun, *Filmmaker*, January 23, 2012, filmmakermagazine.com/38617-four-questions-with-middle-of-nowhere-director-ava-duvernay/.

34. Insight Center for Community Economic Development, "Lifting as We

Climb: Women of Color, Wealth, and America's Future" (Oakland, CA: 2010), 3, http://ww1.insightcced.org/uploads/CRWG/LiftingAsWeClimb-Women Wealth-Report-InsightCenter-Spring 2010.pdf.

35. Grace Kiser, "Study: Single Women of Color Age 36–49 Have Median Wealth of Just $5," HuffingtonPost.com, April 6, 2010, www.huffingtonpost.com/2010/03/11/women-of-color-have-media_n_495238.html.

36. Collins, Black Feminist Thought, 69.

37. Charlene Regester, African American Actresses: The Struggle for Visibility, 1900–1960 (Bloomington: Indiana University Press, 2010), 2.

38. Melissa V. Harris-Perry, Sister Citizen: Shame, Stereotypes, and Black Women in America (New Haven, CT: Yale University Press), Kindle edition, 78.

39. Ibid., 87.
40. Ibid., 54.
41. Ibid., 184.
42. Ibid., 185.

43. Martin, "Conversations with Ava DuVernay: A Call to Action: Organizing Principles of an Activist Cinematic Practice," 74.

44. Tambay A. Obenson, "LAFF 2012 Review—Middle of Nowhere (aka 'Nothing But a Woman')," IndieWire.com, June 21, 2014, https://www.indiewire.com/2012/06/laff-2012–review-middle-of-nowhere-aka-nothing-but-a-woman-144611/.

45. Derrick Bell, "The Sexual Diversion: The Black Man/Black Woman Debate in Context," in Black Men on Race, Gender & Sexuality: A Critical Reader, ed. Devon Carbado (New York: New York University Press), 243–244.

46. DuVernay, "Conversations with Ava DuVernay: A Call to Action: Organizing Principles of an Activist Cinematic Practice," 81.

47. DuVernay and Corinealdi, interview.

48. Office of Policy Planning and Research, United States Department of Labor, "The Negro Family: The Case For National Action," by Daniel Patrick Moynihan, March 1965, https://www.dol.gov/general/aboutdol/history/webid-moynihan.

49. Ava DuVernay, "Middle of Nowhere Live Tweet" (Twitter, August 2, 2014).

50. Harris-Perry, Sister Citizen: Shame, Stereotypes, and Black Women in America, 3–4.

Chapter 7. Who's the Hero of the Piece?: Hollywood's Representation of Jackie Robinson's Legacy

1. Jules Tygiel, "The Great Experiment Fifty Years Later," in The Cooperstown Symposium on Baseball and American Culture, ed. Peter M. Rutkoff (Jefferson, NC: McFarland, 1997), 257.

2. There is a fourth film, entitled Soul of the Game, that aired on HBO in 1996 and starred Delroy Lindo as Satchel Paige, Mykelti Williamson as Josh Gibson, and Blair Underwood as Jackie Robinson. The film is not about Robinson per se as much as it is about the eve of professional baseball's reintegration. A discussion of how Soul of the Game frames race and racism can be found in Lisa Doris Alexander, "But They Don't Want to Play with the White Players, Right?: Depictions of Segregation and Negro League Baseball in Contemporary Popular Film," Black Ball 5, no. 2 (2012): 19–34.

3. Rob Edelman, "The Jackie Robinson

Story: A Reflection of Its Era," NINE: A Journal of Baseball History and Culture 20, no. 1 (Fall 2011): 41.

4. Donald Bogle, Toms, Coons, Mulattoes, Mammies & Bucks: An Interpretive History of Blacks in American Films, 4th ed. (New York: Continuum, 2001), 195.

5. Jaime Schultz, "Glory Road (2006) and the White Savior Historical Sport Film," Journal of Popular Film and Television 42, no. 4 (December 2014): 208, https://doi.org/10.1080/01956051.2014.913001.

6. Alessandra Raengo, "A Necessary Signifier: The Adaptation of Robinson's Body-Image in The Jackie Robinson Story," Adaptation 1, no. 2 (September 2008): 92, https://doi.org/10.1093/adaptation/apn019.

7. Aaron Baker, "Sports Films, History, and Identity," Journal of Sport History 25, no. 2 (Summer 1998): 225.

8. "'You Are the Un-Americans, and You Ought to Be Ashamed of Yourselves': Paul Robeson Appears Before HUAC," June 12, 1956, "History Matters," American Social History Project/Center for Media and Learning (Graduate Center, CUNY) and the Roy Rosenzweig Center for History and New Media (George Mason University), accessed August 4, 2008, http://historymatters.gmu.edu/d/6440.

9. United States House of Representatives Committee on Un-American Activities, "Hearings Regarding Communist Infiltration of Minority Groups—Part 1 (1949)," https://babel.hathitrust.org/cgi/pt?id=umn.31951d034965007;view=1up;seq=3, 481.

10. Angela Y. Davis, Blues Legacies and Black Feminism: Gertrude 'Ma' Rainey, Bessie Smith, and Billie Holiday (New York: Pantheon Books, 1998), 182.

11. Peter Dreier, "The Real Story of Baseball's Integration That You Won't See in 42," The Atlantic, April 11, 2013, http://www.theatlantic.com/entertainment/archive/2013/04/the-real-story-of-baseballs-integration-that-you-wont-see-in-i-42–i/274886/.

12. Jackie Robinson, I Never Had It Made (New York: Putnam, 1972), 22.

13. Arnold Rampersad, Jackie Robinson: A Biography (New York: Alfred A. Knopf, 1997), 104.

14. Ibid.

15. Ibid., 225.

16. Donald Simpson, "Black Images in Film—the 1940s to the Early 1960s," Black Scholar 21, no. 2 (March–April–May 1990): 25; Doug Battema, "Jackie Robinson as Media's Mythological Black Hero," in The Cooperstown Symposium on Baseball and American Culture, ed. Peter M. Rutkoff (Jefferson, NC: McFarland, 1997), 207.

17. Viveca Greene and Chris Tinson, "Do the Right Thing: Still a Racial Rorschach at 20," The Nation, August 18, 2009, http://www.thenation.com/article/do-right-thing-still-racial-rorschach-20.

18. Montgomery Brower, "The Racial Murder of Yusef Hawkins Inflamed New York City, Forcing His Parents to Relive Their Anguish," People, June 4, 1990, http://www.people.com/people/archive/article/0,,20117855,00.html.

19. Mike Downey, "The Jackie Robinson Biopic and Me," CNN, updated April 9, 2013, http://www.cnn.com/2013/04/09/opinion/downey-jackie-robinson/.

20. Daniel Fienberg, "Spike Lee Doesn't Regret Lost Jackie Robinson Opportunity," Screener, July 11, 2008, http://screenertv.com/news-features/spike-lee-doesnt-regret-lost-jackie-robinson-opportunity/.

21. Ethan Anderton, "Robert Redford's Branch Rickey and Jackie Robinson Film Returns," FirstShowing.net, April 6, 2011, http://www.firstshowing.net/2011/robert-redfords-branch-rickey-and-jackie-robinson-film-returns/.

22. "42 (2013)."

23. Mark Kermode, "42—Review," The Guardian, September 14, 2013, http://www.theguardian.com/film/2013/sep/15/42-jackie-robinson-film-review/print.

24. Richard Roeper, "42" (Review), RogerEbert.com, April 11, 2013, http://www.rogerebert.com/reviews/42-2013; Scott Foundas, "Film Review: 42," Variety, April 9, 2013, http://variety.com/2013/film/reviews/film-review-42-1200339020/.

25. A. O. Scott, "That Rookie at First Is in a New Position," New York Times, April 11, 2013, http://www.nytimes.com/2013/04/12/movies/42–with-chadwick-boseman-as-jackie-robinson.html; Wesley Morris, "The Problem with Saints," Grantland.com, April 11, 2013, http://grantland.com/features/the-limp-42–excellent-trance/.

26. Dreier, "The Real Story of Baseball's Integration That You Won't See in 42."

27. Rampersad, Jackie Robinson: A Biography, 119; Jackie Robinson, directed by Ken Burns, Sarah Burns, and David McMahon, PBS, 2016.

28. Howard Bryant, "Righting the Wrongs of 42," ESPN, April 24, 2013, http://espn.go.com/mlb/story/_/id/9207998/42–gets-some-jackie-robinson-history-wrong-starts-conversation.

29. Ta-Nehisi Coates, "Fear of a Black President," The Atlantic, September 2012, http://www.theatlantic.com/magazine/archive/2012/09/fear-of-a-black-president/309064/.

30. "2013 Yearly Box Office," Box OfficeMojo.com, accessed May 3, 2015, http://www.boxofficemojo.com/yearly/chart/?yr=2013&p=.htm.

31. Matthew W. Hughey, The White Savior Film: Content, Critics, and Consumption (Philadelphia: Temple University Press, 2014), 15.

32. Matthew W. Hughey, "Racializing Redemption, Reproducing Racism: The Odyssey of Magical Negroes and White Saviors," Sociology Compass 6, no. 9 (2012): 762, https://doi.org/10.1111/j.1751-9020.2012.00486.x.

33. Derrick Bell, "Wanted: A White Leader Able to Free Whites," U.C. Davis Law Review 33, no. 3 (Spring 2000): 541, 538.

34. John Carlos and Dave Zirin, The John Carlos Story (Chicago: Haymarket Books, 2011), 85; Stuart L. Weiss, The Curt Flood Story: The Man Behind the Myth (Columbia: University of Missouri Press, 2007), 185.

35. Dave Zirin, "A Review of 42: Jackie Robinson's Bitter Pill," The Nation, April 17, 2013, http://www.thenation.com/blog/173905/review-42–jackie-robinsons-bitter-pill.

36. Rampersad, Jackie Robinson: A Biography, 435.

37. Robinson, I Never Had It Made, 266.

Chapter 8. Are We Allowed to Be Children?: Black Teen Films, Trauma, and the Race to Adulthood

1. Stacey Patton, "In America, Black Children Don't Get to Be Children," Washington Post, November 26, 2014, www.washingtonpost.com/opinions/in-america-black-children-dont-get-to-be-children/2014/11/26/a9e24756

-74ee-11e4-a755-e32227229e7b_story.html.

2. bell hooks and Melissa Harris-Perry, "Black Female Voices: Who's Listening—A Public Dialogue Between bell hooks + Melissa Harris-Perry," The New School, November 11, 2013, https://www.youtube.com/watch?v=5OmgqXaoIng.

3. Kat Chow, "What's So 'Cringeworthy' About Long Duk Dong in *Sixteen Candles?*," NPR, February 6, 2015, www.npr.org/sections/codeswitch/2015/02/06/384307677/whats-so-cringe-worthy-about-long-duk-dong-in-sixteen-candles.

4. Reginald and Warrington Hudlin, "Tearing the Roof Off the Sucker: An Interview with Reginald and Warrington Hudlin," by Michael Kantor *Cineaste* 18, no. 1 (1990): 2.

5. Aisha Harris and Dan Kois, "The Black Film Canon," Slate.com, May 30, 2016, www.slate.com/articles/arts/cover_story/2016/05/the_50_greatest_films_by_black_directors.html.

6. Roger Ebert, "*House Party*" (Review), RogerEbert.com, August 22, 1990, www.rogerebert.com/reviews/house-party-1990.

7. Owen Gleiberman, "*House Party*," *Entertainment Weekly*, March 9, 1990, www.ew.com/article/1990/03/09/house-party; Desson Howe, "*House Party*," *Washington Post*, March 9, 1990, www.washingtonpost.com/wp-srv/style/longterm/movies/videos/housepartyrhowe_a0b25b.htm.

8. Bruce Alfred, "*House Party*," *Cineaste* 18, no. 1 (1990).

9. "*House Party* (1990)," IMDb.com, accessed September 5, 2016, www.imdb.com/title/tt0099800/?ref_=nv_sr_1.

10. Matt Barone, "Commentary: You're Remembering *House Party* All Wrong," BET, March 9, 2015, www.bet.com/news/celebrities/2015/03/09/commentary-you-re-remembering-house-party-all-wrong.html.

11. Elizabeth Rhodes, "*House Party* Forever! Christopher "Play" Martin and Bun B Explain Why Classic Hip Hop Movie Endures," CultureMap.com (Houston), November 13, 2015, houston.culturemap.com/news/arts/11-13-15-ihouse-partyi-forever-christopher-play-martin-and-bun-b-explain-why-classic-hip-hop-movie-endures/#slide=0; Emily Tan, "Kid 'n Play to Showcase *House Party* Battle and Break Down 'Invisible Walls' at Everything Is Festival," The Boombox.com, May 27, 2015, theboombox.com/kid-n-play-every thing-is-festival-interview/; Tambay A. Obenson, "Hey NYC! 25th Anniversary Screening of '*House Party*' Followed by Discussion w/ Cast & Crew, Next Week!," *IndieWire.com*, June 18, 2015, www.indiewire.com/2015/06/hey-nyc-25th-anniversary-screening-of-house-party-followed-by-discussion-w-cast-crew-next-week-153708/; "Celebrating 25 Years of Cult Classic *House Party*," "Young Voices," *The Voice*, July 9, 2015, www.voice-online.co.uk/article/celebrating-25-years-cult-classic-house-party.

12. In the film credits and on the film's IMDb page, the officers are simply credited as Cop #1 and Cop #2. In the scene where the officers confront Pop, he identifies the cops as Officers Boyd and Wanarski. Because they are not officially listed by those names and the film is not closed-captioned, I must approximate the spelling.

13. Nicole Smith Futrell, "Vulnerable, Not Voiceless: Outsider Narrative in Advocacy Against Discriminatory

Policing," *North Carolina Law Review* 93, no. 5 (June 2015): 1627.

14. Hudlin, "Tearing the Roof Off the Sucker: An Interview with Reginald and Warrington Hudlin."

15. David Berri, "Here's What It Will Take for Women's Sports to Grow in the U.S.," *Time*, July 6, 2015, time.com/3945762/world-cup-womens-sports/.

16. Jessica Learish, "Why Are the Olympic Games the Only Time We Pay Attention to Female Athletes?," *Bustle.com*, August 20, 2016, www.bustle.com/articles/177814–why-are-the-olympic-games-the-only-time-we-pay-attention-to-female-athletes.

17. Berri, "Here's What It Will Take for Women's Sports to Grow in the U.S."

18. Kelley L. Carter, "How *Love & Basketball* Changed the Way Black Audiences Saw Themselves Onscreen," *BuzzFeed.com*, May 17, 2015, www.buzzfeed.com/kelleycarter/how-love-basketball-changed-the-way-we-see-black-romance-on.

19. Jessica Zack, "*Pariah* Director Dee Rees Confronts Disapproval," SFGate.com (*San Francisco Chronicle*, December 25, 2011, www.sfgate.com/movies/article/Pariah-director-Dee-Rees-confronts-disapproval-2420456.php.

20. Anupa Mistry, "Why Aren't There More Movies Like *Love & Basketball*?," *Vulture.com*, October 22, 2014, www.vulture.com/2014/10/love-and-basketball-appreciation.html.

21. Lucy McCalmont, "Double or Nothing: An Oral History of *Love & Basketball*," *HuffingtonPost.com*, June 16, 2015, www.huffingtonpost.com/2015/06/16/love-and-basketball-oral-history-n_7572140.html.

22. Ibid.

23. See Kirby Dick's 2006 documentary *This Film Is Not Yet Rated* for an in-depth history and discussion of the issue.

24. McCalmont, "Double or Nothing: An Oral History of *Love & Basketball*."

25. Adam Serwer, "Film Review: *Pariah* and the Untold Stories in Black Cinema," *Mother Jones*, December 28, 2011, www.motherjones.com/mixed-media/2011/12/film-review-pariah.

26. Zack, "*Pariah* Director Dee Rees Confronts Disapproval."

27. Ashley Clark, "Burning Down the House: Why the Debate Over *Paris Is Burning* Rages On," *The Guardian*, June 24, 2015, www.theguardian.com/film/2015/jun/24/burning-down-the-house-debate-paris-is-burning.

28. bell hooks, *Reel to Real: Race, Sex, and Class at the Movies* (New York: Routledge, 1996), 218.

29. Bradford Young, "The Visual Aesthetic of *Pariah*—an Interview w/ Cinematographer Bradford Young," by Nijla Mumin, *IndieWire.com*, August 17, 2015, https://www.indiewire.com/2015/08/the-visual-aesthetic-of-pariah-an-interview-w-cinematographer-bradford-young-151844/.

30. A. O. Scott, "*Moonlight*: Is This the Year's Best Movie?" (Review), *New York Times*, October 20, 2016, www.nytimes.com/2016/10/21/movies/moonlight-review.html.

31. Edward Wyckoff Williams, "Black Parents, Gay Sons and Redefining Masculinity," *TheRoot.com*, June 16, 2014, www.theroot.com/articles/culture/2014/06/being_gay_isn_t_the_antithesis_of_becoming_a_strong_black_man/.

32. Ibid.

33. David Leonard, "Refusing Invisibility: *Pariah* Challenges Social and Religious Norms," *UrbanCusp.com*, January 9,

2012, www.urbancusp.com/2012/01/refusing-invisibility-pariah-challenges-social-and-religious-norms/.

34. Nelson George, "New Directors Flesh Out Black America, All of It," *New York Times*, December 23, 2011, www.nytimes.com/2011/12/25/movies/pariah-reveals-another-side-of-being-black-in-the-us.html.

35. Patton, "In America, Black Children Don't Get to Be Children."

Post-Credit Sequence

1. Dennis Sullivan and Fred Boehrer, "Spike Lee's *Do the Right Thing*: Filmmaking in the American Grain," *Contemporary Justice Review* 6, no 2 (2003): 164.

2. Aisha Harris and Dan Kois, "The Black Film Canon," *Slate.com*, May 30, 2016, www.slate.com/articles/arts/cover_story/2016/05/the_50_greatest_films_by_black_directors.htm.

BIBLIOGRAPHY

"42 (2013)." IMDb.com, accessed May 3, 2015. http://www.imdb.com/title/tt0453562/?ref_=fn_al_tt_1.

"1984 Domestic Gross." BoxOfficeMojo.com, accessed July 22, 2016. www.boxofficemojo.com/yearly/chart/?yr=1984&p=.htm.

"2013 Yearly Box Office." BoxOfficeMojo.com, accessed May 3, 2015. www.boxofficemojo.com/yearly/chart/?yr=2013&p=.htm.

Abdul-Jabbar, Kareem, and Alan Steinberg. *Black Profiles in Courage: A Legacy of African-American Achievement.* New York: William Morrow, 1996.

Ade-Brown, Lathleen. "Exclusive: Sanaa Lathan and Omar Epps on the 15th Anniversary of *Love and Basketball*." *Essence*, April 24, 2015. www.essence.com/2015/04/24/love-and-basketball-15th-anniversary-sanaa-lathan-omar-epps.

Alexander, Lisa Doris. "But They Don't Want to Play with the White Players, Right?: Depictions of Segregation and Negro League Baseball in Contemporary Popular Film." *Black Ball* 5, no. 2 (2012): 19–34.

———. *When Baseball Isn't White, Straight, and Male: The Media and Difference in the National Pastime.* Jefferson, NC: McFarland, 2012.

Alfred, Bruce. "House Party." *Cineaste* 18, no. 1 (1990): 23–24.

Altman, Alex. "Person of the Year: The Short List No. 4: Black Lives Matter." *Time*, December 10, 2015. time.com/time-person-of-the-year-2015-runner-up-black-lives-matter/?iid=toc_121015.

Anderton, Ethan. "Robert Redford's Branch Rickey and Jackie Robinson Film Returns." FirstShowing.net, April 6, 2011. http://www.firstshowing.net/2011/robert-redfords-branch-rickey-and-jackie-robinson-film-returns/.

Ansen, David, Jay Carr, Godfrey Cheshire, Mike Clark, Manohla Dargis, David Denby, Morris Dickstein, et al. "Film Criticism in America Today: A Critical Symposium." *Cineaste* 26, no. 1 (2000): 27–45. www.jstor.org/stable/41689315.

Ardolino, Frank. "A Name, a Number, and a Picture: The Cinematic Memorialization of Jackie Robinson." *Journal of Popular Film and Television* 33, no. 3 (Fall 2005): 151–159.

Ashkenas, Jeremy, and Haeyoun Park. "The Race Gap in America's Police Departments." *New York Times*, April 8, 2015. www.nytimes.com/interactive/2014/09/03/us/the-race-gap-in-americas-police-departments.html.

Askar, Jamshid Ghazi. "Jackie Robinson Biographer Arnold Rampersad Applauds 42 Biopic." *Deseret News* (Salt Lake City), April 22, 2013. http://www.deseretnews.com/article/865578770/Jackie-Robinson-biographer-Arnold-Rampersad-applauds-42-biopic.html?pg=all.

Baker, Aaron. "Sports Films, History, and Identity." *Journal of Sport History* 25, no. 2 (Summer 1998): 217–233.

Balko, Radley. "Mass Shooting Hysteria and the Death of John Crawford." *Washington Post*, September 25, 2014. www.washingtonpost.com/news/the-watch/wp/2014/09/25/mass-shooting-hysteria-and-the-death-of-john-crawford/.

Barkley, Whitney. "How For-Profit Colleges Rip Off Students." CNN, October 31, 2014. www.cnn.com/2014/08/28/opinion/barkley-corinthian-for-profit-colleges/index.html.

Barone, Matt. "Commentary: You're Remembering *House Party* All Wrong." BET, March 9, 2015. www.bet.com/news/celebrities/2015/03/09/commentary-you-re-remembering-house-party-all-wrong.html.

Battema, Doug. "Jackie Robinson as Media's Mythological Black Hero." In *The Cooperstown Symposium on Baseball and American Culture*, edited by Peter M. Rutkoff. Jefferson, NC: McFarland, 1997: 199–214.

Bausch, Katharine. "Superflies into Superkillers: Black Masculinity in Film from Blaxploitation to New Black Realism." *Journal of Popular Culture* 46, no. 2 (2013): 257.

Bell, Derrick. *Faces at the Bottom of the Well: The Permanence of Racism*. New York: Basic Books, 1992.

———. "The Sexual Diversion: The Black Man/Black Woman Debate in Context." In *Black Men on Race, Gender & Sexuality: A Critical Reader*, edited by Devon Carbado, 237–247. New York: New York University Press, 1999.

———. "Wanted: A White Leader Able to Free Whites." *U.C. Davis Law Review* 33, no. 3 (Spring 2000): 527–544.

———. "White Superiority in America: Its Legal Legacy, Its Economic Costs." *Villanova Law Review* 33, no. 5 (1988): 767–779.

———. "Who's Afraid of Critical Race Theory?" *University of Illinois Law Review* 1995, no. 4 (1995): 893–910.

Berri, David. "Here's What It Will Take for Women's Sports to Grow in the U.S." *Time*, July 6, 2015. time.com/3945762/world-cup-womens-sports/.

"Black Girls Rock 2015." Directed by Joe DeMaio. BET, April 5, 2015. Television.

"Black Lives Matter." Accessed March 4, 2019. https://blacklivesmatter.com/about/.

Blauvelt, Christian. "*Red Tails* DVD: George Lucas Talks About His 'Real Dogfight Movie.'" *Entertainment Weekly*, May 22, 2012. www.ew.com/article/2012/05/22/red-tails-dvd-george-lucas-rick-mccallum.

Bobo, Jacqueline. *Black Women as Cultural Readers*. New York: Columbia University Press, 1995.

Bogle, Donald. *Prime Time Blues: African Americans on Network Television*. New York: Farrar, Straus and Giroux, 2001.

———. *Toms, Coons, Mulattoes, Mammies & Bucks: An Interpretive History of Blacks in American Films*. 4th ed. New York: Continuum, 2001.

Bonilla-Silva, Eduardo. *White Supremacy and Racism in the Post-Civil Rights Era*. Boulder, CO: Lynne Rienner, 2001.

Boyd, Todd. *Am I Black Enough for You? Popular Culture from the 'Hood and Beyond*. Bloomington: Indiana University Press, 1997.

"A Brief History of the DPOA." Detroit Police Officers Association, accessed June 20, 2016. www.detroitpoa.com/dpoa_history.php.

Brockes, Emma, "Director Michael Roemer on His Seminal 60s Drama *Nothing But a Man*." *The Guardian*, October 1, 2013. www.theguardian.com/film/2013/oct/01/director-michael-roemer-nothing-but.

Brooks, Justin P. "Will Boys Just Be *Boyz N the Hood*—African American Directors Portray a Crumbling Justice System in Urban America." *Oklahoma City University Law Review* 22, no. 1 (1997): 1–12.

Brower, Montgomery. "The Racial Murder of Yusef Hawkins Inflamed New York City, Forcing His Parents to Relive Their Anguish." *People*, June 4, 1990. http://www.people.com/people/archive/article/0,,20117855,00.html.

Bryant, Howard. "Righting the Wrongs of 42." ESPN, April 24, 2013. http://espn.go.com/mlb/story/_/id/9207998/42-gets-some-jackie-robinson-history-wrong-starts-conversation.

Burnett, Charles. "Charles Burnett: *The Glass Shield* Q&A at Lincoln Center 9/10/2016." Reelblack, September 14, 2016. www.youtube.com/watch?v=v2E9eLQ1KJE.

———. "Inner City Blues." In *Questions of Third Cinema*, edited by Jim Pines and Paul Willemen, 223–226. London: BFI Publishing, 1989.

Burns, Ken, director. "Forever Free" (Episode 3), *The Civil War*. PBS, September 24, 1990.

Burr, Ty. "CSA Raises Real Questions with a Bogus Documentary." *Boston Globe*, February 24, 2006. www.boston.com/ae/movies/articles/2006/02/24/csa_raises_real_questions_with_a_bogus_documentary/.

Butler, Bethonie. "Why Ava DuVernay Hired Only Female Directors for Her New TV Show *Queen Sugar*." *Washington Post*, September 15, 2016. www.washingtonpost.com/news/arts-and-entertainment/wp/2016/09/15/why-ava-duvernay-hired-only-female-directors-for-her-new-tv-show-queen-sugar/.

Butler, Paul. "Stop and Frisk and Torture-Lite: Police Terror of Minority Communities." *Ohio State Journal of Criminal Law* 12, no. 57 (2014–2015): 57–69.

Butte, George. "Suture and the Narration of Subjectivity in Film." *Poetics Today* 29, no. 2 (2008): 277. ProQuest.

Calvin, Delores. "Robinson Film Adds Ten Years to Negro Progress in Hollywood." *State Press* (Arkansas), May 26, 1950.

Canby, Vincent. "Review/Film; of Murphy, by Murphy, and Starring . . . Murphy." *New York Times*, November 17, 1989. www.nytimes.com/movie/review?res=950DE7D7133DF934A25752C1A96F948260.

———. "Screen: *Blazing Saddles*, a Western in Burlesque" (Review). *New York Times*, February 8, 1974. https://www.nytimes.com/1974/02/08/archives/screen-blazing-saddles-a-western-in-burlesque.html.

Caple, Jim. "The Jackie Robinson Realism in 42." ESPN, April 12, 2013. http://espn.go.com/mlb/story/_/id/9160031/ex-minor-leaguer-jasha-balcom-adds-jackie-robinson-realism-42.

———. "Robinson Women Preserving Jackie's Legacy." ESPNW, April 12, 2013. http://espn.go.com/espnw/news-commentary/article/9161436/espnw-rachel-sharon-robinson-preserving-jackie-legacy.

Carbado, Devon W. "(E)Racing the Fourth Amendment." *Michigan Law Review* 100, no. 5 (2002): 946–1044.

Carlos, John, and Dave Zirin. *The John Carlos Story.* Chicago: Haymarket Books, 2011.
Carroll, Noel. *Interpreting the Moving Image.* Cambridge: Cambridge University Press, 1998.
Carter, Kelley L. "How *Love & Basketball* Changed the Way Black Audiences Saw Themselves Onscreen." BuzzFeed.com, May 17, 2015. www.buzzfeed.com/kelleyl carter/how-love-basketball-changed-the-way-we-see-black-romance-on.
Cartwright, Samuel A. "Diseases and Peculiarities of the Negro Race." *De Bow's Review,* New Orleans, 1851. Retrieved from *Africans in America,* PBS. www.pbs.org /wgbh/aia/part4/4h3106t.html.
Cawelti, John G. "The Gunfighter and the Hard-Boiled Dick: Some Ruminations on American Fantasies of Heroism." *American Studies* 16, no. 2 (1975): 49–64.
"Celebrating 25 Years of Cult Classic *House Party.*" "Young Voices," *The Voice,* July 9, 2015. www.voice-online.co.uk/article/celebrating-25-years-cult-classic-house -party.
Chan, Kenneth. "The Construction of Black Male Identity in Black Action Films of the Nineties." *Cinema Journal* 37, no. 2 (1998).
Chew, Richard. IMDb.com, accessed March 4, 2019. https://www.imdb.com/news /ni30459520.
Child, Ben. "Italian Posters for *12 Years a Slave* Herald Brad Pitt over Chiwetel Ejiofor." *The Guardian,* December 24, 2013. www.theguardian.com/film/2013/dec/24/12 -years-slave-italy-posters-pitt-ejiofor.
Chow, Kat. "What's So 'Cringeworthy' About Long Duk Dong in *Sixteen Candles?*" NPR, February 6, 2015. www.npr.org/sections/codeswitch/2015/02/06/384307677 /whats-so-cringe-worthy-about-long-duk-dong-in-sixteen-candles.
Churchill, Winston. "If Lee Had Not Won the Battle of Gettysburg." *Wisconsin Magazine of History* 44, no. 4 (Summer 1961): 243–251.
Clark, Ashley. "Burning Down the House: Why the Debate Over *Paris Is Burning* Rages On." *The Guardian,* June 24, 2015. www.theguardian.com/film/2015/jun/24/burn ing-down-the-house-debate-paris-is-burning.
Cleaver, Kathleen Neal. "Racism, Civil Rights, and Feminism." In *Critical Race Feminism: A Reader,* edited by Adrien Katherine Wing, 48–56. New York: New York University Press, 1997.
Coates, Ta-Nehisi. "Fear of a Black President." *The Atlantic,* September 2012. http:// www.theatlantic.com/magazine/archive/2012/09/fear-of-a-black-president /309064/.
———. "The Lost Cause Rides Again." *The Atlantic,* August 4, 2017. www.theatlantic .com/entertainment/archive/2017/08/no-confederate/535512/.
Cohen, Shawn, and Bob Fredericks. "NYPD Is as Diverse as New York City Itself: Study." *New York Post,* September 8, 2014. nypost.com/2014/09/08/nypd-is-as -diverse-as-new-york-city-itself/.
Collins, Patricia Hill. *Black Feminist Thought: Knowledge, Consciousness, and the Politics of Empowerment.* 10th ed. New York: Routledge, 2000.
———. *Black Sexual Politics: African Americans, Gender, and the New Racism.* New York: Routledge, 2004.

———. *Fighting Words: Black Women and the Search for Justice*. Minneapolis: University of Minnesota Press, 1998.
Covey, William. "The Genre Don't Know Where It Came From: African American Neo-Noir Since the 1960s." *Journal of Film and Video* 55, no. 2/3 (2003): 59–72. http://www.jstor.org.proxy.lib.wayne.edu/stable/20688414.
Crasnick, Jerry. "Getting It Right in 42." ESPN, April 12, 2013. http://espn.go.com/mlb/story/_/id/9161338/jackie-robinson-movie-42-labor-love-brian-helgeland.
Crémieux, Anne. "From Queer to Quare: The Representation of LGBT Blacks in Cinema." In *African American Cinema Through Black Lives Consciousness*, edited by Mark A. Reid, 255–274. Detroit: Wayne State University Press, 2019.
Crenshaw, Kimberlé, Neil Gotanda, Gary Peller, and Kendall Thomas. *Critical Race Theory: The Key Writings That Formed the Movement*. New York: New Press, 1995.
Crowther, Bosley. "The Screen in Review." *New York Times*, May 17, 1950, 1.
Culp Jr., Jerome McCristal. "The Michael Jackson Pill: Equality, Race, and Culture." *Michigan Law Review* 92, no. 8 (August 1994): 2613–2644.
Davis, Angela Y. *Blues Legacies and Black Feminism: Gertrude 'Ma' Rainey, Bessie Smith, and Billie Holiday*. New York: Pantheon Books, 1998.
Delgado, Richard, and Jean Stefancic, eds. *The Derrick Bell Reader*. New York: New York University Press, 2005.
DeMaio, Joe. "Black Girls Rock 2015." BET, April 5, 2015. Television.
Denby, David. "Artful Dodgers." *New Yorker*, April 22, 2013.
Desta, Yohana. "Ava DuVernay and *Queen Sugar* Look Like the Future of Television." *Vanity Fair*, September 13, 2016. www.vanityfair.com/hollywood/2016/09/ava-duvernay-queen-sugar-interview.
Diawara, Manthia. "Black American Cinema: The New Realism." In *Black American Cinema*, edited by Manthia Diawara, 3–25. New York: Routledge, 1993.
Díaz, Junot. "The Junot Díaz Episode." *FanBrosShow*. November 18, 2013. Podcast, 48:45. https://forallnerds.com/junot-diaz-episode/.
Dippie, Brian W. "The Winning of the West Reconsidered." *Wilson Quarterly* 14, no. 3 (1990): 70–85.
Doherty, Thomas. "The Sincerest Form of Flattery: A Brief History of the Mockumentary." *Cineaste* 28, no. 4 (Fall 2003): 22–24.
Donalson, Melvin. *Hip Hop in American Cinema*. New York: Peter Lang, 2007.
Dorinson, Joe. "A Life Worth Living: The Jackie Robinson Biopic." In *The Brooklyn Film: Essays in the History of Filmmaking*, edited by John B. Manbeck and Robert Singer, 148–158. Jefferson, NC: McFarland, 2003.
Dowell, Pat. "The Mythology of the Western: Hollywood Perspectives on Race and Gender in the Nineties." *Cineaste* 21, no. 1/2 (1995): 6–10.
Downey, Mike. "The Jackie Robinson Biopic and Me." CNN, updated April 9, 2013. http://www.cnn.com/2013/04/09/opinion/downey-jackie-robinson/.
Dreier, Peter. "The Real Story of Baseball's Integration That You Won't See in 42." *The Atlantic*, April 11, 2013. http://www.theatlantic.com/entertainment/archive/2013/04/the-real-story-of-baseballs-integration-that-you-wont-see-in-i-42-i/274886/.

Dunne, Michael. *Metapop: Self-Referentiality in Contemporary American Popular Culture.* Jackson: University Press of Mississippi, 1992.
DuVernay, Ava. "Conversations with Ava DuVernay: A Call to Action: Organizing Principles of an Activist Cinematic Practice." By Michael T. Martin. *Black Camera, an International Film Journal* 6, no 1 (2014): 57–91.
———. "Four Questions with Middle of Nowhere Director Ava DuVernay." By Dan Schoenbrun. *Filmmaker*, January 23, 2012. filmmakermagazine.com/38617-four-questions-with-middle-of-nowhere-director-ava-duvernay/.
———. "*Middle of Nowhere* Live Tweet." Twitter, August 2, 2014.
———. "Q&A: Director Ava Marie DuVernay on Her Glam New Video for Miu Miu." By Araceli Cruz. *Rolling Stone*, February 8, 2013. www.rollingstone.com/culture/news/q-a-director-ava-marie-duvernay-on-her-glam-new-video-for-miu-miu-20130208.
———. "Selma Director DuVernay Joins 'MHP' for Extensive Interview." By Melissa Harris-Perry. January 13, 2015. www.msnbc.com/melissa-harris-perry/selma-director-duvernay-joins-mhp-extensive-interview.
DuVernay, Ava, and MC Lyte. "Female Emcees Say My Mic Sounds Nice." By Allison Keyes. *NPR News*. August 30, 2010. www.npr.org/templates/story/story.php?storyId=129530573.
DuVernay, Ava, David Oyelowo, Emayatzy Corinealdi, and Omari Hardwick. "Interview: Ava DuVernay, David Oyelowo, Emayatzy Corinealdi and Omari Hardwick (*Middle of Nowhere*)." By Nicholas Bell. *IonCinema.com*, October 10, 2012. www.ioncinema.com/interviews/interview-ava-duvernay-middle-of-nowhere.
Ebert, Roger. "Blazing Saddles" (Review). RogerEbert.com, February 7, 1974. https://www.rogerebert.com/reviews/blazing-saddles-1974.
———. "Harlem Nights" (Review). RogerEbert.com, April 18, 1989. www.rogerebert.com/reviews/harlem-nights-1989.
———. "House Party" (Review). RogerEbert.com, August 22, 1990. www.rogerebert.com/reviews/house-party-1990.
———. "I Will Follow" (Review). RogerEbert.com, March 2, 2011. www.rogerebert.com/reviews/i-will-follow-2011.
———. "*Middle of Nowhere*" (Review). RogerEbert.com, April 10, 2013. www.rogerebert.com/reviews/middle-of-nowhere-2012.
———. "Nothing but a Man" (Review). RogerEbert.com, June 4, 1993. www.rogerebert.com/reviews/nothing-but-a-man-1993.
Edelman, Rob. "The Jackie Robinson Story: A Reflection of Its Era." *NINE: A Journal of Baseball History and Culture* 20, no. 1 (Fall 2011): 40–55.
"ESPN Films: 30 for 30." ESPN, accessed March 29, 2015. espn.go.com/30for30/.
Evans, Howie. "Sports Writer Bombs Original Jackie Robinson Story." *Amsterdam News* (New York), December 3, 1994.
Fain, Kimberly. *Black Hollywood: From Butlers to Superheroes, the Changing Role of African American Men in the Movies.* Santa Barbara, CA: Praeger, 2015.
Fallon, Kevin. "Chris Rock's Brutal Oscars Monologue Was Legendary. But It Wasn't Perfect." TheDailyBeast.com, February 28, 2016. www.thedailybeast.com

/articles/2016/02/28/chris-rock-s-brutal-oscars-monologue-was-legendary-but-it-wasn-t-perfect.html.

Farred, Grant. "Menace II Society: No Way Out for the Boys in the Hood." *Michigan Quarterly Review* 35, no. 3 (1995): 475–492. hdl.handle.net/2027/spo.act2080.0035.003:13.

Faulx, Nadya. "*Blazing Saddles*, the Best Interracial Buddy Comedy, Turns 40." NPR, February 7, 2014. https://www.npr.org/sections/codeswitch/2014/02/07/272452677/blazing-saddles-the-best-interracial-buddy-comedy-turns-40.

Fienberg, Daniel. "Spike Lee Doesn't Regret Lost Jackie Robinson Opportunity." *Screener*, July 11, 2008. http://screenertv.com/news-features/spike-lee-doesnt-regret-lost-jackie-robinson-opportunity/.

Fisher, Celeste A. *Black on Black: Urban Youth Films and the Multicultural Audience*. Lanham, MD: Scarecrow Press, 2006.

Ford, Rebecca. "Golden Globes: *Selma*'s Ava DuVernay Becomes First Black Woman to Receive Director Nomination." *Hollywood Reporter*, December 11, 2014. www.hollywoodreporter.com/news/golden-globes-selmas-ava-duvernay-756511.

Foundas, Scott. "Film Review: 42." *Variety*, April 9, 2013. http://variety.com/2013/film/reviews/film-review-42-1200339020/.

Francis, Terri. "Can't Stay, Can't Go: What Is History to Cinematic Imagination?" *Black Camera, an International Film Journal* 3, no. 2 (Spring 2012): 128–139. https://doi.org/10.2979/blackcamera.3.2.128.

———. "Whose "Black Film" Is This? The Pragmatics and Pathos of Black Film Scholarship." *Cinema Journal* 53, no. 4 (Summer 2014): 146–150.

Fuchs, Cynthia. "*C.S.A.: Confederate States of America* (2004)" (Review). PopMatters.com, March 30, 2006. www.popmatters.com/review/csa_confederate_states_of_america_2004/.

Fuller, Hoyt W. "*Nothing But a Man* Reconsidered." *Negro Digest* 14, no. 7 (May 1965). https://books.google.com/books?id=7zkDAAAAMBAJ&pg=PA3&lr=&source=gbs_toc&cad=2#v=onepage&q&f=false

Fussman, Cal. "What I've Learned: The Comedians: Mel Brooks." *Esquire*, January 1, 2008. https://archive.esquire.com/article/2008/1/1/mel-brooks.

Futrell, Nicole Smith. "Vulnerable, Not Voiceless: Outsider Narrative in Advocacy Against Discriminatory Policing." *North Carolina Law Review* 93, no. 5 (June 2015): 1598–1638.

Gallagher, Catherine. "When Did the Confederate States of America Free the Slaves?" *Representations* 98, no. 1 (Spring 2007): 53–61.

Garrett, Daniel. "Notes on Elevating the Conversation About African American Film." IndieWire.com, May 28, 2013. https://www.indiewire.com/2013/05/notes-on-elevating-the-conversation-about-african-american-film-167727/.

Gates, Philippa. "Always a Partner in Crime: Black Masculinity in the Hollywood Detective Film." *Journal of Popular Film and Television* 32, no. 1 (2004): 20–29. https://doi.org/10.3200/JPFT.32.1.20-30.

Gates, Racquel J. *Double Negative: The Black Image and Popular Culture.* Durham, NC: Duke University Press, 2018.

Gay, Roxane. "I Don't Want to Watch Slavery Fan Fiction." *New York Times,* July 25, 2017. www.nytimes.com/2017/07/25/opinion/hbo-confederate-slavery-civil-war.html.

Gehring, Wes D. *Parody as Film Genre: "Never Give a Saga an Even Break."* Westport, CT: Greenwood, 1999.

George, Nelson. "New Directors Flesh out Black America, All of It." *New York Times,* December 23, 2011. www.nytimes.com/2011/12/25/movies/pariah-reveals-another-side-of-being-black-in-the-us.html.

Gillespie, Michael Boyce. "One Step Ahead: A Conversation with Barry Jenkins." *Film Quarterly* 70, no. 3 (2017): 52–62.

Gladwell, Malcolm. "Malcolm Gladwell on Pioneers, Tokens, and 'the Satire Paradox.'" By Larry Wilmore. *Larry Wilmore Black on the Air,* July 20, 2017. Podcast, 1:06:27. https://www.theringer.com/2017/7/20/16077718/malcolm-gladwell-larry-wilmore-golf-black-on-the-air-podcast-d10d7b45a79c.

"The Glass Shield" (1994). IMDb.com, accessed December 13, 2015. www.imdb.com/title/tt0109906/?ref_=rvi_tt.

Gleiberman, Owen. "*House Party*" (Review). *Entertainment Weekly,* March 9, 1990. www.ew.com/article/1990/03/09/house-party.

Goldstein, Joseph. "'Testilying' by Police: A Stubborn Problem." *New York Times,* March 18, 2018. www.nytimes.com/2018/03/18/nyregion/testilying-police-perjury-new-york.html.

Good, Howard. "The Heart of the Order: The Success Myth in Baseball Biopics." In *Beyond the Stars 5: Themes and Ideologies in American Popular Film,* edited by Paul Loukides and Linda K. Fuller, 187–209. Bowling Green, OH: Bowling Green State University Popular Press, 1996.

Gramlich, John. "The Gap Between the Number of Blacks and Whites in Prison Is Shrinking." Pew Research Center, January 12, 2018. http://www.pewresearch.org/fact-tank/2018/01/12/shrinking-gap-between-number-of-blacks-and-whites-in-prison/.

Greene, Viveca, and Chris Tinson. "*Do the Right Thing*: Still a Racial Rorschach at 20." *The Nation,* August 18, 2009. http://www.thenation.com/article/do-right-thing-still-racial-rorschach-20.

Groen, Rick. "*Middle of Nowhere* Is a Taut Study of a Woman Marooned" (Review). *Globe and Mail,* February 8, 2013. www.theglobeandmail.com/arts/film/film-reviews/middle-of-nowhere-is-a-taut-study-of-a-woman-marooned/article8341882/.

Guerrero, Ed. *Framing Blackness: The African American Image in Film.* Philadelphia: Temple University Press, 1993.

Hagler, Frank. "Kerry Washington's *Vanity Fair* Cover Is Smokin'—But White People Still Might Not Notice It." Mic.com, August 14, 2013. mic.com/articles/59293/kerry-washington-s-vanity-fair-cover-is-smokin-but-white-people-still-might-not-notice-it.

Hall, Stuart. "What Is This 'Black' in Black Popular Culture?" *Social Justice* 20, no. 1/2 (Spring-Summer 1993): 104–114.
"Harlem Nights." BoxOfficeMojo.com, accessed May 16, 2016. www.boxofficemojo.com/movies/?id=harlemnights.htm.
"Harlem Nights." IMDb.com, accessed March 1, 2019. https://www.imdb.com/title/tt0097481/?ref_=nv_sr_1.
"Harlem Nights." The-Numbers.com, accessed July 11, 2016. www.the-numbers.com/movie/Harlem-Nights.
"Harlem Nights Beats the Daylights out of Rivals." *Globe and Mail*, November 22, 1989, C11. ProQuest.
"Harlem Nights Near Record of Fall Box Office Openings." *Ottawa (Ontario) Citizen*, November 22, 1989, Arts/Entertainment. ProQuest.
"Harlem Nights Reviews." RottenTomatoes.com, accessed June 27, 2016. www.rottentomatoes.com/m/harlem_nights/reviews.
Harley, Sharon. "'Working for Nothing but for a Living': Black Women in the Underground Economy." In *Sister Circle: Black Women and Work*, edited by Sharon Harley and the Black Women and Work Collective. New Brunswick, NJ: Rutgers University Press, 2002.
Harris, Aisha, and Dan Kois. "The Black Film Canon." *Slate.com*, May 30, 2016. www.slate.com/articles/arts/cover_story/2016/05/the_50_greatest_films_by_black_directors.html.
Harris, Alexa A., and Adria Y. Goldman. "Black Women in Popular Culture: An Introduction to the Reader's Journey." In *Black Women in Popular Culture: The Conversation Continues*, edited by Adria Y. Goldman, VaNatta S. Ford, Alexa A. Harris, and Natasha R. Howard. Lanham, MD: Lexington Books, 2015.
Harris, Cheryl I. "Whiteness as Property." *Harvard Law Review* 106, no. 8 (June 1993): 1707–1791.
Harris, Trudier. "The Trickster in African American Literature." TeacherServe: National Humanities Center, 2010. http://nationalhumanitiescenter.org/tserve/freedom/1865-1917/essays/trickster.htm.
Harrison, Rick. "*Nothing But a Man*." *Independent Film & Video Monthly* 27, no. 6 (2004): 9. ProQuest.
Harris-Perry, Melissa V. *Sister Citizen: Shame, Stereotypes, and Black Women in America*. New Haven, CT: Yale University Press, 2011. Kindle edition.
Hathaway, Jay. "Video of Sam DuBose's Death Drastically Different from the Police Report." *Gawker.com*, July 29, 2015. gawker.com/video-of-sam-duboses-death-drastically-different-from-t-1720896658.
Henderson, Eric. "Review: *The Glass Shield*." SlantMagazine.com, August 29, 2005. www.slantmagazine.com/film/review/the-glass-shield.
Hinson, Hal. "*Harlem Nights*" (Review). *Washington Post*, November 17, 1989. www.washingtonpost.com/wp-srv/style/longterm/movies/videos/harlemnights.htm.
———. "When Injustice Gets Under the Skin." *Washington Post*, July 10, 1993, ProQuest.

hooks, bell. *Reel to Real: Race, Sex, and Class at the Movies*. New York: Routledge, 1996.
hooks, bell, and Melissa Harris-Perry. "Black Female Voices: Who's Listening—A Public Dialogue Between bell hooks + Melissa Harris-Perry." The New School, November 11, 2013. https://www.youtube.com/watch?v=5OmgqXao1ng.
hooks, bell, and Isaac Julien. "States of Desire." *Transition* 53 (1991): 168–184.
Hornaday, Ann. "C.S.A.: A Bitter State of the Union" (Review). *Washington Post*, March 31, 2006. www.washingtonpost.com/wp-dyn/content/article/2006/03/30/AR2006033000818.html.
———. "*Moonlight* Is Both a Tough Coming-of-Age Tale and a Tender Testament to Love" (Review). *Washington Post*, October 27, 2016. https://www.washingtonpost.com/goingoutguide/movies/moonlight-is-both-a-tough-coming-of-age-tale-and-a-tender-testament-to-love/2016/10/27/45d88eea-9b80-11e6-9980-50913d68eacb_story.html.
"House Party (1990)." IMDb.com, accessed September 5, 2016. www.imdb.com/title/tt0099800.
Howard, Brendan. "Blazing Saddles Up." *Video Store Magazine* 26, no. 14 (2004): 42.
Howe, Desson. "Harlem Nights" (Review). *Washington Post*, November 24, 1989. www.washingtonpost.com/wp-srv/style/longterm/movies/videos/harlemnightshowe.htm.
———. "House Party" (Review). *Washington Post*, March 9, 1990. www.washingtonpost.com/wp-srv/style/longterm/movies/videos/housepartyrhowe_a0b25b.htm.
Howell, Peter. "*Middle of Nowhere* Review: The Ring that Binds, The Bars that Divide." *Toronto Star*, February 7, 2013. www.thestar.com/entertainment/movies/2013/02/07/middle_of_nowhere_review_the_ring_that_binds_the_bars_that_divide.html.
Hudlin, Reginald and Warrington. "Tearing the Roof Off the Sucker: An Interview with Reginald and Warrington Hudlin." By Michael Kantor. *Cineaste* 18, no. 1 (1990).
Hughey, Matthew W. "Racializing Redemption, Reproducing Racism: The Odyssey of Magical Negroes and White Saviors." *Sociology Compass* 6, no. 9 (2012): 751–767. https://doi.org/10.1111/j.1751-9020.2012.00486.x.
———. *The White Savior Film: Content, Critics, and Consumption*. Philadelphia: Temple University Press, 2014.
Ice Cube. "How to Survive in South Central." In *Boyz n the Hood: Music from the Motion Picture*. Burbank, CA: Qwest (Warner), 1991.
Insight Center for Community Economic Development. "Lifting as We Climb: Women of Color, Wealth, and America's Future." Oakland, CA, 2010. http://www.insightcced.org/uploads/CRWG/LiftingAsWeClimb-WomenWealth-Report-InsightCenter-Spring2010.pdf.
Iverem, Esther. *We Gotta Have It: Twenty Years of Seeing Black at the Movies, 1986–2006*. New York: Thunder's Mouth Press, 2007.
Johnson, Albert. "Moods Indigo: A Long View." *Film Quarterly* 44, no. 2 (Winter 1990–1991): 13–27.

———. "The Negro in American Films: Some Recent Works." *Film Quarterly* 18, no. 4 (Summer 1965): 14–30.
Juhasz, Alexandra, and Jesse Lerner, eds. *F Is for Phony: Fake Documentary and Truth's Undoing*. Minneapolis: University of Minnesota Press, 2006.
Kantor, MacKinlay. *If the South Had Won the Civil War*. New York: Tom Doherty Associates, 1960.
Kapsis, Robert E. *Charles Burnett: Interviews*. Jackson: University Press of Mississippi, 2011.
Keeling, Kara, Jennifer DeClue, Yvonne Welbon, Jacqueline Steward, and Roya Rastegar. "Pariah and Black Independent Cinema Today: A Roundtable." *GLQ: A Journal of Lesbian and Gay Studies* 21, no. 2–3 (June 2015): 423–439.
Kempadoo, Kamala. "Women of Color and the Global Sex Trade: Transnational Feminist Perspectives." *Meridians* 1, no. 2 (Spring 2001): 28–51.
Kendall, Steven D. *New Jack Cinema: Hollywood's African American Filmmakers*. Silver Spring, MD: J. L. Denser, 1994.
Kermode, Mark. "42—Review." *The Guardian*, September 14, 2013. http://www.theguardian.com/film/2013/sep/15/42-jackie-robinson-film-review.
King Jr., Martin Luther. "I've Been to the Mountaintop." Speech. Memphis: April 3, 1968, AmericanRhetoric.com. http://www.americanrhetoric.com/speeches/mlkivebeentothemountaintop.htm.
Kiser, Grace. "Study: Single Women of Color Age 36–49 Have Median Wealth of Just $5." *HuffingtonPost.com*, May 25, 2010. www.huffingtonpost.com/2010/03/11/women-of-color-have-media_n_495238.html.
Kleinknecht, William. "Murphy Film Canceled After Shooting Wounds 3 Outside Michigan Theater." *Austin American-Statesman*, November 19, 1989, p. A7. ProQuest.
Krindler, Chris. "Police Look Different Through *The Glass Shield*" (Review). *Baltimore Sun*, June 2, 1995. articles.baltimoresun.com/1995-06-02/entertainment/1995153170_1_michael-boatman-charles-burnett-lori-petty.
Lanouette, Jennine. "Nothing but a Good Tale." *Village Voice* 38, no. 9 (1993): 56. ProQuest.
LaSalle, Mick. "What If the South Had Won the Civil War?" SFGate.com (*San Francisco Chronicle*), February 24, 2006. www.sfgate.com/movies/article/What-if-the-South-had-won-the-Civil-War-2503771.php.
Latchem, John. "*Blazing Saddles*: 40th Anniversary Edition." (Review). *Home Media Magazine* 36, no. 15 (2014): 24.
Lawrence, Charles R, III. "If He Hollers Let Him Go: Regulating Racist Speech on Campus." In *Words That Wound: Critical Race Theory, Assaultive Speech, and the First Amendment*, edited by Mari J. Matsuda, Charles R. Lawrence III, Richard Delgado, and Kimberlé Williams Crenshaw, 53–88. Boulder, CO: Westview Press, 1993.
Lawrence, Novotny. *Blaxploitation Films of the 1970s: Blackness and Genre*. New York: Routledge, 2008.
Learish, Jessica. "Why Are the Olympic Games the Only Time We Pay Attention to

Female Athletes?" *Bustle.com*, August 20, 2016. www.bustle.com/articles/177814-why-are-the-olympic-games-the-only-time-we-pay-attention-to-female-athletes.

Lee, Paula Young. "A White Buddy for Miles Davis: Don Cheadle's Struggle to Get *Miles Ahead* Financed Is Absurd—and Not Surprising." *Salon.com*, April 13, 2016. www.salon.com/2016/02/19/a_white_buddy_for_miles_davis_don_cheadles_struggle_to_get_miles_ahead_financed_is_absurd_and_not_surprising/.

Legum, Judd. "Everything the Police Said About Walter Scott's Death Before a Video Showed What Really Happened." *ThinkProgress.org*, April 8, 2015. thinkprogress.org/justice/2015/04/07/3644189/everything-police-said-walter-scotts-death-video-showed-really-happened/.

Leonard, David. "Refusing Invisibility: *Pariah* Challenges Social and Religious Norms." *UrbanCusp.com*, January 9, 2013. www.urbancusp.com/2012/01/refusing-invisibility-pariah-challenges-social-and-religious-norms/.

Lewis, Hilary. "NYC's Dalton School Apologizes for Showing Movie Satirizing Slavery." *Hollywood Reporter*, January 31, 2014. www.hollywoodreporter.com/news/nycs-dalton-school-apologizes-showing-676218.

Lewis, Zach. "Without Theatres: *Nothing But a Man* Is Unapologetically Political and Deeply Humanistic" (Review). *Popoptiq.com*, accessed March 4, 2019. https://www.popoptiq.com/nothing-but-a-man-review.

Loewen, James W. *Lies My Teacher Told Me: Everything Your American History Textbook Got Wrong*. New York: Simon & Schuster, 2007.

Long, Michael G. *First Class Citizenship: The Civil Rights Letters of Jackie Robinson*. New York: Times Books, 2007.

MacLeod, Lewis. "'A Documentary-Style Film': *Borat* and the Fiction/Nonfiction Question." *Narrative* 19, no. 1 (January 2011): 111–132.

Macnab, Geoffrey. "Blazing Saddles." (Review). *Sight and Sound* (September 2004): 94.

Marable, Manning. *The Great Wells of Democracy: The Meaning of Race in American Life*. New York: Basic Civitas Books, 2002.

Martin, Michael T., and Adele Stephenson. "Close-up Gallery: *Nothing But a Man*." *Black Camera, an International Film Journal* 3, no. 2 (Spring 2012): 194–204.

Martin, Michael T., and David C. Wall. "Introduction." *Black Camera, an International Film Journal* 3, no. 2 (Spring 2012): 85–90.

Martin, Roland. "News One Now." Washington, DC: TVOne, April 18, 2016.

Mask, Mia. *Contemporary Black American Cinema: Race, Gender and Sexuality at the Movies*. New York: Routledge, 2012.

———. *Divas on Screen: Black Women in American Film*. Urbana: University of Illinois Press, 2010.

Massood, Paula. *Black City Cinema: African American Urban Experiences in Film*. Philadelphia: Temple University Press, 2003.

———. "Film Reviews: *Menace II Society*." *Cineaste* 20, no. 2 (1993): 44–45.

May, Robert E. *The Southern Dream of a Caribbean Empire 1854–1861*. Baton Rouge: Louisiana State University Press, 1973.

McCalmont, Lucy. "Double or Nothing: An Oral History of *Love & Basketball*."

HuffingtonPost.com, June 16, 2015. www.huffingtonpost.com/2015/06/16/love-and-basketball-oral-history_n_7572140.html.

McCarthy, Todd. "42: Film Review." Hollywood Reporter, April 9, 2013. http://www.hollywoodreporter.com/movie/42/review/434880.

———. "The Glass Shield" (Review). Variety, May 30, 1994. variety.com/1994/film/reviews/the-glass-shield-1200436941/.

McCurry, Stephanie. "The U.S. Won the Civil War." New York Times, July 2, 2013. www.nytimes.com/roomfordebate/2013/07/02/who-won-the-civil-war/the-us-won-the-civil-war.

McPherson, James M. Battle Cry of Freedom: The Civil War Era. The Oxford History of the United States. Edited by C. Vann Woodward. New York: Oxford University Press, 1988.

"Meet the 2012 Sundance Filmmakers #24: Ava DuVernay, Middle of Nowhere." Indiewire.com, January 10, 2012. www.indiewire.com/article/meet-the-2012-sundance-filmmakers-24-ava-duvernay-middle-of-nowhere.

Mendelson, Scott. "Black Panther Shatters Stereotypes, Breaks Box Office Records with $400M+ Debut." Forbes, February 18, 2018. www.forbes.com/sites/scott-mendelson/2018/02/18/black-panther-crushes-conventional-wisdom-with-record-218m-debut/#4dcf195f64c7.

Metaxas, Eric. "Jackie Robinson's Faith Missing from 42 Movie." HuffingtonPost.com, April 12, 2013. http://www.huffingtonpost.com/2013/04/12/jackie-robinsons-faith-missing-from-42-movie_n_3072672.html.

Metz, Walter. "From Harlem to Hollywood: The 1970s Renaissance and Blaxploitation." In Beyond Blaxploitation, edited by Novotny Lawrence and Gerald Butters, 225–245. Detroit: Wayne State University Press, 2016.

Millar, Jeff. "Harlem Nights and Eddie's Day—Overdose of Obscenity Mars Movies." Houston Chronicle, November 18, 1989, 1. Newsbank. https://infoweb.newsbank.com/apps/news/document-view?p=NewsBank&docref=news/0ED7AF8927E3144B.

Miller, Cynthia J. Too Bold for the Box Office: The Mockumentary from Big Screen to Small. Lanham, MD: Scarecrow Press, 2012.

"(Mis)Representation of the Black Female on Film: The Celluloid Sister; Part II." Michigan Citizen (Highland Park), August 7, 1999, B2. ProQuest.

Mistry, Anupa. "Why Aren't There More Movies Like Love & Basketball?" Vulture.com, October 22, 2014. www.vulture.com/2014/10/love-and-basketball-appreciation.html.

Moore, Ward. "Bring the Jubilee." In The Best Alternate History Stories of the 20th Century, edited by Harry Turtledove and Martin H. Greenberg, 152–249. New York: Del Rey/Ballantine, 2001.

Morris, Wesley. "The Problem with Saints." Grantland.com, April 11, 2013. http://grantland.com/features/the-limp-42-excellent-trance/.

Murphy, Eddie. "Eddie! An Exclusive Interview with Eddie Murphy by Spike Lee." By Spike Lee. Spin, 1990, 33–36; 97–98. books.google.com/books?id=hV6_z7r2zQMC&lpg=PA5&lr&pg=PA98#v=onepage&q&f=true.

Naremore, James. *More Than Night: Film Noir in Its Contexts*. Rev. ed. Berkeley: University of California Press, 2008.

Nastasi, Alison. "25 Delightful Roger Ebert Quotes About Movies." *Flavorwire.com*, July 6, 2014. flavorwire.com/465863/25-delightful-roger-ebert-quotes-about-movies.

Nickel, John. "Disabling African American Men: Liberalism and Race Message Films." *Cinema Journal* 44, no. 1 (Autumn 2004): 25–48.

"Nine for IX: *Venus Vs.*" ESPNW, June 26, 2013. espn.go.com/espnw/w-in-action/nine-for-ix/article/8948839/nine-ix-film-summary-director-venus-vs.

Norton, Chris. "Black Independent Cinema and the Influence of Neo-Realism: Futility, Struggle and Hope in the Face of Reality." *Images: A Journal of Film and Popular Culture*, no. 5 (1997). www.imagesjournal.com/issue05/features/black3.htm.

"Nothing But a Man." *Wikipedia*, accessed March 4, 2019. https://en.wikipedia.org/w/index.php?title=Nothing_But_a_Man&oldid=839751667.

Obenson, Tambay A. "DVD Review—"I Will Follow"—(A Deeply Personal, Reflective Chamber Drama) + Interviews Galore." *IndieWire.com* August 23, 2011. https://www.indiewire.com/2011/08/dvd-review-i-will-follow-a-deeply-personal-reflective-chamber-drama-interviews-galore-151265.

———. "Hey NYC! 25th Anniversary Screening of *House Party* Followed by Discussion W/ Cast & Crew, Next Week!" *IndieWire.com*, June 18, 2015. www.indiewire.com/2015/06/hey-nyc-25th-anniversary-screening-of-house-party-followed-by-discussion-w-cast-crew-next-week-153708/.

———. "LAFF 2012 Review—*Middle of Nowhere* (Aka 'Nothing but a Woman'). In dieWire.com, June 21, 2012. https://www.indiewire.com/2012/06/laff-2012-review-middle-of-nowhere-aka-nothing-but-a-woman-144611/.

O'Connor, Ian. "Jackie Robinson Enlightened a Nation." ESPN, April 9, 2013. http://espn.go.com/new-york/story/_/id/9149601/jackie-robinson-always-took-one-team.

O'Connor, John J. "2 Cable Movies of Substance." *New York Times*, Oct 15, 1990. https://proxy.lib.wayne.edu/login?url=https://search-proquest-com.proxy.lib.wayne.edu/docview/108456743?accountid=14925.

Owsley, Frank Lawrence. *King Cotton Diplomacy: Foreign Relations of the Confederate States of America*. 2nd ed. Chicago: University of Chicago Press, 1931.

Painter, Nell Irvin. "After the Civil War, Memory Took Time to Desegregate." *New York Times*, July 2, 2013. www.nytimes.com/roomfordebate/2013/07/02/who-won-the-civil-war/after-the-civil-war-memory-took-time-to-desegregate.

Patterson, Brandon E. "10 Things You Should Know About the Killing of Laquan McDonald by Police." *Mother Jones*, December 1, 2015. www.motherjones.com/politics/2015/11/laquan-mcdonald-chicago-police-shooting-video-explainer.

Patton, Stacey. "In America, Black Children Don't Get to Be Children." *Washington Post*, November 26, 2014. www.washingtonpost.com/opinions/in-america-black-children-dont-get-to-be-children/2014/11/26/a9e24756-74ee-11e4-a755-e32227229e7b_story.html.

Pinsker, Sanford. "The Instruments of American-Jewish Humor: Henny Youngman on Violin, Mel Brooks on Drums, Woody Allen on Clarinet." *Massachusetts Review* 22, no. 4 (1981): 739–750.

Podhoretz, John. "Saddles Revisited." *Weekly Standard*, June 16, 2014, 43.

Prasch, Thomas. "Between What Is and What If: Kevin Willmott's CSA." In *Too Bold for the Box Office: The Mockumentary from Big Screen to Small*, edited by Cynthia J. Miller, 187–199. Lanham, MD: Scarecrow Press, 2012.

"Prize Money and Finance." Wimbledon.com, 2014, accessed March 31, 2015. https://www.wimbledon.com/en_GB/aboutwimbledon/prize_money_and_finance.html.

Quinn, Eithne. "'Trying to Get Over': Super Fly, Black Politics, and Post–Civil Rights Film Enterprise." *Cinema Journal* 49, no. 2 (2010): 86–105.

Rabbitt, Emily. "This New Movie Is a Landmark Victory for Race—So What's the Problem?" *Groundswell.com*, April 7, 2015. www.groundswell.org/dreamworks_home_diversity/.

"Race Relations on Campus." *Journal of Blacks in Higher Education* 62 (2008): 100–101.

Raengo, Alessandra. "A Necessary Signifier: The Adaptation of Robinson's Body-Image in the Jackie Robinson Story." *Adaptation* 1, no. 2 (September 2008): 79–105. https://doi.org/10.1093/adaptation/apn019.

Rainer, Peter. "Movie Review: Glass Shield: Pursuit of Manifesto Cloaks Cop Drama." *Los Angeles Times*, June 2, 1995.

Rampersad, Arnold. *Jackie Robinson: A Biography*. New York: Alfred A. Knopf, 1997.

Reese, Della. "The Christmas Angel: An Interview with Della Reese." By Jennifer Sikora. *5MinutesForMom.com*, November 24, 2012. www.5minutesformom.com/68235/the-christmas-angel-an-interview-with-della-reese/.

Reese, Diana. "Jackie Robinson's Courage as Civil Rights Pioneer Subject of Film 42." *Washington Post*, April 11, 2013. http://www.washingtonpost.com/blogs/she-the-people/wp/2013/04/11/jackie-robinsons-courage-as-civil-rights-pioneer-subject-of-film-42/.

Regester, Charlene. *African American Actresses: The Struggle for Visibility, 1900–1960*. Bloomington: Indiana University Press, 2010.

Reid, Mark A. *Black Lenses, Black Voices: African American Film Now*. Lanham, MD: Rowman & Littlefield, 2005.

Rhodes, Elizabeth. "House Party Forever! Christopher "Play" Martin and Bun B Explain Why Classic Hip Hop Movie Endures." *CultureMap.com* (Houston), November 13, 2015. houston.culturemap.com/news/arts/11-13-15-ihouse-partyi-forever-christopher-play-martin-and-bun-b-explain-why-classic-hip-hop-movie-endures/#slide=0.

Richardson, L. Song, and Phillip Atiba Goff. "Interrogating Racial Violence." *Ohio State Journal of Criminal Law* 12, no. 115 (2014): 115–152.

Rickey, Carrie. "The 411 on 42." *CarrieRickey.com*, April 11, 2013. http://www.carrierickey.com/blog/the-411-on-42/.

Robb, David. "The Jackie Robinson You Won't See in 42." April 11, 2013, updated July 24, 2014. http://www.thewrap.com/movies/blog-post/jackie-robinson-you-wont-see-42-85351.

Roberts, John W. *From Trickster to Badman: The Black Folk Hero in Slavery and Freedom.* Philadelphia: University of Pennsylvania Press, 1989.

Robertson, Joel G. "FFR—Harlem Nights (1989)." *Forgotten Flix Remembers,* September 5, 2015. Podcast, 1:16:01. https://forgottenflix.com/ffr021/.

Robinson, Jackie. *I Never Had It Made.* New York: Putnam, 1972.

Rock, Chris. "Chris Rock Pens Blistering Essay on Hollywood's Race Problem: 'It's a White Industry.'" *Hollywood Reporter,* December 3, 2014. www.hollywoodreporter.com/news/top-five-filmmaker-chris-rock-753223.

Roeper, Richard. "42" (Review). RogerEbert.com, April 11, 2013. http://www.rogerebert.com/reviews/42-2013.

Rosenbaum, Jonathan. "The Glass Shield" (Review). *Chicago Reader,* accessed September 7, 2018. www.chicagoreader.com/chicago/the-glass-shield/Film?oid=1054074.

———. "The World According to Harvey and Bob." *Chicago Reader,* June 16, 1995. www.jonathanrosenbaum.net/1995/06/the-world-according-to-harvey-and-bob/.

Sachs, Ira. "Interview: Director Ira Sachs Reminds Us *Love Is Strange.*" By Patrick McDonald. HollywoodChicago.com, August 27, 2014. www.hollywoodchicago.com/news/24449/interview-director-ira-sachs-reminds-us-love-is-strange.

Schultz, Jaime. "*Glory Road* (2006) and the White Savior Historical Sport Film." *Journal of Popular Film and Television* 42, no. 4 (December 2014): 205–213. https://doi.org/10.1080/01956051.2014.913001.

Scott, A.O. "Moonlight: Is This the Year's Best Film?" (Review). *New York Times,* October 20, 2016. https://www.nytimes.com/2016/10/21/movies/moonlight-review.html.

———. "That Rookie at First Is in a New Position." *New York Times,* April 11, 2013. http://www.nytimes.com/2013/04/12/movies/42-with-chadwick-boseman-as-jackie-robinson.html.

Seewood, Andre. "Towards Defining the Black Film: The Genuine, the Compromised, and the Token." *ShadowandAct.com,* March 2, 2015, accessed on *IndieWire.com.* https://www.indiewire.com/2015/03/towards-defining-the-black-film-the-genuine-the-compromised-and-the-token-155411/.

Sergio, "Why Sidney Poitier's *A Warm December* Is No 'Click [sic] Flick.'" *IndieWire.com,* August 18, 2014. https://www.indiewire.com/2014/08/why-sidney-poitiers-a-warm-december-is-no-chick-flick-158797/.

Serwer, Adam. "Film Review: *Pariah* and the Untold Stories in Black Cinema." *Mother Jones,* December 28, 2011. www.motherjones.com/mixed-media/2011/12/film-review-pariah.

Setoodeh, Ramin. "Spike Lee on *Da Sweet Blood of Jesus* and Hollywood's Diversity Problem." *Variety,* June 23, 2014. variety.com/2014/film/markets-festivals/spike-lee-da-sweet-blood-of-jesus-hollywood-diversity-problem-1201243416/.

Sieving, Christopher. *Soul Searching: Black-Themed Cinema from the March on Washington to the Rise of Blaxploitation.* Middletown, CT: Wesleyan University Press, 2011.

Silverstein, Melissa. "A Distribution Success Story: *I Will Follow*—Written and

Directed by Ava DuVernay." *IndieWire.com*, March 17, 2011. https://www.indiewire.com/2011/03/a-distribution-success-story-i-will-follow-written-and-directed-by-ava-duvernay-212657/.

Simon-Kerr, Julia. "Systemic Lying." *William & Mary Law Review* 56, no. 6 (2015).

Simpson, Donald. "Black Images in Film—the 1940s to the Early 1960s." *Black Scholar* 21, no. 2 (March-April-May 1990): 20–29.

Sims, Yvonne D. *Women of Blaxpolitation: How the Black Action Film Heroine Changed American Popular Culture*. Jefferson, NC: McFarland, 2006.

Singleton, John. "Can a White Director Make a Great Black Movie?" *Hollywood Reporter*, September 19, 2013. https://www.hollywoodreporter.com/news/john-singleton-can-a-white-630127.

Siskel, Gene, and Roger Ebert. "*Congo, The Glass Shield, Pocahontas, Fluke*" (Review). SiskelEbert.org, December 13, 1995. https://siskelebert.org/?p=3485.

Slezak, Michael. "*Dukes of Hazzard* Dropped by TV Land: Bad Rap for the Good Ol' Boys?" *TVLine.com*, July 1, 2015. tvline.com/2015/07/01/dukes-of-hazzard-tv-land-pulls-reruns-confederate-flag-controversy/.

Smalls, James. "The Past, Present, and Future of Black Queer Cinema." In *African American Cinema Through Black Lives*, edited by Mark A. Reid, 275–296. Detroit: Wayne State University Press, 2019.

Smith, Jonathan. "42 Movie Review: Film Enables Public to Discuss Racism in Entertaining Way." *Mic.com*, April 5, 2013. http://www.mic.com/articles/32663/42-movie-review-film-enables-public-to-discuss-racism-in-entertaining-way.

Smith, Stacy L., Marc Choueiti, and Katherine Pieper. *Inequality in 800 Popular Films: Examining Portrayals of Gender, Race/Ethnicity, LGBT, and Disability from 2007–2015*. Los Angeles: Annenberg School for Communication and Journalism, University of Southern California, September 2016. annenberg.usc.edu/pages/ffi/media/MDSCI/Dr%20Stacy%20L%20Smith%20Inequality%20in%20800%20Films%20FINAL.ashx.

Smith, Stacy L., Marc Choueiti, Katherine Pieper, Traci Gillig, Carmen Lee, and Dylan DeLuca. *Inequality in 700 Popular Films: Examining Portrayals of Gender, Race & LGBT Status from 2007–2014*. Los Angeles: Annenberg School for Communication and Journalism, University of Southern California, August 2015.

Smith-Shomade, Beretta E., Racquel Gates, and Miriam J. Perry. "When and Where We Enter." *Cinema Journal* 53, no. 4 (2014): 121–127.

Smurthwaite, Nick, and Paul Gelder. *Mel Brooks and the Spoof Film*. London: Proteus Books, 1982.

Sobchack, Vivian. "Baseball in the Post-American Cinema, or Life in the Minor Leagues." *East-West Film Journal* 7, no. 1 (January 1993): 1–23.

Somashekhar, Sandhya, Wesley Lowery, Keith L. Alexander, Kimberly Kindy, and Julie Tate. "Black and Unarmed." *Washington Post*, August 8, 2015. www.washingtonpost.com/sf/national/2015/08/08/black-and-unarmed/.

Stark, Susan. "Is This Racist, Sexist Garbage, or Simply Entertainment?" *Detroit Free Press*, December 1, 1998.

Sue, Derald Wing. "Racial Microaggressions in Everyday Life." *Psychology Today*, October 5, 2010. www.psychologytoday.com/blog/microaggressions-in-every day-life/201010/racial-microaggressions-in-everyday-life.

Sullivan, Dennis, and Fred Boehrer. "Spike Lee's *Do The Right Thing*: Filmmaking in the American Grain." *Contemporary Justice Review* 6, no. 2 (2003).

"Sundance 2012: Ava DuVernay Becomes First Black Woman to Win Best Director Prize for *Middle of Nowhere* (Video)." "Black Voices." *HuffingtonPost.com*, January 30, 2012, updated March 31, 2012. www.huffingtonpost.com/2012/01/30/ava -duvernay-sundance_n_1241286.html.

Takaki, Ronald. *A Different Mirror: A History of Multicultural America*. Boston: Back Bay Books, 2008.

Tan, Emily. "Kid 'N Play to Showcase *House Party* Battle and Break Down 'Invisible Walls' at Everything Is Festival [Exclusive Interview]." TheBoombox.com, May 27, 2015. theboombox.com/kid-n-play-everything-is-festival-interview/.

Tartakovsky, Gabi. "Eddie Murphy and the Original Gangsters of Black Comedy." *PopMatters.com*, June 6, 2011. www.popmatters.com/feature/138792-harlem -nights-eddie-murphy-and-the-original-gangsters-of-black-comedy/.

Taubin, Amy. "The South and the Fury." *Village Voice*, 1993, 54. ProQuest.

Thomas, William. "Harlem Nights Review." *Empire*, January 1, 2000, updated October 14, 2015. www.empireonline.com/movies/harlem-nights/review/.

Thompson, Cliff. "The Devil Beats His Wife: Small Moments and Big Statements in the Films of Charles Burnett." *Cineaste* 23, no. 2 (1997): 24–27. www.jstor.org /stable/41689017.

"Title IX of the Education Amendments of 1972." United States Department of Justice, Updated December 31, 2014. www.justice.gov/crt/about/cor/coord/titleix .php.

Tueth, Michael V. *Reeling with Laughter: American Film Comedies: From Anarchy to Mockumentary*. Lanham, MD: Scarecrow Press, 2012.

Turner, Frederick Jackson. *Rereading Frederick Jackson Turner*. New Haven, CT: Yale University Press, 1998.

Turtledove, Harry. *The Guns of the South*. New York: Del Rey, 1992.

——— . *How Few Remain*. New York: Ballantine Books, 1997.

Tygiel, Jules. "The Great Experiment Fifty Years Later." In *The Cooperstown Symposium on Baseball and American Culture*, edited by Peter M. Rutkoff, 257–270. Jefferson, NC: McFarland, 1997.

United States Department of Labor Office of Policy Planning and Research. "The Negro Family: The Case For National Action." By Daniel Patrick Moynihan. 1965. https://www.dol.gov/general/aboutdol/history/webid-moynihan.

United States House of Representatives Committee on Un-American Activities. "Hearings Regarding Community Infiltration of Minority Groups—Part 1." July 1949. https://babel.hathitrust.org/cgi/pt?id=umn.31951d034965007;view=1up ;seq=3.

Van Jordan, A. "Blazing Saddles." *The Virginia Quarterly Review* 88, no. 2 (2012): 196–198.

"Venice Film Festival." IMDb.com, accessed May 10, 2011. www.imdb.com/event/evoooo681/overview.

"Violence Darkens the Bright Opening of Eddie Murphy's Plush, Flush *Harlem Nights*." *People*, December 4, 1989. www.people.com/people/archive/article/0,,20116112,00.html.

Walker, Alice. *In Search of Our Mother's Gardens: Womanist Prose*. New York: Open Road, 2011. Kindle edition.

Wall, David C., and Michael T. Martin, eds. *The Politics and Poetics of Black Film: Nothing But a Man*. Bloomington: Indiana University Press, 2015.

Wallace, Michele. "Why Women Won't Relate to 'Justice': Losing Her Voice." In *Dark Designs and Visual Culture*, 147–148. Durham, NC: Duke University Press, 2004.

Watson, Steven. *The Harlem Renaissance: Hub of African-American Culture, 1920–1930*. New York: Pantheon Books, 1995.

"Weekend Box Office June 2–4, 1995." BoxOfficeMojo.com. https://www.boxofficemojo.com/weekend/chart/?yr=1995&wknd=22&p=.htm.

Weiss, Stuart L. *The Curt Flood Story: The Man Behind the Myth*. Columbia: University of Missouri Press, 2007.

Wells, Veronica. "Bet You Didn't Know: Secrets Behind the Making of *Harlem Nights*." *MadameNoire.com*, November 26, 2012. madamenoire.com/236653/bet-you-didnt-know-secrets-behind-the-making-of-harlem-nights/.

———. "Bet You Didn't Know: Secrets Behind the Making of *House Party*." *Madame Noire.com*, August 22, 2012. madamenoire.com/204941/bet-you-didnt-know-secrets-behind-the-making-of-house-party/.

———. "Simply Beautiful: Ava DuVernay & Fashion Fair Create Short Film 'Say Yes.'" *MadameNoire.com*, August 15, 2013. madamenoire.com/291382/simply-beautiful-ava-duvernay-fashion-fair-create-short-film-say-yes/.

Wertheimer, Linda. "*Blazing Saddles* Makes National Film Registry" (Transcript). NPR, December 30, 2006. https://www.npr.org/templates/story/story.php?storyId=6700144.

West, Cornel. *Democracy Matters: Winning the Fight against Imperialism*. New York: Penguin Books, 2004.

Wheeler, Drew. "Marquee Values—*Nothing But a Man* Starring Ivan Dixon and Abbey Lincoln." *Billboard* 105, no. 52 (1993): 85. ProQuest.

Williams, Edward Wyckoff. "Black Parents, Gay Sons and Redefining Masculinity." TheRoot.com, June 16, 2014. www.theroot.com/articles/culture/2014/06/being_gay_isn_t_the_antithesis_of_becoming_a_strong_black_man/.

Williams, John A., and Dennis A. Williams. *If I Stop I'll Die: The Comedy and Tragedy of Richard Pryor*. New York: Thunder's Mouth Press, 1991.

Willmott, Kevin. "Playing with History: A *Black Camera* Interview with Kevin Willmott." By Derrais Carter. *Black Camera, an International Film Journal* 6, no. 2 (Spring 2015): 42–51.

Willmott, Kevin, and Rick Cowen. "*CSA: The Confederate States of America*" (Transcript).

By Greg Allen. *Day to Day*. NPR. October 28, 2005. www.npr.org/templates/story/story.php?storyId=4979746.

Willoughby, Vanessa. "What I Learned from Token Black Characters in Teen Movies." *Vice.com*, October 16, 2015. www.vice.com/read/what-i-learned-from-the-token-black-characters-in-teen-movies-921.

Wilmington, Michael. "Emotion, Not Violence, Drives *Glass Shield*" (Review). *Chicago Tribune*, June 2, 1995. articles.chicagotribune.com/1995-06-02/entertainment/9506020053_1_glass-shield-deborah-fields-police-movie.

Wilson, Julee. "Miu Miu Debuts Stunning New Short Film 'The Door' Starring Gabrielle Union and Alfre Woodard (Video)." *HuffingtonPost.com*, February 11, 2013. www.huffingtonpost.com/2013/02/11/gabrielle-union-miu-miu-the-door_n_2664312.html.

Wilson, William Julius. *The Declining Significance of Race: Blacks and Changing American* Chicago: University of Chicago Press, 1978.

Wintz, Cary D., ed. *The Emergence of the Harlem Renaissance*. New York: Garland, 1996.

Worland, Rick. *Searching for New Frontiers: Hollywood Films in the 1960s*. Hoboken, NJ: Wiley Blackwell, 2018.

X, Malcolm. "The Ballot or the Bullet." Speech. Detroit: April 12, 1964, American Radio Works.com. http://americanradioworks.publicradio.org/features/blackspeech/mx.html

"'You Are the Un-Americans, and You Ought to Be Ashamed of Yourselves': Paul Robeson Appears Before HUAC." June 12, 1956. "History Matters," American Social History Project / Center for Media and Learning (Graduate Center, CUNY) and the Roy Rosenzweig Center for History and New Media (George Mason University), accessed August 4, 2008. http://historymatters.gmu.edu/d/6440.

Young, Bradford. "The Visual Aesthetic of *Pariah*—an Interview W/ Cinematographer Bradford Young." By Nijla Mumin. *IndieWire.com*, August 17, 2015. https://www.indiewire.com/2015/08/the-visual-aesthetic-of-pariah-an-interview-w-cinematographer-bradford-young-151844/.

Young, Robert. "Close-Up: *Nothing But a Man*: Filmmaker's Perspective." *Black Camera, an International Film Journal* 3, no. 2 (Spring 2012): 91–100.

Zack, Jessica. "Pariah Director Dee Rees Confronts Disapproval." SFGate.com (San Francisco Chronicle), December 25, 2011. www.sfgate.com/movies/article/Pariah-director-Dee-Rees-confronts-disapproval-2420456.php.

Zad, Martie. "Jackie Robinson's Greatest Battle Off the Field." *Washington Post*, October 14, 1990, 1. NewsBank. https://infoweb.newsbank.com/apps/news/document-view?p=NewsBank&docref=news/0EAEA8A166E2DDE8.

Zeitchik, Steven. "With 42, the History-Lesson Movie Strikes Again" (Review). *Los Angeles Times*, April 15, 2013. http://articles.latimes.com/2013/apr/15/entertainment/la-et-mn-box-office-42-movie-reviews-theaters-jackie-robinson-race-lincoln-20130414.

Zirin, Dave. "A Review of 42: Jackie Robinson's Bitter Pill." *The Nation*, April 17, 2013. http://www.thenation.com/blog/173905/review-42-jackie-robinsons-bitter-pill.

Ziyad, Hari. "Empathy Won't Save Us in the Fight Against Oppression. Here's Why."

BlackGirlDangerous.org, August 11, 2015. www.blackgirldangerous.org/2015/08/empathy-wont-save-us-in-the-fight-against-oppression-heres-why/.

Filmography

42. Directed by Brian Helgeland. Burbank, CA: Warner Bros., 2013.
48 Hrs. Directed by Walter Hill. Los Angeles: Paramount Pictures, 1982.
Back in the Saddle. Directed by Wes Rubinstein and Mike Ruiz. Accessed on *Blazing Saddles* (1974). Burbank, CA: Warner Home Video, 2001. Blu-Ray.
Beverly Hills Cop. Directed by Martin Brest. Los Angeles: Paramount Pictures, 1984. Los Angeles: Paramount Home Entertainment, 2002. Blu-Ray.
———. "Commentary Track." By Martin Brest. Los Angeles: Paramount Home Entertainment, 2002. Blu-Ray.
"*Beverly Hills Cop*—the Phenomenon Begins." Accessed on *Beverly Hills Cop*. Los Angeles: Paramount Home Entertainment, 2002. Blu-Ray.
The Black List: Intimate Portraits of Black America. Directed by Timothy Greenfield-Sanders. New York: HBO, 2008.
Blazing Saddles. Directed by Mel Brooks. Burbank, CA: Warner Bros., 1974.
Boyz n the Hood. Directed by John Singleton. Culver City, CA: Columbia Pictures, 1991.
The Court-Martial of Jackie Robinson. Directed by Larry Peerce. Atlanta, GA: TNT, 1990.
C.S.A.: The Confederate States of America. Directed by Kevin Willmott. New York: IFC Films, 2004. Del Mar, CA: Genius Entertainment, 2006. DVD.
The Glass Shield. Directed by Charles Burnett. Los Angeles: Miramax, 1994.
Harlem Nights. Directed by Eddie Murphy. Los Angeles: Paramount Pictures, 1989.
House Party. Directed by Reginald Hudlin. Los Angeles: New Line Cinema, 1990.
Jackie Robinson. Directed by Ken Burns, Sarah Burns, and David McMahon. PBS, April 11–12, 2016.
The Jackie Robinson Story. Directed by Alfred E. Green. Los Angeles: Eagle-Lion Films, 1950.
Love & Basketball. Directed by Gina Prince-Bythewood. Los Angeles: New Line Cinema, 2000.
Menace II Society. Directed by the Hughes Brothers. Los Angeles: New Line Cinema, 1993.
Middle of Nowhere. Directed by Ava DuVernay. Beverly Hills, CA: Participant Media, 2012. Santa Monica, CA: Lionsgate Home Entertainment, 2015. DVD.
New Jack City. Directed by Mario Van Peebles. Los Angeles: Warner Bros., 1991.
Nothing But a Man. Directed by Michael Roemer. New York: DuArt Film and Video, 1964. New York: New Video, 2004. DVD.
Pariah. Directed by Dee Rees. New York: Focus Features, 2011.
Selma. Directed by Ava DuVernay. Los Angeles: Paramount Pictures, 2014. Los Angeles, CA: Paramount, 2015. Blu-Ray.
Trading Places. Directed by John Landis. Los Angeles: Paramount Pictures, 1983.
Venus Vs. Nine for IX. Directed by Ava DuVernay. Bristol, CT: ESPN Films, 2013. DVD.

INDEX

Abdul-Jabbar, Kareem, 54, 67
Academy Awards
    Best Picture, 1–2, 119, 181
    Best Song, 42
    black nominees and winners, 8, 18, 81, 119–120, 186
    Blazing Saddles nominations, 40–41
    Harlem Nights nomination, 60
    #OscarsSoWhite campaign, 2, 6, 186
Acham, Christine, 13
adolescents. *See* teenagers
advertising
    of black films, 10, 19
    fictional commercials in *C.S.A.*, 99, 109–114, 115
African American Film Festival Releasing Movement (AFFRM), 122
American Film Institute (AFI), 38, 185–186
Amistad, 11, 12
Angelou, Maya, *Down in the Delta*, 93, 121
Annenberg School for Communication and Journalism, University of Southern California, 8
Army, US
    Robinson's court-martial, 146, 148–149, 152, 155
    segregation, 148, 149
Ashcroft, John, 113
Aykroyd, Dan, 63–64

Baker, Aaron, 144
Baltimore, Freddie Gray case, 78, 82
Bankhead, Dan, 152
baseball
    Kansas City Monarchs, 150, 153
    power relations, 7
    reintegration supporters, 145–146, 151, 152
    reserve clause, 160
    Soul of the Game, 206n2
    See also Robinson, Jackie

Basie, Count, 43
Baszile, Natalie, 126
Batman, 61
Beasts of the Southern Wild, 2, 121, 163–164
Beavers, Louise, 110, 147
Bell, Derrick, 30, 50, 105, 138, 158
Benjamin, Judah P., 108
Benoit, Andy, 173
Bergman, Andrew, 39, 43
Berri, David, 172
Best Man Holiday, 2
Beulah, 110
Beverly Hills Cop, 64–65
biopic genre, 144, 156–157. *See also* Robinson, Jackie
Birth of a Nation, 4, 38, 52, 120
black audiences, 19, 59–61, 75, 130–131, 187
Black Camera, 19
blackface, 4, 64, 110
black feminist thought
    black matriarchy, 24–25
    in DuVernay's films, 122–123, 188
    fighting words, 49
    intersectionality, 8–9, 123
    See also controlling images
black film festivals, 19
black films
    in 1960s, 17–18, 37, 52, 142–143, 187
    in 1970s, 3, 39–40, 187
    in 1980s, 74–75, 187
    in 1990s, 81–83, 92, 93, 164–165, 174–175, 183–184, 187–188
    in 2000s, 121–122, 188
    in 2010s, 1–3, 186
    advertising, 10, 19
    canon, 5–6, 165, 186
    defined, 12, 41
    evolution, 189
    financing obstacles, 9–10, 174–175
    independent, 122

black films, *continued*
   lack of recognition, 2–4, 6, 185–186
   New Black Realism, 81, 82–83, 92, 200n17
   number of, 3
   producers, 175
   scholarship on, 3–4, 5–7, 13, 186–187, 189
   ten-year cycles, 1, 3, 6, 122
   writers, 11
   See also Blaxploitation films
Black Girls Rock Shot Caller award, 122
BlacKkKlansman, 3
Black Lives Matter, 79, 170, 188
Black Panther, 3, 4, 5, 186
Black Youth Project, 182
Bland, Sandra, 79
Blaxploitation films
   black male sexuality, 42, 52, 53
   Blazing Saddles compared to, 40, 42–43, 44, 55, 57
   conventions, 39
   scholarship on, 3, 39–40
   success, 187
   trickster motif, 41–42, 44, 55
Blazing Saddles
   black main character, 41, 42–46, 45 (photo), 47–51, 49 (photo), 52–54, 187
   black male sexuality, 52–54
   breaks in fourth wall, 47–50, 56
   compared to Blaxploitation films, 40, 42–43, 44, 55, 57
   contemporary urban references, 43, 45–46, 56–57
   ending, 56–57
   gunfights, 55, 56
   historical context, 7
   interest convergence, 50–52
   not seen as black film, 3, 41
   offensive elements, 40
   Oscar nominations, 40–41
   parody and satire, 46–50, 52–54, 103
   plot, 39, 40
   racism ridiculed, 44, 45–46, 47–50, 55, 57–58, 103, 187
   reception, 38–39, 40–41, 47
   trickster motif, 42–46, 50, 53–54, 55
   as Western, 54–58
   white racist characters, 43–46, 47–50, 51–52
Boehrer, Fred, 185
Bogle, Donald, 6, 7–8, 52, 69
Bonilla-Silva, Eduardo, 82
Born on the Fourth of July, 66–67
Boseman, Chadwick, 151, 153 (photo)
Boston Red Sox, 152
Boyz n the Hood, 5, 81–82, 164, 165, 175, 200n17
Bradbury, Ray, "The Sound of Thunder," 98
Braugher, Andre, 145, 147–148, 148 (photo)
Brest, Martin, *Beverly Hills Cop*, 64–65
Brooklyn Dodgers, 142, 143, 145–146, 150, 151. *See also* Rickey, Branch; Robinson, Jackie
Brooks, Mel, 39, 40, 57. *See also Blazing Saddles*
Brown, John, 115
Brown, Michael, 77–78, 163
Brown v. Board of Education, 50
Bruce, Alfred, 167, 168
Bruckheimer, Jerry, 65
Bryant, Howard, 152
buddy films, interracial, 48, 62–64
Burnett, Charles, 5, 80. *See also Glass Shield, The*
Burns, Ken, 99, 108, 152
Burr, Ty, 100
Burton, Tim, *Batman*, 61
Butler, Paul, 82
Butler, The, 2
butterfly effect, 97–98
Butters, Gerald R., Jr., 6–7

Canby, Vincent, 40, 66
Cannes Film Festival, 2
Carroll, Noel, 31
Carter, Derrais, 98
Cartwright, Samuel A., 111
Castile, Philando, 79
Chapman, Ben, 153, 158, 159
Cheadle, Don, *Miles Ahead*, 10
Chew, Richard, 19
Chicago, Laquan McDonald case, 78, 79, 86
children, black, 163–164, 184. *See also* teenagers

Churchill, Winston, 102, 105–106
Cinema Journal, 3–4
civil rights movement
  in 1950s, 142–143, 152
  in 1960s, 17–18
  economic justice and, 27
  Mississippi Burning, 11
  Robinson's contributions to, 150, 160, 161–162
  Selma, 119–120
  women's involvement, 119–120
Civil War
  European powers and, 108
  Glory, 11, 157
  slavery and states' rights as issues, 106
  speculative fiction about, 100–102
  See also *C.S.A.: The Confederate States of America*
class
  in *Beverly Hills Cop*, 64–65
  differences among blacks, 20–21
  in DuVernay's films, 131–135
  interaction with race, 9, 20–21, 22, 27, 133–134
  middle, 20–21, 174–175
  in *Nothing But a Man*, 20–21, 22, 27
  in teen films, 166, 174–175
  in *Trading Places*, 63–64
Cleaver, Kathleen Neal, 120
Clinton, Bill, 115, 116
Clinton, George, 168
Coates, Ta-Nehisi, 102, 152–153
Cold War, 143–145, 155
Collins, Patricia Hill, 7–8, 24–25, 49, 122–123, 134
Color Purple, The, 181
Combs, Sean, 59
comedians, black, 61–62, 70
comedies. See *Blazing Saddles*; *Harlem Nights*
coming-of-age films. See *Moonlight*; teen films
Confederacy, 108–109. See also Civil War; *C.S.A.: The Confederate States of America*
Confederate, 102
controlling images
  angry black women, 32, 70, 134–135
  female sexuality, 75
  jezebels, 8, 33, 135, 137
  mammies, 7, 26, 110, 134
  of men, 7–8
  pervasiveness, 7–8
  rejection by DuVernay, 135–140
  strong black women, 8, 32–33, 135
Coogler, Ryan, 2, 3, 4, 5, 6, 186
Cooley High, 6, 165
COPS, 111, 112
Court-Martial of Jackie Robinson, The, 148 (photo)
  compared to *The Jackie Robinson Story*, 145–150
  historical context, 145–146, 149, 155, 188
  portrayals of racism, 145, 148–149, 153, 162, 188
  release, 142
  Robinson family members, 146–147, 159
Cowen, Rick, 110, 113
Crawford, John, III, 78, 79, 86
Creed, 2, 6
Crenshaw, Kimberlé, 8
criminal characters (gangsters), 81, 82–83, 92
criminal justice system
  critiques of, 9, 83, 88–92, 96
  incarceration rates, 131
  systemic lying, 88–89
  See also law enforcement
critical race theory (CRT)
  analysis of baseball, 7
  characteristics, 104–105
  defined, 9
  economic violence, 30
  on fighting words, 49
  interest convergence, 50–52
  intersectionality, 8–9, 28, 30
  legal analysis, 9
  narratives from vulnerable individuals, 80, 91–92
  on racism, 104
  themes, 9–11
Crutcher, Terence, 79
C.S.A.: The Confederate States of America
  counterfactual history, 105–108, 117
  critical race theory and, 104–105
  documentary frame, 99, 103

C.S.A.: The Confederate States of America, continued
   fictional commercials, 99, 109–114, 112 (photo), 113 (photo), 115
   goals, 105
   as mockumentary, 103–104, 105
   parody and satire, 98, 103–104
   racial identity issue, 112–114, 115–117
   racism ridiculed in, 103
   reviews, 99–100
   similarities to reality, 98, 106, 108–109, 110–111, 117–118, 188
   slave interviews, 114–115
   truth-telling, 98–99
Cube, Ice, 87, 92
Cullors, Patrice, 79
Culp, Jerome McCristal, Jr., 105

Dalton School, 100
Daniels, Lee, *The Butler*, 2
Dash, Julie, 5, 13, 121, 125
Dassin, Jules, *Uptight*, 18
Daughters of the Dust, 5, 121
Davis, Angela Y., 145
Davis, Jefferson, 102, 106, 109
Davis, Miles, 10
Dear White People, 182
Dee, Ruby, 147
Detroit, 65
Diawara, Manthia, 120
Díaz, Junot, 5
Dick, Philip K., *The Man in the High Castle*, 98
Dickerson, Ernest, *Juice*, 6, 81, 164, 165, 200n17
directors, black
   of mainstream films, 12
   men, 120–121
   number of, 6, 10–11, 189
   Oscar nominations, 81
   women, 119–120, 121–122, 126, 175
Dixon, Ivan, 13, 29 (photo), 33, 34 (photo)
Django Unchained, 11, 157
Doby, Larry, 152
documentaries
   30 for 30 series, 125–126
   fake, 104
   My Mic Sounds Nice, 123
   Paris Is Burning, 181
   Standing in the Shadows of Motown, 129

   See also mockumentaries
Do the Right Thing, 5, 67, 149, 167, 185–186
Dowell, Pat, 46
DreamWorks, 10
DuBose, Samuel, 78, 86–87
Dukes of Hazzard, The, 109–110
Dunye, Cheryl, *The Watermelon Woman*, 121
Dutchman, The, 18
DuVernay, Ava
   awards, 2, 122, 127
   black feminist sensibility, 122–123, 188
   class in films, 131–135
   on diversity of black women, 123, 125, 126, 134, 140
   documentaries, 123, 126
   "The Door," 124
   goals, 123, 126
   I Will Follow, 122, 127, 128–130, 132–133, 135–136
   Middle of Nowhere, 2, 127, 130–132, 137–140
   My Mic Sounds Nice, 123
   on *Nothing But a Man*, 33
   Oscar nominations, 119–120
   "Say Yes," 124–125
   Selma, 119–120
   short films, 124–126
   television projects, 126
   Venus Vs., 126
   A Wrinkle in Time, 123, 186

Earp, Wyatt, 46–47
Eastwood, Clint, 47, 157
Ebert, Roger, 39, 60, 66, 127, 128, 167, 187
Edelman, Rob, 142
Ejiofor, Chiwetel, 10
El Dorado, 47
Emancipation Proclamation, 106
ESPN
   30 for 30 series, 125–126
   Jackie Robinson project, 150
   women's sports coverage, 172
Eve's Bayou, 6, 9, 93, 121, 42, 153 (photo)
   exposition, 155–157
   historical context, 152–153, 160–161, 188
   limited scope, 154–155, 162

opening, 160–161
plot, 142, 151–152
portrayals of racism, 152–154, 158, 160, 162, 188
Rachel's portrayal, 159–160
release, 2, 150
reviews, 150–151
white savior trope, 151, 157–158, 188
See also Robinson, Jackie
48 Hrs., 48, 62–63
Fashion Fair Cosmetics, 124–125
fashion industry, 124–125
Fassbender, Michael, 10
Faulx, Nadya, 40
Ferguson, Missouri, 77–78
film canons, 5–6, 38, 165, 185–186
Fisher, Celeste A., 92
Flood, Curt, 160
Flynn, Ray, 61
Ford, Harrison, 151
Foundas, Scott, 151
Foxx, Redd, 61, 68 (photo), 70
Foxy Brown, 39, 42
Franklin, Carl, 12, 93
Fruitvale Station, 2
Fuchs, Cynthia, 99
Fuller, Hoyt W., 36
Fuqua, Antoine, 12
Futrell, Nicole Smith, 80

gangsta films, 81–82, 92, 164–165, 174, 175, 183–184, 187–188
Garner, Eric, 78
Garza, Alicia, 79
Gates, Philippa, 65
Gates, Racquel J., 62
Gay, Roxane, 102
Gehring, Wes D., 47
gender
    disparities in sports, 171–174
    in *Harlem Nights*, 69–74, 75–76
    interaction with race, 9, 28, 30
    in *Nothing But a Man*, 30–35, 69
    patriarchy, 30, 72, 181
    policing, 172, 178–180
    See also men; women
George, Nelson, 183
Gerima, Haile, 5–6, 13

Girls Trip, 186
Glass Shield, The
    black deputy character, 80–81, 84–85, 87, 88–89, 90, 94, 95 (photo), 187–188
    context, 79–80, 83, 86–87
    limited release, 95
    marketing, 92–93, 95
    opening comic book images, 84, 85 (photo)
    plot, 87–91, 92, 93–95
    police relations with community, 85–86, 87–88, 90, 96, 188
    reviews, 80, 92–93
    themes, 80
    violence in, 92–95
Gleiberman, Owen, 167
Glory, 11, 157
Gold Dust Washing Powder, 110
Golden Globes, 119
Gone with the Wind, 4, 134
Grant, Ulysses S., 100, 106
Gray, F. Gary, *Set It Off*, 81, 182, 200n17
Gray, Freddie, 78, 82
Green Book, 11, 12, 157
Grier, Pam, *Foxy Brown*, 39, 42
Griffith, D. W., *Birth of a Nation*, 4, 38, 52, 120
Guerrero, Ed, 63, 121
Guess Who's Coming to Dinner, 18
Guest, Christopher, 103
Gunfight at the O.K. Corral, 46–47, 56

Hall, Stuart, 4
Harlem Nights, 68 (photo), 71 (photo)
    black audiences, 59–61, 75
    box-office success, 66, 75
    as caper film, 61, 75, 76
    female characters, 62, 69–74, 75–76
    gender politics, 69–74, 75–76
    Harlem setting and time period, 67–68
    Oscar nomination, 60
    plot, 61
    profanity, 66–67
    reception, 59–61, 62, 66, 75, 187
    reviews, 60, 62, 66, 75
    stuttering character, 198–199n33
    video tribute, 59

Harlem Nights, continued
   violent incidents at showings, 61, 66
   violent scenes, 69–73, 74
Harlem Renaissance, 67
Harley, Sharon, 71
Harris, Aisha, 186
Harris, Cheryl I., 114, 116
Harris, Leslie, *Just Another Girl on the I.R.T.*, 121
Harris-Perry, Melissa V., 119–120, 134–135, 140, 163–164
Haskell, Molly, 122
Hawk, Kali, 125
Hawkins, Yusef, 149
Hayes, Isaac, 42
HBO, 102, 206n2
Helgeland, Brian, 150. See also 42
Help, The, 11, 12, 134, 157
Hemingway, Anthony, 2
Hepburn, Katherine, 18
High Noon, 46
Hinson, Hal, 19, 60
hip-hop music, 92, 123, 166
history, counterfactual, 98, 100–102, 201n1
Holiday, Billie, "Strange Fruit," 145
Home, 10
hooks, bell, 72, 73, 163–164, 181
Hornaday, Ann, 99
House Party
   all-black spaces, 174
   awards, 168
   box-office success, 168
   class differences, 166, 175
   as cult classic, 168
   father-son relationship, 168, 177, 184
   interactions with police, 168–171, 169 (photo), 175
   plot, 165–166
   rappers, 166
   reviews, 166–167
   romantic relationship, 176, 180
House Un-American Activities Committee (HUAC), 143 (photo), 144, 155
Howe, Desson, 60, 167
HUAC, 143 (photo), 144, 155
Hudlin, Reginald, 166, 171, 186. See also *House Party*

Hughes, Albert and Allen, *Menace II Society*, 81, 82–83, 164, 175, 200n17
Hughes, John, 164
Hughes, Langston, 67, 131
Hughey, Matthew W., 157
Hunt, Darrien, 78, 79
Hurston, Zora Neale, 67, 140
Hutcheon, Linsa, 103
hypermasculinity, 62, 73. See also masculinity

If Beale Street Could Talk, 186
I Like It Like That, 121
Imus, Don, 172
incarceration rates, 131
independent films, 122, 130–131, 182
Insight Center for Community Economic Development, 133
interest convergence, 50–52
intersectionality, 8–9, 28, 30, 123
In the Heat of the Night, 18
Irish immigrants, 51–52
Iverem, Esther, 100
I Will Follow
   class differences, 132–133
   flashbacks, 129–130
   main character, 135–136, 136 (photo)
   plot, 127
   release, 122
   reviews, 127, 128
   role of race, 128–129, 133

Jackie Robinson: A Biography (Rampersad), 141–142, 150, 156
Jackie Robinson Story, The, 143 (photo)
   compared to *The Court-Martial of Jackie Robinson*, 145–150
   historical context, 142–143, 155, 188
   length, 157
   limited scope, 141, 155, 162, 188
   message, 142
   Robinson family members, 147, 159
   role of race and racism, 144–145, 160
   white savior trope, 143, 188
Jackson, Jesse, 27
James, Quentin, 59
Jarmusch, Jim, 93
Jazz Singer, The, 4

J. Edgar, 157
Jenkins, Barry, 2, 181, 186
Jethroe, Sam, 152
Jewison, Norman, In the Heat of the Night, 18
Jolson, Al, 4
Jordan, A. Van, 53
Journal of Personality and Social Psychology, 184
Juhasz, Alexandra, 102–103
Juice, 6, 81, 164, 165, 200n17
Julien, Isaac, 72
Just Another Girl on the I.R.T., 121

Kansas City Monarchs, 150, 153
Kantor, MacKinlay, If the South Had Won the Civil War, 100–101
Kempadoo, Kamala, 74
Kennedy, John F., 107–108
Kermode, Mark, 151
Kid 'n Play, 166
Kidron, Beeban, To Wong Foo, Thanks for Everything! Julie Newmar, 182
Killer of Sheep, 5
King, Coretta Scott, 120
King, Martin Luther, Jr., 27. See also Selma
King, Rodney, 79–80, 84
Kois, Dan, 186
Ku Klux Klan, 4. See also Birth of a Nation; BlacKkKlansman
Kurosawa, Akira, Seven Samurai, 47

L.A. Confidential, 150
Lacy, Sam, 146, 151
La Guardia, Fiorello, 146
Landis, John, Trading Places, 62, 63–64
LaSalle, Mick, 99
law enforcement
   in black films, 81–82, 83
   black officers, 80–82, 90, 96, 175
   harassment of black teenagers, 168–169, 170–171
   misconduct and corruption, 89–92, 96
   racial profiling, 87–89, 149
   relations with black communities, 77–80, 81–82, 85–86, 87–88, 90, 91, 96, 168–171, 188
   stop-and-frisk rules, 82
   violence against black bodies, 77–80, 83, 86–87, 96, 163, 184
   See also Glass Shield, The
Lawrence, Charles R., III, 30
Lawrence, Martin, 70
Lawrence, Novotny, 6–7, 39
Learish, Jessica, 172–173
Learning Tree, The, 5, 18
Lee, Malcolm D., 2, 3, 186
Lee, Robert E., 102, 106
Lee, Spike
   on black films, 1
   BlacKkKlansman, 3
   Do the Right Thing, 5, 67, 149, 167, 185–186
   as executive producer, 175
   on Harlem Nights scene, 70
   Jackie Robinson project, 150
   Malcolm X, 150
   scholarship on films of, 13
   School Daze, 180
   She Hate Me, 182
   She's Gotta Have It, 135
   Summer of Sam, 12
legal system. See criminal justice system; law enforcement
Legum, Judd, 86
Lemmons, Kasi
   in The Court-Martial of Jackie Robinson, 147
   Eve's Bayou, 6, 9, 93, 121
Leonard, David, 183
Lerner, Jesse, 102–103
LGBTQ characters
   black, 180–183
   lesbian, 172, 178–180, 181, 182–183
Lilies of the Field, 18
Lincoln, Abbey, 29 (photo), 34 (photo). See also Nothing But a Man
Lincoln, Abraham, 106
Little, Cleavon, 40, 45 (photo), 49 (photo)
Livingston, Jennie, Paris Is Burning, 181
Loewen, James, 4
Lorenz, Edward, 98
Los Angeles
   films set in, 81–83, 84
   Rodney King beating, 79–80, 84
Louis, Joe, 146, 148

Love & Basketball, 122, 165, 171–174, 173 (photo), 175–178, 179
Lucas, George, Red Tails, 2, 10

MacLeod, Lewis, 104
Magnificent Seven, The (1960), 47
Magnificent Seven, The (2016), 47
Malcolm X, 150
Mandela: A Long Walk to Freedom, 157
Marable, Manning, 113
Martin, Darnell, I Like It Like That, 121
Martin, Michael T., 136
Martin, Roland, 59–60, 61
Martin, Trayvon, 79, 163
masculinity, 27, 30, 46, 62, 72–73
Massood, Paula, 82–83
matriarchs, 24–25
McCraney, Tarell Alvin, 181
McDaniel, Hattie, 110, 134
McDonald, Laquan, 78, 79, 86
McPherson, James M., 108
McQueen, Steve, 1–2, 10, 186
Meeropol, Abel, 145
men
    controlling images, 7–8
    fathers in teen films, 168, 176–178, 179, 184
    masculinity, 27, 30, 46, 62, 72–73
    producers, 175
    racial stereotypes, 7–8, 52–54, 57–58
    sexuality, 42, 52–54
    See also gender
Menace II Society, 81, 82–83, 164, 175, 200n17
Mendelson, Scott, 5
Micheaux, Oscar, 5, 120
microaggressions, 31, 103
Middle of Nowhere, 132 (photo)
    awards, 2, 127
    class differences, 131–133, 134
    family relationships, 138–140
    plot, 127
    reviews, 127
    role of race, 130–131
    romantic relationships, 137–138
Miles Ahead, 10
Miller, Cynthia J., 103
Miramax, 93, 95
misogynoir, 71, 199n39

Mississippi Burning, 11
Miu Miu, 124
mockumentaries, 102–104, 121. See also C.S.A.: The Confederate States of America
Mo'Nique, 59
Monster's Ball, 135
Moonlight, 2, 181
Moore, Ward, Bring the Jubilee, 100
Morris, Wesley, 151
Morrison, Toni, 161
Moynihan, Daniel Patrick, 24, 139
MPAA ratings, 176
Murphy, Eddie, 61–65, 67, 68 (photo), 70, 71 (photo), 74–75, 187. See also Harlem Nights
music
    in Harlem, 67
    heavy metal, 129
    rap and hip-hop, 92, 123, 166
    session musicians, 128–129
    of U2, 130
My Mic Sounds Nice, 123
Mystic River, 150

9/11 aftermath, 113
NAACP, 67, 146
Naked Spur, The, 46
Nama, Adilifu, 7
National Film Registry, 19, 39
New Black Realism, 81, 82–83, 92, 200n17
New Jack City, 81, 200n17
News One Now, 59–60, 61
New York Police Department (NYPD), 78, 82
Nickel, John, 25
Nolte, Nick, 62–63
Nothing But a Man
    advertising, 19
    as art film, 18–19
    class differences, 20–21, 22, 27
    effects of white supremacy, 25, 26–31, 32, 34–37, 187
    ending, 35–37
    gender relations, 30–35, 69
    generational divides, 21–26
    main characters, 20, 26, 29 (photo), 31–35, 34 (photo), 44
    masculinity, 27, 30

political context, 21–23
power relations, 30
race relations, 22–23
rediscovery, 19
as romance film, 33–36, 137–138
white characters, 26–27, 36, 37
Notorious, 156
Nuri, Joia Jefferson, 59
NYPD, 78, 82

Obama, Barack, 11, 133, 152–153, 157, 162, 188
Obama, Michelle, 124
Obenson, Tambay A., 127
Owens, Jesse, 11, 54
OWN Network, 126

Painter, Nell Irvin, 117
Pariah, 179 (photo)
    father-daughter relationship, 177, 179
    financing, 174–175
    gender policing, 178–180
    plot, 178–180, 182–183
    release, 122
    reviews, 165, 178, 183
    sexual relationship, 180
Paris Is Burning, 181
Parks, Gordon, 3, 5, 18, 39, 42, 52
parody
    in *Blazing Saddles*, 46–50, 52–54, 103
    in *C.S.A.: The Confederate States of America*, 98, 103–104
    defined, 46
patriarchy, 30, 72, 181
Patton, Stacey, 163
Peck, Gregory, 18
Pennock, Herb, 158
Peters, Brock, 18
Petrie, Douglas, *A Raisin in the Sun*, 18
Pew Research Center, 131
Pharrell, 59
Pitt, Brad, 10
Pittsburgh Courier, 145, 146, 152
Poitier, Sidney, 18, 52
police. *See* criminal justice system; law enforcement
Porter, Cole, 45–46
"postracial" ideology, 152–153, 162, 188

Prasch, Thomas, 103–104
Preston, J. A., 145
Prince-Blythewood, Gina
    Beyond the Lights, 122
    Love & Basketball, 122, 165, 171–174, 173 (photo), 175–178, 179
    The Secret Life of Bees, 122
prisons. *See* criminal justice system
Pryor, Richard, 3, 39, 40, 61, 62, 66, 68 (photo), 71

Queen Sugar, 126

race
    interaction with class, 9, 20–21, 22, 27, 133–134
    interaction with gender, 9, 28, 30
    interracial buddy films, 48, 62–64
    in mainstream films, 4–5, 7–10
    as social construct, 114, 116–117
Race, 11
racism
    economic violence and, 30
    effects of Obama's election, 152–153
    fighting words, 48–49
    in Jackie Robinson films, 142, 144–145, 148–149, 151, 152–154, 158, 159, 160–161, 162, 188
    microaggressions, 31, 103
    in military, 149
    in 1960s films, 18
    "postracial" ideology, 152–153, 162, 188
    public discussions, 149
    ridiculed in *Blazing Saddles*, 44, 45–46, 47–50, 55, 57–58, 103, 187
    ridiculed in *C.S.A.*, 103
    Robinson on, 144
    in speech, 30
    systemic, 144, 149, 154, 160–161, 162
    See also segregation; white supremacy
Raengo, Alessandra, 144
Rafferty, Terrence, 80
Raisin in the Sun, A, 18
Rampersad, Arnold, *Jackie Robinson: A Biography*, 141–142, 150, 156
Randolph, A. Philip, 13, 23
Random House, 161
rap music, 92, 166

Razzie Awards, 60
Redford, Robert, 150
Red Tails, 2, 10
Ree, Dee
    Mudbound, 3
    Pariah, 122, 165, 174–175, 177, 178–180, 182–183
Reese, Della, 61, 69–72, 71 (photo)
Reese, Pee Wee, 155–156
Reich, Elizabeth, 13
Reid, Mark A., 81
Reiner, Rob, 103
Rhimes, Shonda, 126
Rhymes, Busta, 59, 61, 69
Rice, Tamir, 78–79, 163
Rickey, Branch, 143, 145–146, 150, 151, 153–154, 155–156, 157–158
Riggs, Marlon, 6, 182
Rihanna, 10
Roberts, Damone, 133
Robeson, Paul, 144
Robinson, Jackie
    biography, 141–142, 150, 156
    court-martial, 146, 148–149, 152, 155
    family, 146–147, 156, 159–160
    HUAC testimony, 144–145, 155
    I Never Had It Made, 146, 156, 161–162
    legacy, 149–150, 154–155, 160, 161–162
    retellings of story, 141–142, 160
    Soul of the Game, 206n2
    See also 42; Court-Martial of Jackie Robinson, The; Jackie Robinson Story, The
Robinson, Mallie, 146–147, 159
Robinson, Rachel, 146, 147, 150, 151 152, 154, 156, 159–160
Rochon, Lela, 59, 73–74
Rock, Chris, 2, 9–10
Rodney, Lester, 146, 151
Roemer, Michael, 19, 30. See also Nothing But a Man
Roeper, Richard, 151
Roth, Philip, The Plot Against America, 98
Rotten Tomatoes, 60, 167

Sachs, Ira, 19, 25
Sambo image, 110
satire
    in Blazing Saddles, 46–50, 52–54, 103
    in C.S.A.: The Confederate States of America, 98, 103–104
    defined, 47
    truth-telling, 103
Scandal, 122, 126
School Daze, 180
Schultz, Michael, Cooley High, 6, 165
science fiction/fantasy films, 4–5
Scott, A. O., 181
Scott, Randolph, 56
Scott, Walter, 78, 79, 86
Secret Life of Bees, The, 122
Seewood, Andre, 12, 41
segregation
    of film audiences, 130–131
    Jim and Jane Crow, 21, 107, 114, 145
    in military, 148, 149
    official support, 36
    residential, 21
    school, 24, 50
    See also baseball
Selma, 119–120
Serwer, Adam, 178
Set It Off, 81, 182, 200n17
Setoodeh, Ramin, 1–2
Seven Samurai, 47
Seward, William H., 109
sexuality
    black male, 42, 52–54
    in teen films, 176
sexual orientation. See LGBTQ characters
sex workers, 71, 73–74, 75–76
Shaft, 3, 42, 52
Shane, 46
Shaw, George Bernard, 98–99
She Hate Me, 182
She's Gotta Have It, 135
Shipp, Thomas, 145
Shirley, Don. See Green Book
Simien, Justin, Dear White People, 182
Simon-Kerr, Julia, 88
Singleton, John
    Boyz n the Hood, 5, 81–82, 164, 165, 175, 200n17
    on Hollywood hiring practices, 11
Singleton, Shermichael, 59–60
Siskel, Gene, 93, 94–95

Sixteen Candles, 164
Slate magazine, 6, 165, 166–167, 186
slavery, 11, 106, 117–118. See also C.S.A.: The Confederate States of America; 12 Years a Slave
Sliders, 201n1
Smith, Abram, 145
Smith, Judith E., 36–37
Smith, Wendell, 145–146, 151–152, 159
Smith, Will, 5, 166
Smith-Shomade, Beretta E., 3–4, 5, 6
social media, 78, 79
Soul of the Game, 206n2
"Space Traders" (Bell), 105
Spaulding, Bill, 143
Spielberg, Steven, 12, 181
Spook Who Sat by the Door, The, 13
sports
    documentaries, 125–126
    female athletes, 125–126, 171–174, 178
    gender disparities, 171–174
    Love & Basketball, 122, 165, 171–174, 175–178, 179
    professional, 176–177, 178
    See also baseball; Robinson, Jackie
Standing in the Shadows of Motown, 129
Stark, Susan, 60
Steiger, Rod, 18
Steinberg, Norman, 39
stereotypes
    racial, 4, 7–8, 9, 52–54, 57–58, 130
    tragic mulatto, 116
    See also controlling images
Stone, Oliver, Born on the Fourth of July, 66–67
"Strange Fruit," 145
strong black woman image, 32–33, 135
Sue, Derald Wing, 31
Sullivan, Dennis, 185
Summer of Sam, 12
Sundance Film Festival, 2, 99, 127, 168
Super Fly, 3, 39, 42
superhero films, 4–5
Sweet Sweetback's Baadasssss Song, 5, 39, 42, 52

12 Years a Slave, 1–2, 10
30 for 30 series, 125–126

Takaki, Ronald, 51–52
Taubin, Amy, 84
teenagers
    black, 163–164, 165, 184
    police treatment of, 77–78, 79, 163, 184
teen films
    in 1980s, 164
    all-black spaces, 174
    black characters in white films, 164, 180–181
    class differences, 166, 174–175
    Cooley High, 6, 165
    father-child relationships, 168, 176–178, 179, 184
    gangsta films, 81–82, 92, 164–165, 174, 175, 183–184, 187–188
    gender policing, 172, 178–180
    interactions with police, 168–171, 175
    LGBTQ characters, 180–181, 182–183
    Love & Basketball, 122, 165, 171–174, 175–178, 179
    messages, 165, 183–184
    mothers, 179
    Pariah, 122, 165, 174–175, 177, 178–180, 182–183
    sexual relationships, 176, 180
    social context, 188–189
Tensing, Ray, 86–87
Thomas, William, 66
Thompson, Cliff, 80
To Kill a Mockingbird, 18, 143
Tometi, Opal, 79
Top Five, 9–10
To Wong Foo, Thanks for Everything! Julie Newmar, 182
Tracy, Spencer, 18
Trading Places, 62, 63–64
tricksters, 41–46
Truman, Harry S., 149
Tueth, Michael V., 46
Turner, Frederick Jackson, 54
Turtledove, Harry, Southern Victory series, 100, 101
Tuskegee Airmen, 2, 10
Tygiel, Jules, 141, 160

U2, 130
Uger, Alan, 39

universal narrative, 9–10, 11–12
Uptight, 18
U.S. Department of Education, 184
U.S. Justice Department, 78
U.S. Supreme Court, 50

Van Dyke, Jason, 86
Van Peebles, Melvin, 5, 39, 42, 52, 81, 200n17
Venice Film Festival, 18
violence
    economic, 30
    by law enforcement, 77–80, 83, 86–87, 96, 163, 184
    lynchings, 23, 24, 31, 36, 145
    mass shooting in movie theater, 197n10
    physical, 30–31
    racial, 149
    at showings of Harlem Nights, 61, 66
    in Westerns, 46, 47, 55
    against women, 30–31, 32, 69–70, 74

Waithe, Lena, 125
Walker, Alice, The Color Purple, 181
Wallace, Christopher (Notorious B.I.G.), 156
Wallace, George, 36
Wallace, Michele, 122
Washington, Denzel, 2–3, 47
Washington, Kerry, 122, 124, 182
Watermelon Woman, The, 121
Waters, Ethel, 110
Waters, Maxine, 135
Wayne, John, 47
Welles, Orson, War of the Worlds, 103
Wells, Mary, 33–34
West, Cornel, 9
Western frontier, 54
Westerns
    cultural importance, 54–55
    gunslinger characters, 46–47
    masculinity in, 46
    recent, 47
    violence in, 46, 47, 55
    See also Blazing Saddles
whiteness
    patriarchal, 181
    privileges, 114, 158

whites
    characters in black films, 10, 11–12, 18, 37, 157
    film audiences, 10, 11–12, 19, 37, 63, 75, 167
    passing as, 113–114, 115–117
    writers and directors, 11, 39–40
white savior trope, 143, 151, 157–158, 188
white supremacy
    effects shown in Nothing But a Man, 25, 26–31, 32, 34–37, 187
    gendered effects, 28, 30
    in legal system, 9
    patriarchal, 30
    in popular culture, 9, 117
    resisting, 35–36, 37
    victory of, 117–118
    See also Birth of a Nation; C.S.A.: The Confederate States of America; racism
Wilder, Gene, 40, 49 (photo), 57. See also Blazing Saddles
Williams, Marvin, 152
Williams, Serena, 172
Williams, Venus, 126
Willmott, Kevin, 98, 108, 114, 117. See also C.S.A.: The Confederate States of America
Wilmore, Larry, 103
Wilson, Darren, 77–78
Wilson, Julee, 124
Wilson, William Julius, 20
Wimbledon Grand Slam Tournament, 126
Winfrey, Oprah, 120, 126
Winner, Ben, Underground Airlines, 101–102
WNBA, 172–173
women
    athletes, 125–126, 171–174, 178
    in civil rights movement, 119–120
    directors, 119–120, 121–122, 126, 175
    fashion industry and, 124–125
    in hip-hop, 123
    households headed by, 24–25
    matriarchs, 24–25
    mothers in teen films, 179
    musicians, 128–130
    as protagonists of black films, 121, 122–123, 140, 188
    roles for black, 62

sex workers, 71, 73–74, 75–76
television series centered on, 122
violence against, 30–31, 32, 69–70, 74
wealth disparities, 133–134
See also black feminist thought;
   controlling images; DuVernay, Ava;
   gender
women's films, 122
Women's Tales, The, 124
Wrinkle in Time, A, 123, 186

X, Malcolm, 27, 120, 150

Young, Bradford, 181
Young, Robert, 19, 34

Zack, Jessica, 179–180
Zeitlin, Benh, *Beasts of the Southern Wild*, 2, 121, 163–164
Zimmerman, George, 79
Zirin, Dave, 161